THE DIVINITY OF THE WORD

Publications of the Thomas Instituut te Utrecht

(Tilburg School of Catholic Theology, Tilburg University, Netherlands)

New Series, Volume XX

Vol. I Henk J.M. Schoot, Christ the 'Name' of God. Thomas Aquinas on Naming Christ, 1993

Vol. II Jan G.J. van den Eijnden ofm, Poverty on the Way to God. Thomas Aquinas on Evangelical Poverty, 1994

Vol. III Henk J.M. Schoot (ed.), Tibi soli peccavi. Thomas Aquinas on Guilt and Forgiveness, 1996

Vol. IV Harm J.M.J. Goris, Free Creatures of an Eternal God. Thomas Aquinas on God's Infallible Foreknowledge and Irrisistible Will, 1996

Vol. V Carlo Leget, Living with God. Thomas Aquinas on the Relation between Life on Earth and 'Life' after Death, 1997

Vol. VI Wilhelmus G.B.M. Valkenberg, Words of the Living God. Place and Function of Holy Scripture in the Theology of St. Thomas Aquinas, 2000

Vol. VII Paul van Geest, Harm Goris, Carlo Leget (eds.), Aquinas as Authority. A Collection of Studies presented at the Second Conference of the Thomas Instituut te Utrecht, December 14-16, 2000, 2002

Vol. VIII Eric Luijten, Sacramental Forgiveness as a Gift of God. Thomas Aquinas on the Sacrament of Penance, 2003

Vol. IX Mark-Robin Hoogland c.p., God, Passion and Power. Thomas Aquinas on Christ Crucified and the Almightiness of God, 2003

Vol. X Stefan Gradl, Deus Beatitudo Hominis. Eine evangelische Annäherung an die Glückslehre des Thomas von Aquin, 2004

Vol. XI Barbara Roggema, Marcel Poorthuis, Pim Valkenberg (eds.), The Three Rings. Textual Studies in the Historical Trialogue of Judaism, Christianity and Islam, 2005

Vol. XII Fáinche Ryan, Formation in Holiness. Thomas Aquinas on *Sacra doctrina,* 2007

Vol. XIII Harm Goris, Herwi Rikhof, Henk Schoot (eds.), Divine Transcendence and Immanence in the Work of Thomas Aquinas, 2009

Vol. XIV Matthew Kostelecky, Thomas Aquinas's *Summa contra Gentiles*: a mirror of human nature, 2012

Vol. XV Kevin E. O'Reilly, o.p., The Hermeneutics of Knowing and Willing in the Thought of St. Thomas Aquinas, 2013

Vol. XVI Harm Goris, Lambert Hendriks, Henk Schoot (eds.), Faith, Hope and Love. Thomas Aquinas on Living by the Theological Virtues, 2015

Vol. XVII Harm Goris and Henk Schoot (eds.), The Virtuous Life. Thomas Aquinas on the Theological Nature of Moral Virtues, 2016

Vol. XVIII Anton ten Klooster, Thomas Aquinas on the Beatitudes. Reading Matthew, Disputing Grace and Virtue, Preaching Happiness, 2018

Vol. XIX Henk Schoot, Jacco Verburgt and Jörgen Vijgen (eds.), Initiation and Mystagogy in Thomas Aquinas. Scriptural, Systematic, Sacramental and Moral, and Pastoral Perspectives, 2019

STEFAN MANGNUS, O.P.

THE DIVINITY OF THE WORD

Thomas Aquinas Dividing and Reading the Gospel of John

PEETERS
LEUVEN – PARIS – BRISTOL, CT
2022

A catalogue record for this book is available from the Library of Congress.

ISBN 978-90-429-4821-1
eISBN 978-90-429-4822-8
D/2022/0602/1

CONTENTS

ABBREVIATIONS

CCSL	*Corpus Christianorum Series Latina*
CSEL	*Corpus Scriptorum Ecclesiasticorum Latinorum*
PG/PL	J.-P. MIGNE (ed.), *Patrologiae Cursus Completa*, Series Graeca/Series Prima – Patres Latinae
SC	*Sources Chrétiennes*
Catena Aurea in Io	*Catena Aurea Super Ioannis Evangelium*
Comp. Theol.	*Compendium Theologiae*
De Trin	*Super Boetium De Trinitate*
In Rom	*Expositio super epistolam ad Romanos*
In I Cor	*Super I ad Corinthios*
In II Cor	*Super II ad Corinthios*
In Is	*Expositio super Isaiam ad litteram*
In Job	*Expositio super Job ad litteram*
In Io	*Lectura super Ioannem*
In Matt	*Lectura super Matthaeum*
In Peryerm	*Expositio libri Peryermenias*
In Ps	*Postilla super Psalmos*
In I Sent	*Scriptum super libros Sententiarum,* Liber I
ScG	*Summa contra Gentiles*
STh I-II	*Summa Theologiae*, Prima Secundae
Tract. in Io	Augustine, *In Evangelium Ioannis Tractatus*
a.	articulus
bk.	book
c.	corpus articuli
ch.	chapter
d.	distinctio
e.g.	exempli gratia
ibid.	ibidem
intr.	introduction
lect.	lectio
obj.	objectio
n.	number
nt.	note
p.	page

proe.	proemium
prol.	prologus
q.	quaestio (plural: qq.)
qc.	quaestiuncula
s.c.	sed contra

ACKNOWLEDGEMENTS

To those who taught me

During the long process of which this study is the result, I have been blessed with the support of many people. Among them are a few that I would like to mention by name.

Prof. Henk Schoot took over as first supervisor when the project was well under way. His theological insights, challenging questions and constant support were both indispensible and a great source of motivation. I am most grateful for his encouragement, his patience and his example.
Without prof. Herwi Rikhof, this project might have never started. As my first supervisor, he spent many an hour with me learning to read Thomas Aquinas and learning to write a thesis. His understanding of and contagious love for theology continue to be an inspiration for me to this day, and I happily remain indebted to him for his unwavering encouragement and patience.
I am grateful to Prof. Marcel Sarot , the second supervisor for this project, for his helpful questions, his precise reading of the manuscript, and his encouragement during the final stages of the project.
I wish to thank Dr. Harm Goris, Dr. Lambert Hendriks, Dr. Anton ten Klooster, Frank Steijger, Prof. Rudi te Velde, Dr. Jörgen Vijgen and Dr. Syds Wiersma, current and former members of the Research Group Thomas Aquinas of the Thomas Instituut Utrecht for their feedback on parts of this study.

This project was made possible by the support of the Archdiocese of Utrecht, for which I wish to thank former vicar-general Piet Rentinck. My provincial René Dinklo OP generously gave me time and space to finish the project. I thank him for this opportunity and for his trust. During my year in Blackfriars Oxford, Richard Conrad OP provided very helpful insights, and my brothers in the community in Rotterdam, Richard Steenvoorde OP, Michael-Dominique Magielse OP, Paweł Gużyński OP and Augustinus Aerssens OP were a great support. I thank them all.

During different periods of the project Heleen Gombert and Connie de Vos made room in their lives for me to be able to study and write. I remain immensely grateful for their generosity. I thank Suzanna Varszegi for her help during the final stages of the project.

Jan van Beek, Dorenda Gies, Jacco Calis, and Bernadette van Dijk have been close friends from the beginning of my journey in theology: during this project they were kind enough sometimes to inquire about it and at other times to sensitively refrain from doing so. I give thanks for their friendship.

In the dedication above I remember my teachers. I commemorate my parents, my first teachers in faith and love. I wish to express gratitude to prof. Jozef Wissink who by his words and example has taught me more than I can express, and whose unwavering support for this project has been an enduring source of inspiration. In my life, I have been blessed to have had many excellent teachers; I remain exceedingly grateful to them all.

INTRODUCTION

Whoever starts to read biblical commentaries that had their origin in medieval universities, commentaries like those by Albert the Great, Thomas Aquinas or Bonaventure, awaits a number of surprises. There are surprises as to the content of these biblical commentaries. One finds exegetical remarks next to dogmatic ideas, and notions of what we would now call a moral theological nature go side by side with direct pastoral advice. It is as if these commentaries are supposed to teach their readers the entire width of Christian theology and the Christian life. To a medieval mind, that, of course, is precisely what they are supposed to do. Many medieval commentaries started out as classroom texts in the universities: commenting on Scripture was the first task that a medieval *Magister in Sacra Pagina* had as part of his job to teach theology. Together with this *legere*, reading of Scripture with the students, came the tasks of *disputare* (holding theological debates) and *praedicare* (preaching). There was, therefore, a clear distinction in the functions of a *magister*, but not one in terms of the different theological disciplines that we know now (like systematic theology, exegesis, pastoral or moral theology): the differentiation of theological disciplines is from a later date.

A first-time reader of medieval biblical commentaries also awaits surprises of a more methodological nature. The way Scripture is read and interpreted differs significantly from biblical commentaries in our time. There are hermeneutical presuppositions lying underneath these commentaries, predominantly those about different senses of Scripture, that are not as self-evidently present in most of the biblical commentaries that are written nowadays. There are differences in technique, in the way sources are used or the biblical text is structured by the commentator.

This study is the result of a double sense of wonder. The first sense of wonder is about a technique Thomas Aquinas uses to read Scripture, which is known as the *divisio textus*. This is a technique typical for medieval biblical commentaries that have their origin in the university. It is a method of structuring the text by dividing the whole of the text in big parts, and subsequently subdividing it into ever smaller parts, sometimes even to the level of the single word.

That structure is essential in the works of Thomas has been known for a long time. Ever since Marie-Dominique Chenu presented his famous study of the structure of the *Summa Theologiae* in 1939, the theological meaning of this structure has been debated among scholars.[1] It also was Chenu who in his *Introduction à l'Étude de Saint Thomas d'Aquin* of 1950 mentioned the *divisio textus* as one of the characteristics of scholastic exegesis.[2] Even though more study into the *divisio textus* as a methodical instrument of the medieval masters has often been mentioned as a *desideratum*, only very few studies of it have been published, and there are no studies that take the *divisio textus* as their starting point for studying one of Thomas's biblical commentaries.

This study will analyse the *divisio textus* Thomas makes of the Gospel of John, showing thereby what Thomas sees as the structure of the Gospel and showing how this structure is directing his interpretation both of the Gospel as a whole and of its parts. By doing so, the relevance of the *divisio textus* as a hermeneutical and didactical method for understanding Scripture will be presented. The thesis that will be central to this study is that close consideration of the *divisio textus* is a *conditio sine qua non* for a good understanding of Thomas's commentary on the Gospel of John.

The second sense of wonder that is at the base of this study concerns the strong statement Thomas makes in the prologue to his commentary on John: that while the Gospels of Matthew, Mark and Luke principally speak of the human nature of Christ, John makes known his divinity.[3] This is not an original remark. It goes back to Augustine, who, writing about the sublime nature of the fourth Gospel remarked that John had spoken about the divinity of Christ like none other had.[4] Many medieval commentators take this remark by Augustine as an argument that the Gospel of John is mainly about the divinity of Christ, though not all medieval commentators read John in this way, as we will see.

A remark like this does, however, raise questions: what does it mean for Thomas to say that the fourth Gospel is primarily about the divinity of Christ, even if he does add the nuance that John does not ignore the mysteries of Christ's humanity?[5] Presuming that this is neither just a

---

[1] M.-D. Chenu, 'Le plan de la Somme Théologique de S. Thomas', *Revue Thomiste,* 47 (1939), p. 93-107.

[2] M.-D. Chenu, *Introduction à l'étude de Saint Thomas d'Aquin*, Montréal, Institut d'Études Médiévales, 1984, p. 213-214.

[3] *In Io* Prol., §10.

[4] Augustine, *Tract. in Io* 36,1.

[5] *In Io* Prol., §10.

strong statement nor just an obligatory reverential bow to Augustine, but the lens through which Thomas reads the fourth Gospel, what does he find in this Gospel that speaks to him in a unique way about the divinity of Christ? How does he understand the fourth Evangelist speaking about Christ's divine nature?

The questions about the function of the *divisio textus* in the commentary and about the divinity of Christ as the subject matter of the commentary are related. If the *divisio textus* is as significant as my thesis suggests, it will be a sure guide to understand what the Gospel has to say about the divinity of Christ. *Vice versa*, if the remark in Thomas's prologue that John speaks primarily about the divinity of Christ is more than a reverential bow to Augustine, it is to be expected that the divinity of Christ will be the preeminent matter of the *divisio textus*.

Thomas Aquinas lived nor wrote in a vacuum: no one does. The sources of Thomas's work are especially relevant to his biblical commentaries, which contain so much traditional material. The widespread use of the *Glossa Ordinaria* and the reliance on patristic sources make it understandable why at first sight biblical commentaries that have their origin in the medieval academy seem to be so much alike. In order to get a better idea of what were shared insights among these medieval academic commentators, and what is unique about any single commentary, it is paramount to study more than one commentary. In this thesis, the commentaries on John by Albert the Great and Bonaventure (that are roughly contemporary with Thomas's commentary) are used in comparison with Thomas's commentary (which is usually dated around 1270-1272).[6] It will become clear that Albert, Bonaventure and Thomas have very different *divisiones textus* of the Gospel, and that these different ways of structuring show their different approaches to the Gospel. In other

[6] Robert J. Karris dates the commentary by Bonaventure to ca. 1256: R.J. Karris (ed.), *Commentary on the Gospel of John: Introduction, Translation and Notes by Robert J. Karris,* Works of Bonaventure Vol XI, Saint Bonaventure, Franciscan Institute Publications, 2007, p. 21. There is more debate about the question when Albert wrote his commentary on John: there might have been different versions of the commentary, and the estimations of date of the text we have now differ from 1256-1257 to as late as 1276. For an overview of the discussion about the dating of Albert's commentary on John, cf. J. Casteigt, *Albertus Magnus, "Super Iohannem" (Ioh. 1, 1-18)*, Leuven, Peeters, 2019, p. xxv-lvi. For dating Thomas's commentary, I follow J.-P. Torrell, *Saint Thomas Aquinas: The Person and his Work*, Washington D.C., Catholic University of America Press, 1996, p. 339.

words: the differences in the *divisiones textus* are of hermeneutical importance.

Structure of this book

This thesis is structured into five chapters. Chapter one discusses the *divisio textus* in general. First, an introduction to the *divisio textus* as both a didactical and hermeneutical instrument of medieval exegesis will be given. In a second step, I will study the *divisiones textus* that Albert, Bonaventure and Thomas give of the Gospel of John. It will be shown that the divisions these masters give are quite different from one another and that these differences are significant for their interpretations of the Gospel: the different *divisiones textus* show the different interpretative frameworks within which these three masters read the Gospel of John. The differences between the *divisiones textus* Albert, Bonaventure, and Thomas give of the Fourth Gospel will lead me to the thesis that for Thomas, Jn 1 is the Gospel in a nutshell.

For Thomas, Jn 1 functions as a kind of prospectus for the whole of the Gospel. It is in this chapter that the main subject of the Gospel, the divinity of Christ, is introduced and that the groundwork is laid for further development in the rest of the Gospel. Thomas's *divisio textus* of the Gospel points towards this. For this reason, the next three chapters of my thesis consist of a reading of Thomas's commentary on Jn 1.

In our time Jn 1:1-18, commonly known as 'the prologue' of the Gospel, is often read as a textual unity. Medieval commentaries usually do not see Jn 1:1-18 that way. In fact, none of the three commentators Albert, Bonaventure, and Thomas do. Both for Bonaventure and Albert the main division in the Gospel comes after Jn 1:5, and while it is different in Aquinas, for him too, Jn 1:1-5 is a textual unity that speaks of the divinity of the Word. Therefore, in chapter 2, I will present a reading of Thomas's commentary on Jn 1:1-5.

According to Thomas, Jn 1:6-14 should be read as a textual unity that speaks of the divine Word made flesh. In chapter 3 we will give a reading of Thomas's commentary on these verses, which according to him show different aspects of the incarnation, like the reasons for it, the benefits from it, and the way the Word became incarnate. As will be shown, the *divisio textus* helps understand this part of the commentary and gives insight in how Thomas understands its cohesion.

Thomas reads the Gospel from Jn 2 onwards as relating the effects and actions by which the divinity of the incarnate Word was made known to the world. In chapter 4, I will suggest the commentary on Jn 1:14b-51 should be read as the bridge between what went before and the chapters that will follow. In his *divisio textus* of these verses, Thomas states that the manifestation of the Word happens in two ways: by seeing and by hearing. This might sound innocent enough, but this part of the commentary discusses some fundamental points about how the divinity of the Word incarnate is made known and brings about a knowledge that is salvific.

Chapter 5 shows how what Thomas presented in his commentary on Jn 1 is developed in the commentary on the rest of the Gospel. It does this by studying three things. First, studying the *divisio textus* of Jn 3-11 shows how it directs Thomas's focus on the divinity of Christ in these chapters of the Gospel. Secondly, the many places in the commentary where Thomas, following the Gospel, speaks of the relation of the Son with the Father, show how equality here is used by Thomas as a category to develop what has been said before about the divinity of the Word, and as a way to approach the mystery of God. Finally, Thomas's interpretation of 'glorification' in the commentary on Jn 12-21 will be presented as a helpful way into understanding how Thomas sees the divinity of Christ at work in the chapters of John's Gospel that speak of the suffering, death and resurrection of Christ.

Editions

Finally, a word needs to be said about the text of Thomas's commentary on St. John. The commentary is a *reportatio* made by Reginald of Piperno. In the past, it has been suggested that Thomas reviewed at least part of the text himself, but that seems unlikely.[7] That the text was accepted for publication by the university of Paris is a clear indication that the commentary was regarded as a work by Thomas, and there has never been any doubt about that.

More problematic than the author is the text itself. It has long been known that the text of the Marietti-edition is not reliable.[8] Léon Reid prepared corrections for the Leonina edition, and while his corrections lead to a much more reliable text, they were not a complete text-critical

[7] Cf. J.-P. Torrell, *Saint Thomas Aquinas: The Person and His Work*, Washington, D.C., The Catholic University of America Press, 1996, p. 198-201.

[8] Thomas Aquinas, *Super evangelium S. Ioannis lectura*, edited by R. Cai, fifth revised edition, Roma, Marietti, 1952. The Marietti-edition is based on the *editio princeps* (Venice, 1508), which differs substantially from the manuscripts of the commentary that have survived. Cf. M.-D. Philippe, 'Avertissement', in: Thomas d'Aquin, *Commentaire sur l'Évangile de Saint Jean*, Vol. 1, Préface par M.-D. Philippe, Traduction et notes sous sa direction, Paris, Les Éditions du Cerf, 2002, p. 29.

text that the *Commissio Leonina* could publish in its series.[9] Instead, at the moment, Timothy Bellamah is working on the critical edition of the commentary, to be published by the *Commissio Leonina.* I was lucky to receive a copy of the corrections L. Reid prepared, and T. Bellamah has kindly confirmed to me that Reid's text of the commentary on Jn 1 is reliable.[10] The text prepared by L. Reid is not publicly available, however. I have decided nevertheless to use the text by L. Reid as the text I work from and to consistently mention in footnotes when his text has corrected the widely available Marietti-edition. Whenever that happens, the reader will find the full Latin text suggested by L. Reid in the footnote, followed by the remark "text corrected by L. Reid".

For the text of the commentary on John by Bonaventure, I used the Quaracchi edition, which can be found in volume 6 of the *opera omnia.*[11] For Albert's commentary, there is a recent textcritical edition of the commentary on Jn 1:1-18, but not for the rest of the commentary. I used the textcritical edition by Julie Casteigt for the commentary on the first eighteen verses of the Gospel, and the text made available by A. and E. Borgnet in Albert's *opera omnia* for the rest of the commentary.[12] To clarify references, in the footnotes I will refer to Albert's commentary as *Super Io* when I am referring to Casteigt's edition, and as *In Io* when I am referring to the edition by A. and E. Borgnet.

As for the English translation of Thomas's commentary, I follow the translation made by Fabian Larcher and James Weisheipl, unless otherwise indicated.[13] Biblical quotations in English, when not taken from translations of the commentaries, are from the New Revised Standard Version.

[9] I am grateful to Adriano Oliva, president of the *Commissio Leonina*, for providing me with this information.

[10] I am grateful to Timothy Bellamah for providing information and helping me out with questions I had regarding the text of the commentary.

[11] A. Parma (ed.), S. Bonaventura, *Opera Omnia*, vol. 6, Quaracchi, Collegium S. Bonaventurae, 1893, p. 237-530.

[12] A. Borgnet, E. Borgnet (eds.), Albertus Magnus, *Opera Omnia*, vol. 24: *Enarrationes in Joannem*, Paris, Vivès, 1899

[13] St. Thomas Aquinas, *Commentary on the Gospel of John*, Translated by F. Larcher and J. Weisheipl, with introduction and notes by D. Keating and M. Levering, Washington D.C., Catholic University of America Press, 2010.

CHAPTER 1
THE *DIVISIO TEXTUS*

A reader of Thomas's commentary on John will notice that the further one gets, the more concise Thomas's comments become. The commentary on the first verses is the most detailed part of the work. Not only does Thomas comment on the Gospel verse by verse, in the commentary on the first verses Thomas gives a word for word analysis of the Gospel text. The commentary on Jn 1:1-2 which Thomas reads as four clauses, is rich both in its detailed discussions of patristic commentaries and of heretical readings of these clauses, and in Thomas's own analysis of the text.

However, Thomas does not just give a verse by verse or word by word analysis of the text. In the *divisio textus* Thomas gives his reading of the whole of the text and suggests how the different parts of the text hang together. The *divisio textus* is an underappreciated tool of medieval biblical scholarship. In this chapter, I will introduce this hermeneutical and didactical method in more general terms and then discuss the *divisio* Thomas gives of John's Gospel. I will do this in three steps, beginning with the *divisio* of the whole of the Gospel, then zooming in on the *divisio* of Jn 1, and finally zooming in even further on the *divisio* of Jn 1:1-5. In all three steps, I will compare Thomas's *divisio* with those by Albert and Bonaventure.

After this discussion of the *divisio textus*, I will interpret Thomas's commentary on Jn 1:1-5. I will focus on the theology of the Word that appears from this part of the commentary, and show how for Thomas it is the *nexus mysteriorum* that brings together theological considerations on the Trinity, Christ, creation, revelation and grace. Thomas will develop these considerations further in the rest of the commentary. The commentary on the first five verses of the Gospel is the theological foundation for the commentary, however, and in a nutshell shows what will be developed later on.

1. The *Divisio Textus*: Introduction

When Thomas is studying Paul's letter to the Romans with his students, he comes across a short remark that Paul makes in the context of his discussion of a Christian attitude towards political authorities: *Ea quae sunt, a Deo ordinata sunt* (Rom 13:1). Thomas reads this sentence as a theological remark on the ordering of creation:

> God made all things through his wisdom, according to Ps 103:24: 'He made all things in wisdom'. It belongs to wisdom to dispose all things in a well-ordered way. Ws 8:1: '... and he gently disposes all things'. The divine effects must therefore be ordered: 'Do you know the order of heaven, and do you give its arrangement to the earth?' (Jb 38:33).[1]

This quotation from Thomas's commentary on Romans is an excellent example of a medieval theological way of looking at our world: medieval theologians look at the world for the order in which things are both distinguished from and related to each other by all kinds of arrangements and distinctions.[2] This view includes the world of the Bible, the word of God who "gently disposes all things". When lecturing on biblical books, the medieval *magister* usually starts by giving a division of the text he has in hands, beginning with the larger structure of the text and proceeding to ever smaller parts, generally up to the level of the single verse, sometimes upon the level of single words within a verse. This procedure's origin is said to lie in the faculty of arts, where it was used before it was adopted in the faculty of theology. This adoption had started already in the twelfth century, mainly in the commentaries on the Psalms. By the second half of the thirteenth century, it was used to study all kinds of texts, including the works of Aristotle, the *Sentences* of Peter Lombard, and the books of Holy Scripture.[3]

---

[1] "Secundo ponit, quod 'ea quae sunt, a Deo ordinata sunt', cuius ratio est quia Deus omnia per suam sapientiam fecit, secundum illud Ps 103:24: 'Omnia in sapientia fecisti'. Est autem proprium sapientiae ordinate omnia disponere. Sap 8:1: 'Attingit a fine usque ad finem fortiter, et disponit omnia suaviter'. Et ideo oportet effectus divinos ordinatos esse. Iob 38:33: 'Numquid nosti ordinem caeli, et pones rationem eius in terra?'" *In Rom* 13:1 §1024.

[2] It has often been suggested that the medieval theological search for order was a reaction to a world full of social and political instability. An example of this view can be found in G. Ward, *How the Light Gets in: Ethical Life I*, Oxford, Oxford University Press, 2016, p. 35-39.

[3] That the *divisio textus* finds its origin in the faculty of arts is usually concluded from Roger Bacon who, writing on the seven sins of theology, remarks: "Quae fiunt in textu, principaliter legendo et praedicando, sunt tria principaliter, scilicet divisiones

Margherita Maria Rossi has identified three phases in each *divisio*. First, the text is divided into smaller parts; secondly, each part is defined; thirdly the parts are reconnected to provide a unified reading of the text.[4] The *divisio textus* is a hermeneutical and didactical method directed at understanding the text in its unity and parts.

First of all, it is a hermeneutical method: the naming of a central theme in the prologue and the division of the text in more or less small parts related to the central theme of the text helps to understand the text as a unity. Secondly, the *divisio textus* helps to see what the heart of the text is. When Thomas lectures on the story of the Samaritan woman at the well he describes this part of John as about "how the grace of Christ is given to the gentiles through teaching".[5] He then goes on to describe John 4:1-9 as the preliminaries for the teaching, v. 10 as the summary of the instruction, v. 11-26 as the unfolding in parts of the instruction, and v. 27-42 as the effects of the teaching.[6] Thus it is clear that for Thomas, an understanding of John 4:1-42 must focus on v. 10 as the heart of the story.

A *divisio textus* not only points to the heart of a text, but it also weighs different parts of the text in relation to one another. John Boyle has pointed to an example of this in Thomas's commentary on John 2: according to Thomas, this chapter shows the divinity of Christ in relation to the power he had over nature. Christ's divine power over nature may be obvious in the miracle of the water turned into wine. But it is not so evident in the cleansing of the temple in the second half of Jn 2. Thomas interprets the temple's cleansing in the light of the subsequent discussion

---

per membra varia, sicut artistae fiunt, concordantiae violentes, sicut legistae utuntur, et consonantiae rythmicae, sicut grammatici. Et istis tribus stat praecipuus modus artificum exponendi Scripturam. Et haec licet utilia sint, tamen tracta sunt de philosophia". J.S. Brewer (ed.), *Fr. Rogeri Baconis opera quaedam hactenus inedita,* London, Longman, Green, Longman and Roberts, 1859, p. 322-323. For the history of the *divisio textus*, cf. M.-D. Chenu, *Introduction à l'étude de Saint Thomas d'Aquin*, Montréal, Institut d'Études Médiévales, 1984, p. 213-214; G. Dahan, *L'Exégèse chrétienne de la Bible en occident médiéval - XIIe-XIVe siècle*, Paris, Les Éditions du Cerf, 1999, p. 271-272; A. Even-Ezra, 'Visualizing Narrative Structure in the Medieval University: *Divisio Textus* Revisited, in: *Traditio* 72 (2017), p. 341-376, here p. 4342-346. For a study which argues for the importance of the *divisio textus* in Thomas's commentaries on the works of Aristotle, cf. L. Gili, 'Thomas Aquinas's Commentary on Aristotle's *Metaphysics*: Prolegomena to the Study of the Text', in: *Divus Thomas* 118 (2015), p. 185-217.

[4] M.M. Rossi, 'La "divisio textus" nei commenti scritturistici di S. Tommaso d'Aquino: Un procedimento solo esegetico?', *Angelicum* 71 (1994), p. 540-541.

[5] *In Io* 4:1 §549.

[6] *In Io* 4:1 §549 and *In Io* 4:10 §575.

about the destruction of the temple and its rebuilding in three days. This discussion speaks of Christ's resurrection, Thomas argues, which is a sign of Christ's dominion over nature. Thomas understands the cleansing of the temple as the occasion at which this discussion on the resurrection takes place. Thus, not only is Thomas's characterisation of John 2 fitting for the whole of the chapter, but it also clarifies that the story of the cleansing of the temple points to the discussion on the resurrection.[7] That this structure of the text is not the only possibility can easily be seen when one compares it to Bonaventure's *divisio*. For him, John 1:43-4:54 must be read as Christ's manifestation to his disciples, the Jews, the Samaritans and the Galileans respectively. John 2:12-3:36 tells the story about the manifestation to the Jews *per signum* (2:12-25), *per verbum* (3:1-21), and *per sacramentum* (3:22-36). Bonaventure reads the first part as a twofold sign: a sign of authority (2:12-17) and a sign of power (2:18-25). Thus the story of the cleansing of the temple and the discussion on the resurrection are put on a par structurally, whereas Thomas subordinates the first to the second. Thus, the *divisio textus* shows how different parts of the text are related to each other. Instead of scattering the small parts of the text, it gives each verse its proper place in relation to the other verses.

The *divisio textus* also is a didactical method, in three ways.[8] First of all, its abstract logical form of proceeding helps the student grasp the text being studied: the text's coherence is clarified. This logical way of dividing the material to be studied can be seen in many medieval theological texts, not only in biblical commentaries: the way Thomas structures the biblical text is comparable to the way he structures the *Scriptum* or the *Summa Theologiae*.[9] Secondly, it is a method that teaches itself: by the use the *magister* makes of it, the student sees a way of closely reading a text that helps his own independent studies. Thirdly, it helps to remember the text studied: Rossi calls it "a mental blackboard".[10]

---

[7] *In Io* 2:1 §355, *In Io* 2:12 §366, and *In Io* 2:18 §393. Cf. J.F. Boyle, 'The Theological Character of the Scholastic "Division of the Text" with Particular Reference to the Commentaries of Saint Thomas Aquinas', in: J. Dammen McAuliffe, B.D. Walfish, J.W. Goering (eds.), *With Reverence for the Word: Medieval Scriptural Exegesis in Judaism, Christianity, and Islam*, Oxford, Oxford University Press, 2010, p. 276-83, here p. 279.

[8] M.M. Rossi, *Teoria e metodo esegetici in S. Tommaso d'Aquino: Analisi del super epistolas Sancti Pauli lectura ad Romanos, C. I, L. 6*, Roma, Pontificia Studiorum Universitas a S. Thomas Aq. in Urbem, 1992, p. 157-158.

[9] W.G.B.M. Valkenberg, *Words of the Living God: Place and Function of Holy Scripture in the Theology of St. Thomas Aquinas,* Leuven, Peeters, 2000, p. 167.

[10] "... come una sorte di lavagna mentale". M.M. Rossi, *Teoria e metodo esegetici*, p. 158.

In his book, *Thomas Aquinas as Reader of the Psalms* Thomas Ryan gives an elaborate plea for understanding the *divisio textus* as a mnemonic device.[11] He sketches the importance of memory in the medieval Church: the Dominicans were well known for their stress on *memoria*, both Albert and Thomas wrote on it,[12] it played an important role in preaching, the heart of the *raison d'être* of the Dominican order. Memory had always played an important role in prayer life, and especially the memory of the psalms. Already as a Benedictine oblate at the monastery of Monte Cassino, Thomas certainly would have learned the psalms by heart. Ryan gives two reasons for understanding the *divisio textus* as a mnemonic device. First, he stresses the resemblance to the mnemonic method that Hugh of St. Victor presents as an example in the prologue to his *De tribus maximis circumstantiis gestorum*. The procedure starts with memorising the numbers of the psalms with their first words so that each psalm number evokes the first words and vice versa. Then within a psalm, the first words of each verse are remembered in the same way. In a third step, the complete texts are memorised. This structure can be recognised in Thomas's commentary on the psalms, especially in the *divisio* at the beginning of psalm 2. Next to this resemblance, three other features show the mnemonic intentions of the *divisio* according to Ryan: the giving of themes for the psalms instead of only the numbers, as Hugh had done; secondly, the repetition of phrases such as "Above the Psalmist shows that ...; here, however...;" and finally, the simple use of only the terms *ad litteram* and *mystice* instead of the many other words Thomas has for distinguishing the different levels of Scripture, like *allegorice*, *moraliter*, and *anagogice*.

According to Ryan, scholars have underestimated the importance of memory in understanding the meaning of the *divisio textus*.[13] However, in his wish to equalise this lack of balance, Ryan overstates his case, as becomes clear from the arguments he gives. First, the division in the commentary on the psalms only partly resembles Hugh of St. Victor's mnemonic method. When one looks at the division at the beginning of psalm 2, the prime example Ryan gives, it becomes clear that numbers and first words indeed are given, but that it is the thematic ordering that comes in first place. That is why Thomas does not present the psalms in

---

[11] T.F. Ryan, *Thomas Aquinas as Reader of the Psalms*, Notre Dame, University of Notre Dame Press, 2000, p. 29-38.

[12] Thomas wrote a commentary on Aristotle's *De memoria et reminiscentia* as the second treatise in his *Sentencia Libri de sensu et sensato*.

[13] T. Ryan, *Thomas Aquinas as Reader of the Psalms*, 30-31.

the numerical order, but according to his thematic arrangement. In this thematic ordering, Ps 2 is firstly distinguished from Ps 8-10, then from Ps 7, next from Ps 5-6 and finally from Ps 3-4.[14] The division thus has a centripetal direction, as Rossi has called it.[15] Had Thomas given this division mainly for mnemonic reasons, he probably would have named the psalms in their numerical order, as Hugh does. Thus the hermeneutical division of the text undermines rather than strengthens Hugh's method. As for the repetition of words, Rossi gives a terminology of the *divisio textus*.[16] This terminology makes a division easily recognisable, and it helps memory as well. But the sheer existence of a terminology for the *divisio* does not prove its first meaning to be a mnemonic device. Finally, as for the reduction of all the layers of Scripture to only two senses, the literal and the mystical, there is an important theological reason why Thomas only gives a distinction in two parts for the senses of Scripture. This reason has to do with the twofold way that according to Thomas, God speaks to us in Holy Scripture: God speaks through words (the literal sense) and through things and events (the spiritual sense). Finally, it is important not to look at the commentary's *divisio textus* on the psalms apart from the divisions used by Thomas in his other commentaries. The division in the commentary on John, for example, is that complicated (sometimes there is a division of more than 20 levels deep!) that it is hard to believe that it would mainly function as a mnemonic device. It suffices to conclude that the aid to memory that a structure of the text such as the *divisio textus* gives, is one of the didactical reasons why it was this widely used in scholastic commentaries, albeit not the primary one.

It is useful to stress that not all *divisiones textus* carry the same theological weight. A commentator might give a purely formal *divisio* at the beginning of his commentary. This kind of *divisio* often is of a "disarming simplicity",[17] like the *divisio* one can find at the beginning of many commentaries that states: "This book has two parts, the title and the treatise".[18] In Thomas's works, one sees these formal divisions at the beginning of the commentary on almost each of the Pauline letters, where Thomas divides the greetings from the treatise.[19] Another kind of more

---

[14] *In Ps* 2:1.

[15] M.M. Rossi, *Teoria e metodo esegetici*, p. 150-151.

[16] Ibid., 150-151.

[17] "... d'une simplicité désarmante". G. Dahan, *L'exégèse chrétienne de la Bible en occident médiéval*, p. 273.

[18] Examples in ibid., 273-274.

[19] There are two exceptions. First, the commentary on Ephesians, where Thomas uses a more extended formal division: he divides this letter into greetings, narrative,

formal division can be found within the chapters of the commentary. Thomas often uses divisions in which he distinguishes the occasion for something (a miracle or teaching) from the thing itself, or in which he distinguishes the thing from its effect.[20] A third type of formal *divisio textus* is the narrative division. These are divisions that have what we might call a semiotic view of the text. In Thomas's commentary on John, one finds examples of this, such as divisions according to the *dramatis personae* or the place of the story.[21]

Many *divisiones textus* carry a lot more theological weight: they state the text's theological theme as seen by the commentator and are often put in the commentator's own words. An example from the commentaries by Albert and Bonaventure is the *divisio* they make between Jn 1:1-5, which according to both speaks of the divine Word *in se*, and the rest of the Gospel, which speaks of the Word incarnate.[22] An example from Thomas's commentary on John would be the *divisio* in which he states that Jn 2 shows the divinity of Christ in relation to the power Christ had over nature, while Jn 3-11 shows the divinity of Christ in relation to the effects of grace.[23] It is to these theological divisions that the attention primarily must go: these *divisiones* are the place where the voice of the *magister* can most clearly be heard.

Whose structure?

There is a final question to be posed about the *divisio textus*. Whose structure is the *magister* showing to his students? Is it the structure that

---

exhortation and conclusion. *In Eph* 1:1 §3. Secondly, the letter to the Hebrews, which does not begin with greetings. Thomas divides this letter into two parts. The first part is about the excellence of Christ, the second (beginning in Hebr 11:1) is about faith: *In Hebr* 1:1 §6.

[20] For the first, the words *praeambula* and *occasio* are signals, such as in *In Io* 4:1 §549 or *In Io* 5:1 §699; for the second, Thomas often uses the words *effectus* and *fructus*, e.g. in *In Io* 6:1 §838 or *In Io* 1:1 §1471.

[21] An example of a *divisio* according to the *dramatis personae* is the *divisio* of Jn 18, which according to Thomas tells how Christ was betrayed by a disciple (v. 1-18), brought before the high priests (v. 19-27) and accused before Pilate (v. 28-40): *In Io* 18:1 §2271. *Divisiones textus* according to a place can be found often when the Gospel speaks about Jesus travelling from one place to another, e.g. in Jn 4:1-5. Cf. *In Io* 4:1 §549. These semiotic *divisiones textus* are common in other medieval commentators as well. Cf. the way Bonaventure structures John 1:43-4:54 according to the four groups Christ gives testimony to: Disciples, Jews, Samaritans and Galileans. Bonaventure, *In Io* 1:43 n. 89. Cf. also Albert's *divisio* according to the different groups Christ is instructing in Jn 12: Albert, *In Io* 12:1 p. 467.

[22] Albert, *Super Io* 1:1 p. 12. Bonaventure, *In Io* 1:1 n. 1.

[23] *In Io* 2:1 §335.

the biblical author has used for his text, and that the *magister* tries to find? Or is it the *magister* himself who structures the text, dependent on the situation of the commentary? In other words: is there one definitive *divisio textus* of John that all the medieval masters were looking for, or is there an infinitive number of ways to structure the fourth Gospel, dependent on the *magister*? Commentators of Thomas have stressed either possibility.[24]

The *divisio textus* is a didactical method used by the *magister* to structure his lessons, and this didactical method can be used with considerable freedom. Thomas's commentary on Job is helpful because it is the only biblical commentary where Thomas does not use an elaborate division of the text. Instead, he explains the critical verses one by one. The reason for this striking absence of the *divisio textus* in Job might well be the audience for whom the lectures on Job were given. Whereas Thomas wrote all his other biblical commentaries either at the universities of Cologne and Paris or at the theological *studium generale* that he organised in Naples, the commentary on Job was written during Thomas's period as conventual lector in Orvieto.[25] A conventual lector's task was to give regular teaching to what later would be called the *fratres communes*, the friars that had not been able to study in the *studia provincialia* or *generalia*.[26] On the subject of the biblical education in the

[24] Authors who stress that the *divisio* emerges from the biblical text include C.C. Black II, 'St. Thomas's Commentary on the Johannine Prologue: Some Reflections on Its Character and Implications', *The Catholic Biblical Quarterly* 48 (1986), p. 681-98, here p. 683-684; M. Yaffe, 'Interpretive Essay' in: A. Damico, M.D. Yaffe, *Thomas Aquinas: The Literal Exposition on Job, A Scriptural Commentary Concerning Providence*, Scholars Press, 1989, p. 12; R. Ferri, *Gesù e la verità: Agostino e Tommaso interpreti del vangelo di Giovanni*, Roma, Città Nuova, 2007. On the other hand, G. Dahan, *L'exégèse chrétienne de la Bible en occident médiéval,* p. 273; and C.T. Baglow, *"Modus et Forma": A New Approach to the Exegesis of Saint Thomas Aquinas with an Application to the Lectura Super Epistolam ad Ephesios*, Roma, Editrice Pontificio Istituto Biblico, 2002, p. 68 look at it as a didactical means that can change with the situation.

M. Yaffe uses the metaphor of the *divisio* as a Gothic cathedral and then remarks that "the design is no ordinary product of art, but is dictated by that of the Book of Job itself, as Thomas reads it". A. Damico, M. Yaffe, *Thomas Aquinas: The Literal Exposition on Job*, p. 12. I interpret this remark as saying that the *divisio* emerges from the biblical text itself, not from the commentator, contrary to Baglow, who does quote Yaffe's remark but then goes on to picture Thomas as the prime designer. Cf. C. Baglow, *"Modus et Forma",* p. 68.

[25] J.-P. Torrell, *Saint Thomas Aquinas: The Person and His Work*, Washington, D.C., The Catholic University of America Press, 1996, p. 120-121.

[26] Ibid., 118-119. For a description of the Dominican conventual education in the thirteenth and fourteenth century, cf. M.M. Mulchahey, *"First the Bow Is Bent in*

Dominican convents, M.M. Mulchahey cites a text of Humbert of Romans, who was master of the Dominican order from 1254 to 1263. In this text, written around the time when Thomas lectured on Job, Humbert instructed the conventual lectors to comment on Scripture "in a much simpler and more straightforward manner than they would in advanced *studia*".[27] The lecturer should refrain from too many divisions and subdivisions or from giving an overabundance of arguments for his position.[28] Depending on the audience and purpose, the method of *divisio textus* could thus be used in more or less elaborate ways, and it even was possible to abstain from it altogether, according to the master's estimation. This seems to be what Thomas did when he lectured on Job in Orvieto.

There are more reasons to see the *divisio textus* as a merely didactical means for the medieval master. G. Dahan describes it as a hermeneutical orientation for the lesson that will follow.[29] In an earlier article on the medieval exegesis of the story of Cain and Abel, Dahan compared the *divisiones* of the first chapters of Genesis of six different masters. They show apparent similarities, but they are never the same: each commentator has made his own *divisio*. Apart from the differences regarding content, there are differences regarding the use of the *divisio*. Whereas William of Alton and Nicholas of Gorran have very detailed *divisiones* up to the level of the verse, Petrus Olivi only gives one division at the beginning of the chapter, never to return to it later on. The other three authors examined by Dahan (Nicholas of Lyra, Thomas Waleys and Dominic Grima) are somewhere in between these extremes.[30] When one looks at *divisiones textus* from different masters on the same biblical text, the differences catch the eye more than the similarities.[31] What is more, not only are there significant differences in dividing the text between the

---

Study": Dominican Education before 1350, Toronto, Pontifical Institute of Mediaeval Studies, 1998, p. 130-218.

27 M. Mulchahey, *"First the Bow Is Bent in Study"*, p. 138.

28 "Cavendum est etiam ei a nimis divisionibus, et rationibus reddendis de sufficientia et numero", Humbert of Romans, *Instructionis de officiis ordinis*, 138.

29 "De la sorte, la *divisio textus* donne d'emblée l'orientation herméneutique de la leçon". G. Dahan, *L'exégèse chrétienne de la Bible en occident médiéval,* p. 273.

30 G. Dahan, 'L'exégèse de l'histoire de Caïn et Abel du XIIe au XIVe siècle en occident I: Notes et textes', *Recherches de théologie ancienne et médiévale* 49 (1982), p. 21-89, here p. 56-58; G. Dahan, 'L'exégèse de l'histoire de Caïn et Abel du XIIe au XIVe siècle en occident II', *Recherches de théologie ancienne et médiévale* 50 (1983), p. 5-68.

31 M.M. Rossi comes to the same conclusion: M.M. Rossi, *Teoria e metodo esegetici*, p. 159-161.

commentators, there are hardly any traces of discussions about the *divisio*.[32] Especially in a world so profoundly formed by debate as the medieval theological world was, one would have expected fierce debates on the right *divisio textus* if it would have been understood to be an approximation of the structure the biblical author had in mind.

What does seem unlikely is another thesis that states that the use of a *divisio textus* is dependent on the genre of the biblical text under commentary. J. Boyle has argued that in the case of Job, Thomas uses the movement of the arguments in the narrative and therefore does not need a *divisio*. He fails to take into consideration not only the historical circumstances of the commentary on Job but also the fact that when commenting on other texts where the give and take of an argument could function as structure, Thomas nevertheless uses a detailed *divisio textus*, as for example through the whole of the commentary on the *corpus Paulinum*.[33] A second argument in this sense, that "perhaps the scholastic division is not particularly useful in articulating the give and take of a narrative argument", strands on the observation that Thomas does use the *divisio textus* in the commentary on the narrative parts in John.[34]

All this suggests that the *divisio textus* is mainly a didactical method freely used by a medieval master to structure his lectures. It is not just that, however. It is, after all, a *divisio textus*, a division of the text. That text is the text of Scripture. The *divisio* forces the commentator to follow the text word for word. Therefore, it is an important progress to various types of paraphrase, which "could bend the text to any purpose whatever".[35] The biblical text is, therefore, the most important factor in making the division. That is why several modern commentators have suggested that "the genius of the commentaries is often in the division of

---

[32] In the biblical commentaries of Thomas Aquinas, there are two exceptions that I know of. First, there is the discussion about the structure of the book of Psalms: should it be read as having two parts (70 and 80 psalms), as having five parts of different length, each ending with "Amen, amen", or as three groups of fifty psalms? Cf. *In Ps* proe. Secondly, there is the commentary on John 1:3-4a where Thomas chooses not to subdivide the three *clausulae* that he sees there. I will come back to this text later.

[33] J.F. Boyle, 'St. Thomas Aquinas and Sacred Scripture', *Pro Ecclesia* 4 (1995), p. 92-104.

[34] J.F. Boyle, 'The Theological Character of the Scholastic "Division of the Text"', p. 281.

[35] O.H. Pesch, 'Exegese des Alten Testaments bei Thomas', in: *Die Deutsche Thomas Ausgabe, Summa Theologica*, Band 13; Heidelberg, Gemeinschaftsverlag, 1977, p. 590.

the text".[36] In her identification of the *divisio* in three steps, Rossi states that the most important phases are the second, in which each part is named, and the third, in which the relation of each part to a greater whole is expressed.[37] This unity is not based on the textual unity of the text, nor on the human author of it, but solely on the divine author. In his commentary on John 14:26 Thomas writes: "How could John the evangelist after forty years have remembered all the sayings of Christ he wrote in his Gospel unless the Holy Spirit had brought them to his mind?"[38] The unity of the divine authorship is not only crucial for understanding a biblical book as a whole but as a consequence, it asks for an understanding of the whole of Scripture as a unity.[39] Therefore, the conclusion must be that a *divisio textus* is both: it is, first of all, a hermeneutical instrument, a first interpretation of how in the biblical text things hang together. As M.M. Rossi wrote: "So, though necessarily an exercise of hermeneutics, the *divisio* never forced any content into the Bible nor did it impose an extrinsic dialectics on it, but rather tried to mirror it, and to let it emerge in a clearer way in all its riches".[40] Secondly, it also is a didactical method that the master can use with a certain freedom. Anton ten Klooster put it well when he wrote: "A *divisio textus* was a tool in a search for meaning, structuring the human effort to recognize the divine order of the Bible".[41]

Given its hermeneutical importance, it is surprising to notice how little research has been done on the division of the text in medieval biblical commentaries: there is no monograph on this subject. It is often named as

---

[36] J.F. Boyle, 'St. Thomas Aquinas and Sacred Scripture', p. 99. Cf. M.M. Rossi, *Teoria e metodo esegetici,* p. 161.

[37] M.M. Rossi, 'La "divisio textus" nei commenti scritturistici di S. Tommaso d'Aquino', p. 540-541.

[38] "Quomodo enim Evangelista Ioannes post quadraginta annos potuisset omnium verborum Christi, quae in Evangelio scripsit, habere memoriam, nisi ei Spiritus Sanctus suggessisset?" *In Io* 14:26 §1960.

[39] This idea of Scripture as a unity makes it possible for Thomas to state the usefulness of the whole of Scripture in a single sentence: "Ponitur et huius utilitas, quia effectus fidei, quia 'haec scripta sunt ut credatis quia Iesus Christus est Filius Dei, et ut credentes vitam habeatis in nomine eius'. Ad hoc enim est tota Scriptura Novi et Veteris Testamenti". *In Io* 20:31 §2568.

[40] M.M. Rossi, 'Mind-Space: Towards an 'Environ-Mental Method' in the Exegesis of the Middle Ages', in: P. Roszak, J. Vijgen (eds.), *Reading Sacred Scripture with Thomas Aquinas: Hermeneutical Tools, Theological Questions and New Perspectives*, Turnhout, Brepols, 2015, p. 171-198, here p. 176.

[41] A.M. ten Klooster, *Thomas Aquinas on the Beatitudes: Reading Matthew, Disputing Grace and Virtue, Preaching Happiness*, Leuven, Peeters, 2018, p. 27.

something that should be studied more, but more often than not, scholars of medieval biblical commentaries have left it at that.[42] In Thomas's case, it is all the more surprising that so little attention has been paid to the division of the text. Ever since M.-D. Chenu wrote his article '*Le plan de la Somme Théologique de saint Thomas*' in 1939, the debate about the structure of the *Summa Theologiae*, about whether or not Thomas follows a neo-platonic scheme of *exitus-reditus* and about the place of the Christology in the *Tertia pars* has been a heated debate that continues to this day.[43] That debate is important indeed, for it is clear that Thomas has structured his *Summa Theologiae* very carefully, and a good understanding of this structure is both "door and key to the theology of Thomas".[44] Apart from the discussion about the overarching plan of the *Summa Theologiae*, there have been many discussions about how different parts of the *Summa* are to be understood in relation to each other and to the wider context within the *Summa*. Examples of these would have to include the understanding of the so-called treatises *De Deo Uno* and *De Deo Trino*,[45] Thomas's teaching on human happiness, *beatitudo*,[46]

---

[42] Notable exceptions are G. Dahan, who devotes a section of his general study on medieval exegesis to the subject, J.F. Boyle, who has written several articles on the *divisio textus*, and especially M.M. Rossi who, both in her doctoral dissertation and in a later article, pays careful attention to the *divisio textus*: G. Dahan, *L'exégèse chrétienne de la Bible en occident médiéval,* p. 271-275; J.F. Boyle, 'Authorial Intention and the *Divisio Textus*', in: M. Dauphinais, M. Levering (eds.), *Reading John with St. Thomas Aquinas: Theological Exegesis and Speculative Theology*, Washington D.C., Catholic University of America Press, 2005, p. 3-8; J.F. Boyle, 'The Theological Character of the Scholastic "Division of the Text"'; M.M. Rossi, *Teoria e metodo esegetici;* M.M. Rossi, 'La "divisio textus" nei commenti scritturistici'.

[43] M.-D. Chenu, 'Le plan de la Somme Théologique de S. Thomas', *Revue Thomiste,* 47 (1939), 93-107. For an overview of the literature on this discussion cf. J.-P. Torrell, *Saint Thomas Aquinas: The Person and His Work*, p. 150-153 and B.V. Johnstone, 'The Debate on the Structure of the Summa Theologiae of St. Thomas Aquinas: From Chenu (1939) to Metz (1998)', in: P. van Geest, H. Goris, C. Leget (eds.), *Aquinas as Authority*, Leuven, Peeters, 2000, p. 187-200. For two recent contributions cf. R. Te Velde, *Aquinas on God: The 'Divine Science' of the Summa Theologiae,* Aldershot, Ashgate Publishing, 2006, p. 9-35, and M.D. Jordan, 'Structure', in: P. McCosker, D. Turner (eds.), *The Cambridge Companion to the Summa Theologiae*, Cambridge, Cambridge University Press, 2016, p. 34-47.

[44] The characterisation "Tür und Schlüssel zur Theologie des Thomas" is from O. H. Pesch, *Thomas Von Aquin: Grenze und Grösse mittelalterlicher Theologie, Eine Einführung*, Mainz, Matthias Grünewald Verlag, 1989, p. 394.

[45] H.W.M. Rikhof, 'Aquinas' Authority in the Contemporary Theology of the Trinity', in: P. van Geest e.a. (eds.), *Aquinas as Authority*, p. 213-34, here p. 216-219.

[46] S. Gradl, *Deus Beatitudo Hominis: Eine Evangelische Annäherung an die Glückslehre des Thomas von Aquin*, Leuven, Peeters, 2004, p. 57-158.

and the relation of the theology of the hypostatic union in IIIa, q. 1-26 to the thirty-three questions on the mysteries of Christ's life that follow it.[47]

Compared to these discussions about structure in the *Summa Theologiae*, the absence of discussions about the structure of the biblical commentaries is remarkable. Both in the *Summa Theologiae* and the commentary it is Thomas who provides the structure of the text. Since the debate about the structure of the *Summa Theologiae* has shown how carefully Thomas has structured that book and how vital an understanding of its structure is for its interpretation, there is every reason to pay just as much careful attention to the *divisio textus* of the commentary.

One might even go one step further. For while the *divisio textus* a medieval master gives of a biblical book is his and might differ significantly from one commentator to the next (as we will see later on in this chapter when we compare the *divisiones* Albert, Bonaventure and Thomas give of the Fourth Gospel), the structure Thomas gives is the structure he thinks the inspired biblical author has given to his text.

In 1974 Otto Hermann Pesch expressed his surprise that Thomas, giving his division of the whole of the *corpus Paulinum*, reads the fourteen letters of Paul together as a systematic treatise on grace, as if St. Paul had written a dogmatical monograph about the grace of Christ in the form of fourteen letters.[48] In the commentary on John as well, Thomas's *divisiones textus* usually start with phrases like "Before the Evangelist did a, here he starts to do b".[49] One does find these phrases in Albert and Bonaventure as well, but not as systematical as in Thomas. Albert usually starts with more modest phrases like "Here begins the part which deals with..."[50] In Bonaventure one finds a mixture of the two. I am not convinced that these differences in terminology are strong enough to suggest that Albert, Bonaventure and Thomas have a different understanding of what they are doing when using a *divisio textus*. However, the terminology Thomas uses indicates that the *divisio textus* Thomas gives is not just a structure that might be made for any practical or didactical reason, but that it is the structure of what Thomas thinks John is doing in his Gospel. The *divisio textus* is Thomas's reconstruction of the structure the inspired author has given to his text. Because it is a reconstruction of the structure John has given to his Gospel, one would expect Thomas to be more rather than less interested in how different

---

[47] J.-P. Torrell, *Le Christ en ses mystères: La vie et l'oeuvre de Jésus selon Saint Thomas d'Aquin*, vol.1, Paris, Desclée, 1999, p. 13-20.

[48] O.H. Pesch, 'Paul as Professor of Theology: The Image of the Apostle in St. Thomas's Theology', *The Thomist* (1974), p. 584-605.

[49] E.g. *In Io* 1:1 §23; *In Io* 1:3 §68; *In Io* 1:6 §108 *et passim*.

[50] "Hic incipit pars qua est de...", Albert, *In Io* 2:1 p. 87 *et passim*.

parts of the text relate to each other and to the text as a whole and to how each part is to be named and characterised, as compared to a division he makes for a text of his own making such as the *Summa Theologiae*.

Moreover, since in Thomas's time it was relatively new to use the method of the *divisio textus* in biblical commentaries, and there were therefore hardly any authoritative *divisiones* to fall back on, the *divisio textus* is an excellent place to see a master's hermeneutical and didactical approach to Holy Scripture.

This newness of the *divisio* as a method of reading Scripture might explain why there are no traces of discussions among medieval theologians about which divisions are better. J. Boyle gives another possible explanation. He notes how "Medieval interpreters of scripture are strikingly comfortable with different literal interpretations of a given passage; so too they seem quite comfortable with differing divisions". He goes on to suggest: "This is so perhaps because such divisions were not understood as definitive but rather as illuminative. The division of the text provides insight into a text presumed to be rich, mysterious, multivalent, and ultimately inexhaustible".[51]

In contemporary research, thematic studies of Thomas's biblical commentaries tend to focus on individual passages in a particular commentary in which Thomas discusses the chosen topic. The danger of reading Thomas's biblical commentaries in this way is that thematic passages are taken out of their context in the commentary, rearranged in a way more conducive to a systematic theological approach and discussed as if they form a coherent theological treatise that unfortunately has been shattered randomly throughout the commentary. When that happens, something essential is disregarded: the genre of the text as biblical commentary.[52]

J. Boyle suggests that a lack of appreciation for the *divisio textus* might be a reason why some of those who study scholastic theology are disappointed in the biblical commentaries: "they seem limp or thin or simply pedestrian". Boyle gives the example of a theologian who wants

---

[51] J.F. Boyle, 'The Theological Character of the Scholastic "Division of the Text"', p. 279.

[52] An admirable exception is M. Hammele, *Das Bild der Juden im Johannes-Kommentar des Thomas von Aquin: Ein Beitrag zu Bibelhermeneutik und Wissenschaftsgeschichte im 13. Jahrhundert,* Stuttgarter Biblische Beiträge 71, Stuttgart, Verlag Katholisches Bibelwerk, 2012. Hammele is consistently precise in locating the fragments of the commentary he discusses in their proper context by following Aquinas's *divisio textus*.

to study Thomas on the Eucharist and decides to read Thomas's commentary on the bread of life discourse in Jn 6, only to find a commentary that is "relatively short, moving quickly from phrase to phrase". Boyle writes: "The problem is in looking simply to the commentary on specific verses. The genius of the scholastic division of the text is that every lemma has a context, or better, a set of nested contexts. It never stands alone. The comments presume all that has come before, and indeed, what comes after. The skilled commentator need not say as much at the particular lemma, because he has already said so much getting there". With regard to Jn 6, Boyle explains what the *divisio textus* has to offer a reader of this chapter in Thomas's commentary: "An appreciation of Thomas's interpretation requires minimally that one appreciate that this chapter is in the context of spiritual food as a spiritual benefit conferred on those divinely regenerated, which in turn is part of Christ's manifestation of his divinity through those things he did while living in the world".[53]

To conclude: the *divisio textus* is both a didactical and a hermeneutical instrument of the biblical commentator. It is a didactical method that the commentator uses to structure his lessons, and that he, depending on the situation, can use with more or less detail. As such, it helps the student to get a grip on the text.

It is a hermeneutical instrument because it helps to understand the text as a unity and weigh different parts of the text to one another. The language Thomas uses in his *divisiones textus* both of the *corpus Paulinum* and of the Gospel of John shows that he understands these biblical books as carefully constructed texts. In the *divisio textus*, Thomas reconstructs what he sees as the structure the divinely inspired author has given to his text. For that reason, and even more so than in works like the *Summa Theologiae* in which Thomas is himself the one who structures the text, a close consideration of the *divisio textus* is a *conditio sine qua non* for a good understanding of the commentary.[54]

In what follows, I will compare Thomas's *divisio textus* of the fourth Gospel to those of Albert and Bonaventure, and thereby show the

---

[53] J.F. Boyle, 'The Theological Character of the Scholastic "Division of the Text"', p. 278.

[54] T. Reist makes a similar remark about the commentaries of Bonaventure: "It is precisely the structure of Bonaventure's writings which is at times difficult to appreciate. Nevertheless a grasp of the structure is absolutely essential to the understanding of his method and thought". T. Reist, *Saint Bonaventure as a Biblical Commentator: A Translation and Analysis of His Commentary on Luke, XVIII, 34-XIX, 42*, Lanham, University Press of America, 1985, p. 141.

differences between these commentaries. For these reasons, in this study, I will closely follow the order of the commentary.

2. The *Divisio Textus* of the Gospel of John

The technique of the *divisio textus* is relatively new in the time of Thomas, Albert and Bonaventure. There is no tradition for it, no authorities to refer to. That may be a reason why in these medieval masters, one will not find two identical *divisiones* of a book of Scripture.[55] Each master has to make his own division. When a patristic source has made a remark about structure, the master might use this, but it is his vision on the whole and the parts of the text that determines the *divisio* that he will use. In the words of Rossi: "It is the final hermeneutical hand of the master".[56]

<table>
<tr><td>1:1-5</td><td colspan="4">De proprietatibus Verbi increati in se</td></tr>
<tr><td rowspan="12">1:6-21:25</td><td colspan="4">De proprietatibus Verbi in creaturam rationalem ad sanctificandum eam procedentis</td></tr>
<tr><td>1:6-51</td><td colspan="3">Testimonium per alium</td></tr>
<tr><td rowspan="10">2:1-21:25</td><td colspan="3">Testimonium per seipsum</td></tr>
<tr><td rowspan="4">2:1-11:57</td><td colspan="2">De Verbi manifestatione prout est operativum et eruditivum</td></tr>
<tr><td>2:1-6:71</td><td>De potestate Verbi prout ipsum est virtus Patris</td></tr>
<tr><td>7:1-10:42</td><td>De illuminatione Verbi prout ipsum est sapiential Patris</td></tr>
<tr><td>11:1-57</td><td>De Verbo prout ipsum est vita hominum</td></tr>
<tr><td rowspan="4">12:1-19:42</td><td colspan="2">Creaturae rationalis sanctificatio per verbum incarnatum</td></tr>
<tr><td>12:1-13:38</td><td>Praeparatio ad sanctificationem</td></tr>
<tr><td>14:1-17:26</td><td>Verbum sanctificans</td></tr>
<tr><td>18:1-19:42</td><td>Sanctificatio in passione</td></tr>
<tr><td>20:1-21:25</td><td colspan="2">De glorificatione per resurrectionem et ascensionem</td></tr>
</table>

Figure 1 Albert, Divisio Textus of the Gospel of John

[55] M.M. Rossi, *Teoria e metodo esegetici*, p. 159.
[56] "Essa era il tocco ermeneutico finale del maestro". Ibid., p. 161.

It is crucial to have an idea of the general *divisio textus* that a master gives of the book he is commenting on. Here I will present the *divisiones textus* that Albert, Bonaventure, and Thomas provide of John's Gospel down to the level of the single chapter. I will present the *divisiones* of Albert and Bonaventure first, and then Thomas's (see *figure 1*).[57]

From a modern perspective, the most surprising aspect of Albert's *divisio textus* might well be his primary division. According to Albert the primary division in the Fourth Gospel is not between a 'Book of Signs' and a 'Book of Glory' (to use Raymond Brown's now-classic terminology), but for Albert, the central division comes after Jn 1:5. The first five verses in the Gospel speak of the uncreated Word in itself, the rest of the Gospel speaks of the properties of the Word made flesh, with which incarnate Word sanctifies the rational creature. In other words, that Albert uses a little further on: "the order of these parts is like the order of eternity to time".[58]

A second characteristic of Albert's *divisio* is the centrality of the notion of sanctification. Albert mentions it as the goal of the incarnation in the first *divisio*, and it becomes the dominant notion of his reading of the passion narrative (see *figure 2*). "The sanctification of the rational creature by the incarnate Word" is the title he gives to Jn 12-19, and in the division of that part of the Gospel in three parts, each part is explicitly related to the sanctification: Jn 12-13 is the preparation for the sanctification, Jn 14-17 speaks of the sanctifying Word, and Jn 18-19 is the sanctification in the passion. Albert's choice to place the beginning of the passion narrative at Jn 12 might surprise modern readers. Modern commentators often put Jn 11-12 together, and remark how in these chapters there are both links with Jesus's public ministry in the chapters before and the passion narrative that follows. Commentators then will give different weight to these considerations and either see Jn 12 as the end of Jesus's public ministry with Jn 12:44-50 as the last words Jesus speaks to the people in general, and 13:1 as the beginning of the last

[57] When returning to a *divisio* that was made earlier (at the beginning of the second part of a two-fold division, for instance), a master might rephrase the *divisio*. The wording of the *divisiones* that I present here is based on the first time a master presents a *divisio*. For *figure 1*, I have used the *divisiones* Albert gives at *Super Io* 1:1 p. 12; *Super Io* 1:6 p. 104-106; *In Io* 2:1 pg 87-88; *In Io* 7:1 p. 296; *In Io* 8:1 p. 327; *In Io* 12:1 p. 466-467; *In Io* 14:1 p. 525-526; *In Io* 18:1 p. 626; and *In Io* 20:1 p. 669.

[58] "Et patet ordo istarum partium, sicut est ordo eternitatis ad tempus". Albert, *Super Io* 1:1 p. 12.

discourse, spoken to his disciples,[59] or read Jn 11-12 as the introduction to the passion, pointing to the fact that it is from the raising of Lazarus that the themes of life and death become especially prominent in the Gospel and that to raise Lazarus from the dead, Jesus had to go to Judea,[60] or find a middle way and read Jn 11-12 as two chapters that together form the bridge between the chapters about Jesus's public ministry and those about his passion.[61]

12:1-19:42	Creaturae rationalis sanctificatio per Verbum incarnatum			
	12:1-13:38	Praeparatoria ad sanctificationem		
		12:1-50	Instructio	
		13:1-38	Significatio sacramentalis	
	14:1-17:26	Verbum sanctificans		
		14:1-16:33	Sermo exhortationis	
			14:1-31	fides
			15:1-16:4	caritas
			16:5-33	spes
		17:1-26	oratio	
	18:1-19:42	Sanctificatio in passione		
		18:1-12	De captivitate	
		18:13-19:15	De condemnatione	
		19:16-37	De passione	
		19:38-42	De sepulturae conditione	

Figure 2 *Albert, Divisio Textus of John 12-19*

Albert's structure of the passion narrative depends on his reading of the chapters that have gone before (see *figure 3*). He sees the portrayal of Jesus's public ministry as having three parts: the first part shows the power of the Word, in so far as the Word is the strength of the Father (Jn 2-6); the second part shows the illumination of the Word, in so far as the Word is the Wisdom of the Father (Jn 7-10), and the third part shows the Word as the life for the people (Jn 11). Jn 12 is then interpreted as the

---

[59] So R.E. Brown, *The Gospel According to John I-XII*, New Haven, Yale University Press, 1966, cxxxviii; F.J. Moloney, *The Gospel of John*, Collegeville, Liturgical Press, 1998, p. 23; M.M. Thompson, *John: A Commentary*, Louisville, Westminster John Knox Press, 2015, p. 116-117.

[60] So C.S. Keener, *The Gospel of John: A Commentary*, Vol. 2, Grand Rapids, Hendrickson Publishers, 2003, p. 833.

[61] So G. Mlakuzhyil, *The Christocentric Literary Structure of the Fourth Gospel*, Analecta Biblica, Roma, Editrice Pontificio Istituto Biblico, 1987, p. 215-221.

instruction Jesus gives to different groups to prepare them for his passion: first to the Jews, the small group of intimate friends at the house of Lazarus (Jn 12:1-8) and the large crowd that follows him at his entry into Jerusalem (Jn 12:12-19), then to the Gentiles (Jn 12:20-36) and finally to those who do not wish to prepare for their sanctification by listening to his teaching (Jn 12:37-50).

<table>
<tr><td rowspan="15">2:1-11:57</td><td colspan="4">De Verbi manifestatione prout est operativum et eruditivum</td></tr>
<tr><td rowspan="7">2:1-6:71</td><td colspan="3">De potestate Verbi prout ipsum est virtus Patris</td></tr>
<tr><td>2:1-11</td><td colspan="2">De potestate mutandi creaturas</td></tr>
<tr><td>2:12-25</td><td colspan="2">In cultis divini ordinatione</td></tr>
<tr><td>3:1-4:42</td><td colspan="2">De operatione in sacramento</td></tr>
<tr><td>4:43-5:18</td><td colspan="2">De reformatione naturae corruptae in corpore</td></tr>
<tr><td>5:19-47</td><td colspan="2">Dominus et ordinator sabbati</td></tr>
<tr><td>6:1-71</td><td colspan="2">Creaturarum transsubstantiatio ad seipsum</td></tr>
<tr><td rowspan="6">7:1-10:42</td><td colspan="3">De illuminatione Verbi prout ipsum est sapientia Patris</td></tr>
<tr><td>7:1-52</td><td colspan="2">Illuminatoris manifestatio</td></tr>
<tr><td rowspan="3">8:1-9:41</td><td colspan="2">Illuminatio per doctrinam</td></tr>
<tr><td>8:1-59</td><td>Illuminationis documentum</td></tr>
<tr><td>9:1-41</td><td>Confirmatio per miraculum</td></tr>
<tr><td>10:1-42</td><td colspan="2">Illuminatio per exemplum</td></tr>
<tr><td>11:1-57</td><td colspan="3">De Verbo prout ipsum est vita hominum</td></tr>
</table>

Figure 3 *Albert, Divisio Textus of John 2-11*

Related to the notion of sanctification in Albert's *divisio* is the frequent use of sacramental language. It is one of the powers of the Word "to work in a sacrament to sanctify the soul" says Albert, and he gives this as his title for Jn 3:1-4:42. Therefore, the reader can rightfully expect Albert to read the conversations Jesus has with Nicodemus and the Samaritan woman at the well as a single text about the sacrament of baptism.[62] Sacramental language also is prominent in Albert's description of Jn 6. In the *divisio textus* at the beginning of Jn 2 in which he gives an overview of the first half of the Gospel, Albert writes with reference to Jn 6 that a power of the Word, greater than any other power, is "the

---

[62] "Tertia autem Verbi potestas est, qua operatur in sacramento ad sanctificationem animae: et hanc potestatem manifestat in tertio et in prima parte capituli quarti". Albert, *In Io* 2:1 p. 87.

transubstantiation of the creatures to himself". [63] The stress on the transubstantiation of the faithful is repeated at the beginning of the commentary on Jn 6 itself.[64] The third place where we find sacramental language in Albert's general division of the Gospel is in his description of Jn 13. In Albert's vision, Jn 12-13 speak about the preparation for the sanctification; Jn 12 shows the preparation by way of instruction, Jn 13 by way of sacramental signification.[65]

Another point worth noticing is the importance of testimony. Not only is it the word with which Albert characterises Jn 1:6-51 as the testimony of someone else, but it also is the word he uses to describe the rest of the Gospel, from Jn 2 onwards. What Christ does in his public life, in his passion, death and resurrection, is giving testimony of himself. As Albert explains in the *divisio textus* at the beginning of Jn 2, it is through his testimony that the Word incarnate shows his divinity.[66]

Finally, a modern reader might be surprised to see Albert structuring Jn 14-16 in Jesus's farewell discourse using the theological virtues. Albert reads Jn 14 as a chapter in which Jesus, preparing the disciples for his departure, speaks to them about faith. Jn 14:12 ("Very truly, I tell you, the one who believes in me will also do the works that I do and, in fact, will do greater works than these, because I am going to the Father") is for Albert the central verse of this chapter. In a small aside he remarks that Jesus wishes to speak to the disciples about faith, but allows their doubts to interrupt his speech to make a digression, only to

---

[63] "Est autem adhuc una Verbi potestas, quae est super omne potestas, quae est creaturarum transsubstantiatio ad seipsum, per cujus effectum sibi fideles incorporantur, et unum cum ipso efficiuntur: et hanc manifestat in capitulo sexto". Albert, *In Io* 2:1 p. 88.

[64] "Hic incipit agere de manifestatione Verbi secundum potestatem, quae creaturas transmutat ad seipsum". After having subdivided Jn 6 in two parts, Jn 6:1-25 that shows the miracle and Jn 6:26-71 that gives the doctrine taken from the miracle, Albert goes on to subdivide the first part as follows: "Adhuc, anterior istarum partium dividitur in duas: in quarum prima ponitur miraculum panem, qui sacramentum Eucharistiae signat. In secunda autem declarat suam potestatem ad hoc faciendum in electis, ibi 'Jesus ergo cognovisset, quia venturi essent' etc. (v. 15)" Albert, *In Io* 6:1 p. 237. In other words: the coming to faith of the disciples after seeing Jesus walk on the sea (Jn 6:15-25) is interpreted by Albert as the coming to fruition in the disciples of the sacramental sign that is the feeding of the five thousand in Jn 6:1-14.

[65] "Per modum significationis sacramentalis" Albert, *In Io* 12:1 p. 466-467. In the commentary on Jn 13 itself, the emphasis seems to shift a little bit from the sacrament itself to Christ teaching the disciples about the preparation for the sacrament in humility (the washing of the feet in Jn 13:1-21) and charity (the new commandment that Albert reads as central in Jn 13:22-38). Albert, *In Io* 13:1 p. 499.

[66] "In qua suiipsius manifestat deitatem". Albert, *In Io* 2:1 p. 87.

return to the topic of faith after answering their questions. [67] Albert interprets Jn 15 as the chapter on charity, with Jn 15:1-11 speaking about the love for God and Jn 15:12-16:4 speaking about the love for the neighbour.[68] Albert reads Jn 16:5-33 as a chapter in which Christ gives hope to the disciples, a hope that is Trinitarian in character: he promises them the consolation of the Holy Spirit (Jn 16:5-15), his own return (Jn 16:16-22) and the certainty that the Father will grant them everything they ask for (Jn 16:23-33).[69]

<table>
<tr><td>1:1-5</td><td colspan="5">De Verbo in se</td></tr>
<tr><td rowspan="15">1:6-21:25</td><td colspan="5">De Verbo inquantum est carni unitum</td></tr>
<tr><td rowspan="7">1:6-11:46</td><td colspan="4">Incarnatio</td></tr>
<tr><td>1:6-14a</td><td colspan="3">Incarnatio</td></tr>
<tr><td rowspan="5">1:14b-11:46</td><td colspan="3">Manifestatio incarnationis</td></tr>
<tr><td>1:14b-18</td><td colspan="2">In generali</td></tr>
<tr><td rowspan="3">1:19-11:46</td><td colspan="2">In speciali</td></tr>
<tr><td>1:19-42</td><td>Per Ioannem</td></tr>
<tr><td>1:43-11:46</td><td>Per seipsum</td></tr>
<tr><td rowspan="6">11:47-19:42</td><td colspan="4">Passio</td></tr>
<tr><td rowspan="4">11:47-17:26</td><td colspan="3">Praeambula</td></tr>
<tr><td>11:47-12:19</td><td colspan="2">Iudaeorum conspiratio</td></tr>
<tr><td>12:20-12:50</td><td colspan="2">Passionis praedicatio</td></tr>
<tr><td>13:1-17:26</td><td colspan="2">Discipulorum confirmatio</td></tr>
<tr><td>18:1-19:42</td><td colspan="3">Circumadiacenta</td></tr>
<tr><td>20:1-21:25</td><td colspan="4">Resurrectio</td></tr>
</table>

Figure 4 Bonaventure, Divisio Textus of the Gospel of John

[67] "In capitulo isto toto intendit consolari discipulos, ne in fide propter transitum suum ab eis vacillent. Et hoc quidem fecit in principio capituli. Sed interpositis paucis de illuminatione dubiorum, fecerat quamdam digressionem: et illa digressione jam exposita, revertitur ad propositum, et ostendit iterum consolationem: quia per fidem operantem per dilectionem, perfectum robur accipiunt sequendo Christum". Albert, *In Io* 14:15 p. 538.

[68] Albert, *In Io* 15:1 p. 554.

[69] Albert, *In Io* 16:5 p. 583.

Figure 4 shows the general *divisio textus* as Bonaventure gives it in his commentary on John.[70] There are both similarities and differences with Albert's structure. Bonaventure agrees with Albert that the primary division of the Gospel comes after Jn 1:5, and gives a similar interpretation: Jn 1:1-5 speaks about the Word *in se*, whereas the rest of the Gospel speaks about the Word incarnate. Like Albert, Bonaventure reads Jn 12 as part of the passion narrative. He even begins it a little bit earlier, with Jn 11:47, the meeting of the chief priests and Pharisees in which they plot to kill Jesus. Likewise, just as Albert, Bonaventure uses the three theological virtues to structure Jn 14-16 (see *figure 5*).[71]

<table>
<tr><td rowspan="16">11:47-
19:42</td><td colspan="5">Passio</td></tr>
<tr><td rowspan="10">11:47-
17:26</td><td colspan="4">Praeambula</td></tr>
<tr><td>11:47-
12:19</td><td colspan="3">Iudaeorum conspiratio</td></tr>
<tr><td>12:20-
12:50</td><td colspan="3">Passionis praedicatio</td></tr>
<tr><td rowspan="7">13:1-
17:26</td><td colspan="3">Discipulorum confirmatio</td></tr>
<tr><td>13:1-38</td><td colspan="2">Humilitatis exemplo</td></tr>
<tr><td rowspan="4">14:1-
16:33</td><td colspan="2">Eruditionis et consolationis verbo</td></tr>
<tr><td>14:1-31</td><td>Fides</td></tr>
<tr><td>15:1-16:4</td><td>Dilectio</td></tr>
<tr><td>16:5-33</td><td>Spes</td></tr>
<tr><td>17:1-26</td><td colspan="2">Orationis subsidio</td></tr>
<tr><td rowspan="5">18:1-
19:42</td><td colspan="4">Circumadiacenta</td></tr>
<tr><td>18:1-12</td><td colspan="3">Comprehensio</td></tr>
<tr><td>18:13-
19:15</td><td colspan="3">Condemnatio</td></tr>
<tr><td>19:16-37</td><td colspan="3">Passio</td></tr>
<tr><td>19:37-42</td><td colspan="3">Sepulturae subsidio</td></tr>
</table>

Figure 5 *Bonaventure, Divisio Textus of John 11:47-19:42*

[70] For *figure 4*, I have used the remarks about the *divisio textus* that Bonaventure makes at *In Io* 1:1 n. 1; *In Io* 1:6 n. 17; *In Io* 1:14 n. 35; *In Io* 1:19 n. 44; *In Io* 1:43 n. 89; *In Io* 5:1 n. 1; *In Io* 7:1 n. 1; *In Io* 11:47 n. 64; *In Io* 13:1 n. 1; *In Io* 14:1 n. 1; *In Io* 18:1 n. 1 and *In Io* 20:1 n. 1.

[71] The identical *divisio textus* (up to the level of the verse: both Albert and Bonaventure give a *divisio textus* of the second part, about charity, that runs from Jn 15:1-16:4) raises the question whether they had a common source. If there was a common source, I have not been able to identify it.

Although neither Albert nor Bonaventure mentions it, the central division after Jn 1:5 seems to have its origin in a remark Augustine makes in his treatises on John. Beginning his commentary on Jn 1:6, Augustine writes: "Truly, beloved brethren, those things which were said before, were said regarding the ineffable divinity of Christ, and almost ineffably".[72] After a reflection on the wood of the cross as the ship that carries us over the sea to our heavenly country, Augustine asks rhetorically how God comes to us, and answers: "He appeared as a man".[73] That then is his starting point to reflect on Jn 1:6vv. It seems that medieval theologians like Albert and Bonaventure took this remark by Augustine as a suggestion for structuring the text and used it for their *divisio textus*. It might be worth reminding that neither Albert nor Bonaventure nor, as we will see, Thomas, see Jn 1:1-18, the text that in our times is commonly referred to as 'the Johannine Prologue' as a textual unity. P.J. Williams has shown that it was not until the late eighteenth century that Jn 1:1-18 was regarded as a distinct section of the text and called 'prologue'. Punctuation of the earliest manuscripts suggests Jn 1:1-5 was viewed as a first paragraph, and from the third century on commentators like Irenaeus, Cyprian, Chrysostom and Augustine treat it that way. Eastern lectionaries treat Jn 1:1-17 as a unit, while the Latin church treated Jn 1:1-14 as such.

None of our three commentators uses the word 'prologue' for a section in Jn 1. The term 'prologue' is used for the commentator's own introduction to the commentary and for Jerome's prologue to the Gospel as it is customarily copied in the manuscripts of the Gospel but is not used for any part of the Gospel itself, let alone for Jn 1:1-18. To prevent misunderstandings, I will not speak about the 'Johannine prologue' in this study.[74]

The main difference between Albert and Bonaventure is the central category used by these commentators. In Albert, sanctification is central, as we saw. Bonaventure states in the prologue to his commentary that the "sublime matter" the Fourth Gospel deals with is not the divinity

[72] "Et enim ea quae dicta sunt superius, fratres carissimi, de divinitate Christi dicta sunt ineffabili, et prope ineffabiliter". Augustinus, *Tract. in Io* II.2.

[73] "Sed secundum quod uenit? Quod apparuit homo". Augustinus, *Tract. in Io* II.4.

[74] P.J. Williams, 'Not the Prologue of John', in: *Journal for the Study of the New Testament* 33 (2011), p. 375-386. In his historical overview of the division of Jn 1, Williams goes straight from the Venerable Bede, John Scotus and Rupert of Deutz to the early printed Bibles in the sixteenth century. His assumption seems to be that medieval commentaries after Rupert follow the lectionary units and take Jn 1:1-14 as a section, just like Bede, John Scotus and Rupert of Deutz did. The commentaries of Albert, Bonaventure, and Aquinas show that this is not the case.

of Christ per se, but the incarnate word according to both natures.[75] In Bonaventure therefore, the incarnation is the central focus in his reading of the Fourth Gospel, as is clear from the *divisio textus*. The whole of the Gospel from Jn 1:6 onwards is given the title *De verbo carni unitum*, and especially the first half of the Gospel speaks about the incarnation and the way the incarnation was made known.

Next to the incarnation, *manifestatio* is the other central structuring category for Bonaventure (see *figure 6*). He reads Jn 1:14b-11:46 as speaking of the manifestation of the incarnate Word, and he uses manifestation as the category to describe the two large parts that make up the first half of the Gospel: Jn 1:43-4:54 is structured according to the different groups to whom the Word incarnate is manifested (disciples, Judeans, Samaritans and Galileans), while Jn 5:1-11:46 concentrates on the Word that is manifested, showing it to be healer, conserver, director and vivifier. Manifestation also is the central category Bonaventure uses for the resurrection stories in Jn 20:10-21:23: the resurrection must be made known.[76]

<table>
<tr><td rowspan="14">1:43-11:46</td><td colspan="4">Manifestatio incarnationis per seipsum</td></tr>
<tr><td rowspan="5">1:43-4:54</td><td colspan="3">Conditiones a parte eorum quibus fit manifestatio</td></tr>
<tr><td>1:43-2:11</td><td colspan="2">Discipulis</td></tr>
<tr><td>2:12-3:36</td><td colspan="2">Iudaeis</td></tr>
<tr><td>4:1-42</td><td colspan="2">Samaritanis</td></tr>
<tr><td>4:43-54</td><td colspan="2">Galileis</td></tr>
<tr><td rowspan="8">5:1-11:46</td><td colspan="3">Conditiones a parte verbum manifestati</td></tr>
<tr><td>5:1-47</td><td colspan="2">Curator</td></tr>
<tr><td>6:1-71</td><td colspan="2">Conservator</td></tr>
<tr><td rowspan="4">7:1-10:42</td><td colspan="2">Director</td></tr>
<tr><td>7:1-8:59</td><td>Verbum doctrinae</td></tr>
<tr><td>9:1-41</td><td>Miraculum potentiae</td></tr>
<tr><td>10:1-42</td><td>Exemplum bonae vitae</td></tr>
<tr><td>11:1-46</td><td colspan="2">Reparator</td></tr>
</table>

Figure 6 *Bonaventure, Divisio Textus of John 1:43-11*

[75] Bonaventure, *In Io* prol. n. 5.

[76] R. Karris names 'manifestation' as Bonaventure's dominant interpretive theme as well: R.J. Karris, 'Introduction', in: R.J. Karris (ed.), *Commentary on the Gospel of John: Introduction, Translation and Notes by Robert J. Karris*, St. Bonaventure, Franciscan Institute Publications, 2007, p. 7.

Another difference with Albert is the absence of sacramental language in Bonaventure's *divisio.* Where Albert reads the discourses with Nicodemus and the Samaritan woman as a continued narrative on baptism, Bonaventure structures these chapters according to the different audiences Jesus manifests himself to. Where Albert uses the sacramental language of 'transubstantiation' for the whole of Jn 6, Bonaventure reads it primarily as a chapter about how the Word manifests itself as conserver. And where Albert in his *divisio* stresses the Eucharistic context of Jn 13, Bonaventure calls it an example of humility. This is not to say that there are no sacramental interpretations in Bonaventure's commentary, but they are far less prominent than in Albert's, and the *divisio textus* reflects that.

Looking at Thomas's *divisio textus* of the Fourth Gospel (*figure 7*), there are essential similarities and differences with those of Albert and Bonaventure.[77] Like them, Thomas reads Jn 12 as part of the passion narrative; he agrees with Albert that the passion narrative begins with 12:1, whereas according to Bonaventure, it begins with 11:47. Just like Bonaventure, Thomas uses the categories of example, word and prayer to characterise the three parts of Jn 13-17.

More than the similarities, however, the differences catch the eye. The most important difference can be found right at the beginning, at the principal division of the Gospel. As we have seen, both Albert and Bonaventure give the central division after Jn 1:5 and say that Jn 1:1-5 speaks of the Word in God, in eternity, whereas the rest of the Gospel from Jn 1:6 onwards speaks of the Word incarnate. Thomas gives a different reading. For him, the central division comes between the first two chapters of the Gospel. Jn 1 as a whole states the divinity of Christ, whereas the rest of the Gospel shows it by the things Christ did in the flesh.

This difference in Thomas's *divisio* compared to those of Albert and Bonaventure is not a coincidence; it is a difference in interpretation. Contrary to the other two masters, it shows that Thomas reads Jn 1 as a unified whole. Whatever *divisiones* and distinctions Thomas will make in Jn 1, and they will be many, fundamentally Jn 1 is a unity that as a whole speaks of the divinity of Christ. In Thomas's interpretation, it is only from Jn 2:1 onwards that the Evangelist begins to speak of "the effects and

[77] For *figure 7*, I have used the comments about the *divisio textus* Aquinas makes at *In Io* 1:1 §23; *In Io* 2:1 §335; *In Io* 3:1 §423; *In Io* 4:1 §549; *In Io* 5:1 §699; *In Io* 6:1 §838; *In Io* 7:1 §1010; *In Io* 8:1 §1118; *In Io* 10:1 §1364; *In Io* 12:1 §1589; *In Io* 13:1 §1727; *In Io* 14:1 §1848; *In Io* 18:1 §2271 and *In Io* 20:1 §2470.

actions by which the divinity of the incarnate Word was made known to the world".[78]

<table>
<tr><td>1:1-51</td><td colspan="5">Divinitas</td></tr>
<tr><td rowspan="24">2:1-21:25</td><td colspan="5">Effectus et opera</td></tr>
<tr><td rowspan="10">2:1-11:57</td><td colspan="4">Vita</td></tr>
<tr><td>2:1-25</td><td colspan="3">Dominium supra naturam</td></tr>
<tr><td rowspan="8">3:1-11:57</td><td colspan="3">Effectus gratiae</td></tr>
<tr><td rowspan="3">3:1-4:54</td><td colspan="2">Spiritualis regeneratio</td></tr>
<tr><td>3:1-36</td><td>Quantum ad Iudaeos</td></tr>
<tr><td>4:1-54</td><td>Quantum ad externas nationes</td></tr>
<tr><td rowspan="4">5:1-11:57</td><td colspan="2">Beneficia spiritualia</td></tr>
<tr><td>5:1-47</td><td>Vita</td></tr>
<tr><td>6:1-71</td><td>Nutrimentum</td></tr>
<tr><td>7:1-11:57</td><td>Doctrina</td></tr>
<tr><td rowspan="13">12:1-21:25</td><td colspan="4">Passio et mors</td></tr>
<tr><td rowspan="9">12:1-19:42</td><td colspan="3">Passio et mors</td></tr>
<tr><td>12:1-50</td><td colspan="2">Causa</td></tr>
<tr><td rowspan="4">13:1-17:26</td><td colspan="2">Praeparatio discipulorum</td></tr>
<tr><td>13:1-38</td><td>Exemplo</td></tr>
<tr><td>14:1-16:33</td><td>Verbo</td></tr>
<tr><td>17:1-26</td><td>Oratio</td></tr>
<tr><td rowspan="3">18:1-19:42</td><td colspan="2">Passio et mors</td></tr>
<tr><td>18:1-40</td><td>Per Iudaeos</td></tr>
<tr><td>19:1-42</td><td>Per gentiles</td></tr>
<tr><td rowspan="3">20:1-21:25</td><td colspan="3">Resurrectio</td></tr>
<tr><td>20:1-18</td><td colspan="2">Manifestatio mulieribus</td></tr>
<tr><td>20:19-21:25</td><td colspan="2">Manifestatio discipulis</td></tr>
</table>

Figure 7 *Thomas, Divisio Textus of the Gospel of John*

This fundamental division shows that the reference Thomas makes in his prologue to the commentary to Augustine's remark that while the other Gospels speak principally about the humanity of Christ, John speaks about his divinity, is not there for ornamentation. Thomas

[78] *In Io* 2:1 §335.

has made it his own and will make it the central category for his reading of the Gospel.[79] In this and the following chapters, I will show how this difference in the first and most fundamental division of the Gospel between our three biblical masters has consequences for the way they interpret Jn 1.

There is a difference between Thomas and the other two commentators in their use of the *divisio textus* that might, at first sight, seem to put the different structure that Thomas gives in another perspective. Both in Albert's and in Bonaventure's *divisiones textus,* there are several instances where a textual unity starts in one chapter and goes on into the next. To give a few examples of this: Albert reads Jn 4:43-5:18 as a textual unity that speaks about the reformation of corrupted nature in the body. Bonaventure reads Jn 1:43-2:11 as a textual unity that treats the disciples as the first group to which the incarnation of the Word is made manifest. Both Albert and Bonaventure in structuring the farewell discourse according to the theological virtues, present the part on charity as not only covering Jn 15, but continuing to Jn 16:4, and both Albert and Bonaventure see Jn 18:13-19:15 as a textual unity that treats the condemnation of Christ.

Divisions like this, however, are absent from Thomas's commentary on John. In Thomas's commentary, the beginning of a new chapter always implies a significant next step in the *divisio textus* as well. Sometimes a division within a chapter might come before a division between chapters (an example of this would be Thomas's division of Jn 20-21, where Jn 20:1-18 is distinguished from Jn 20:19-21:25), but the beginning of a new chapter always coincides with a step in the *divisio* as well. Nowhere in his commentary on John do we find a *divisio* that runs over into the next chapter without including the whole of that chapter.

---

[79] My interpretation of the commentaries from Bonaventure and Thomas differs from that of John F. Boyle, who writes: "Beginning with the same unifying theme, Saint Bonaventure and Saint Thomas divide the Gospel according to Saint John in quite different ways…", and refers in a footnote to the first page of Bonaventure's commentary on Jn 1: J.F. Boyle, 'The Theological Character of the Scholastic "Division of the Text"', p. 279. At the place that Boyle refers to, however, Bonaventure writes: "Iste liber, qui est de Verbo incarnato, in quo duplex consideratur natura, divina scilicet et humana…" Bonaventure, *In Io* 1:1 n.1. Already in his prologue, Bonaventure states: "Evangelium beati Ioannis sublime est, quia de sublimis agit, quia de Verbo incarnato secundum utramque naturam". Bonaventure, *In Io* prol., n. 5. For Thomas, however, the divinity of Christ is the theme of John's Gospel, as he states at several places in his commentary, starting from this remark in the prologue: "Ioannes specialiter et praecipue divinitatem Christi in Evangelio suo insinuat". *In Io* Prol., §10.

This observation might seem to challenge the thesis that the fact that Thomas sees Jn 1 as a textual unity is important for his interpretation of the text. Might it not be that this has to be understood as showing a particular feature of the way Thomas uses the hermeneutical tool that the *divisio textus* is, rather than something that has meaning for his interpretation? Might it not be that Thomas, for whatever reason, always first makes a division between the chapters of the biblical text, and only then gives a further division of the text within the chapter and that therefore Thomas's *divisio* of Jn 1 as a textual unity says more about his use of the *divisio textus* as a technique than about his interpretation of Jn 1?

Indeed, Thomas in the *divisiones textus* in his biblical commentaries generally follows the division into chapters that at the time of his commentary on John probably was about a century old and is used to this day.[80] There are exceptions to this rule, but if we leave aside the obvious exceptions in the commentaries on the Pauline *corpus* where Thomas usually will start with distinguishing the greeting at the beginning of the letter from the body of the letter, the exceptions are rare. An example of a *divisio* that does not coincide with the division into chapters can be found in the letter to the Ephesians. Thomas interprets Eph 4:17-6:9 as a textual unity in which Paul teaches the Ephesians the way to remain within the Church's unity. Thomas then subdivides this into a part that sets down precepts for everyone (Eph 4:17-5:21) and a part that gives precepts pertaining to particular classes within the Church (Eph 5:22-6:9): husband and wife (Eph 5:22-33), father and child (Eph 6:1-4) servants and masters (Eph 6:5-9).[81] Another example that shows that the division into chapters is not sacrosanct for Thomas is the obvious one at the end of Paul's letter to the Colossians. Thomas recognises that Col 4:1 is part

---

[80] In the past this chapter division has often been attributed to Stephen Langton during his time as master in Paris around 1200. More recent scholarship suggests that it is at least a few decades older, that it was produced in England and inspired by Hebrew codices. P. Saenger, L. Bruck, 'The Anglo-Hebraic Origins of the Modern Chapter Division of the Latin Bible', in: F.J. Burguillo, L. Meier (eds.), *La fractura historiográfica: Edad media y renacimiento desde el tercer milenio*, Salamanca, Seminario de Estudios Medievales y Renacentistas, 2008, p. 177-202. The division of chapters into verses as we know it today was introduced by Etienne Robert in 1534. By the end of the thirteenth century, the Dominicans in Paris had devised a system of dividing each chapter into seven parts, named "a" to "g" or four parts, named "a" to "d" for the shorter chapters. Cf. F. van Liere, *An Introduction to the Medieval Bible*, Cambridge, Cambridge University Press, 2014, p. 44-45. Albert, Bonaventure and Thomas do not use that system yet; they usually refer by naming book, chapter and the first words of the verse.

[81] *In Eph* 4:17 §230; cf. *In Eph* 5:22 §316.

of Paul's directions about masters and slaves that started in Col 3:22 and that only with Col 4:2 something new begins.[82]

An example of an important *divisio* that begins in the middle of the chapter can be found in Thomas's commentary on Romans. Thomas interprets Romans 12-16 as Paul's teaching on how grace should be used. He subdivides this into two parts, a part that sets out a general moral teaching (Rom 12:1-15:13) and a part in which Paul goes into more particular questions related to the recipients of the letter that starts "around the middle of chapter 15".[83] Another example of a *divisio* that cuts a chapter in half can be found in the commentary on Hebrews. In the *divisio* that begins the commentary on Hebr 7, Thomas states that the apostle first will show the excellence of Christ's priesthood as compared to the priesthood of the Old Testament, and then will show that believers should subject themselves reverently to the priesthood of Christ. According to Thomas, that second part begins "in the middle of chapter 10", at Hebr 10:19.[84]

These examples are exceptions, however. In general, the *divisiones textus* that Thomas makes in his biblical commentaries follow the division into chapters of the biblical book he is commenting on, in the sense that a new chapter coincides with a major division in Thomas's *divisio textus*. However, the exceptions are important: while Thomas will almost always follow the division into chapters, this is not automatic. His *divisio textus* has to be taken seriously as an interpretative instrument at the level of the chapters, just like any other level. For the commentary on John, this means that the fact that in contrast to Albert and Bonaventure Thomas does not make the principal division after Jn 1:5 but instead says that Jn 1 should be read as a textual unity that as a whole speaks about the divinity of Christ should be given its full interpretative weight. It is a first hermeneutical sign that Thomas's interpretation of Jn 1 will differ substantially from the interpretations of Albert and Bonaventure.

There are other differences between Thomas's structure of the Gospel and those of Bonaventure and Albert. Thomas reads Jn 2-11 as the manifestation of the divinity of the incarnate Word while living in the world (see *figure 8*). That is not that different from Bonaventure's reading, even though Bonaventure lets this part of the Gospel start at Jn 1:14b, as we saw. What is different is that Thomas structures Jn 2-11 in two parts, and looks at them through the lens of nature and grace: Jn 2

---

[82] *In Col* 3:18 §182.

[83] "Circa medium XV cap". *In Rom* 12:1 §953.

[84] "In medio decimi capitis" *In Hebr* 7:1 §326.

shows the divinity of Christ in relation to the power he had over nature. Jn 3-11 shows the divinity of Christ in relation to the effects of grace.[85] Thomas confirms the centrality of grace in his reading of the fourth Gospel in the *divisio textus* with which he opens the commentary on Jn 3: "Above, the Evangelist showed Christ's power in relation to changes affecting nature; here he shows it in relation to our reformation by grace, which is his principal subject".[86] Small sentences like these tend to get overlooked when Thomas's biblical commentaries are read without sufficient attention for the *divisio textus*, but they do make all the difference. What is the fourth Gospel about? It is about the divinity of Christ. How does John show us the divinity of Christ? Before everything else, he shows it in the way grace transforms us.

5:1-11:57	Beneficia spiritualia				
	5:1-47	Vita			
	6:1-71	Nutrimentum			
	7:1-11:57	Doctrina			
		7:1-52	Origo		
		8:1-11:57	Utilitas/Virtus		
			8:1-9:41	Vis illuminativa	
				8:1-59	Verba
				9:1-41	Miracula
			10:1-11:57	Vis vivificativa	
				10:1-42	Verba
				11:1-57	Miracula

Figure 8 *Thomas, Divisio Textus of John 5-11*

The subdivision of Jn 3-11 develops this further. Thomas writes: "Reformation by grace comes about through spiritual regeneration and by the conferring of benefits on those regenerated".[87] This determines the *divisio* of what follows: Jn 3-4 speak of the spiritual regeneration, first concerning the Jews (Jn 3) and then the nations (Jn 4). The chapters that

[85] "Primo enim ostendit Christi divinitatem quantum ad dominium quod habuit supra naturam; secundo quantum ad effectus gratiae, et hoc in III cap. Ibi 'erat homo ex Pharisaeis' et cetera". *In Io* 2:1 §335 (text corrected by L. Reid).
[86] "Supra ostendit Evangelista virtutem Christi quantum ad immutationem naturae; hic vero ostendit eam quantum ad reformationem gratiae, de qua principaliter intendit". *In Io* 3:1 §423 (text corrected by L. Reid).
[87] "Reformatio autem gratiae fit per spiritualem regenerationem, et per beneficiorum regeneratis collationem". *In Io* 3:1 §423 (text corrected by L. Reid).

follow will speak of the benefits given to those who are regenerated.[88] Thomas presents these as gifts that are parallel to the gifts parents give to their children: "we see that parents give three things to those who are physically born from them: life, nourishment, and instruction or discipline. And those who are spiritually reborn receive these three from Christ: spiritual life, spiritual nourishment, and spiritual teaching".[89] This gives Thomas the structure for Jn 5-11: in Jn 5 the Evangelist speaks about the gift of spiritual life, in Jn 6 about spiritual food, and in Jn 7-11 about spiritual teaching.

Finally, it is worth noticing the parallels in Thomas's *divisio textus*. The structure of Jn 3-4, the spiritual regeneration given to the Jews and the other nations, finds a parallel in the passion narrative: Jn 18 speaks of what Christ suffered from the Jews, Jn 19 about what he suffered from the gentiles. Of greater importance, however, are the structural parallels in the commentary on Jn 8-11. We saw that Thomas interprets Jn 7-11 as speaking of the gift of spiritual teaching, the third gift given to those who are spiritually regenerated. Jn 7 speaks of the origin of this teaching, Thomas suggests, and Jn 8-11 of its usefulness.[90] Thomas draws on Jn 6:63 to characterise Christ's teaching: "The words that I have spoken to you are spirit and life". Because this is true, Thomas argues, the doctrine of Christ has the power both to enlighten and to give life.[91] This gives Thomas the structure of Jn 8-11: Jn 8-9 focuses on the illuminative power of Christ's teaching, Jn 10-11 on its life-giving power. Light and life, key words in John that the Evangelist introduces to his reader in the first verses of his Gospel and that he returns to again and again, are thus picked up by Thomas to structure Jn 8-11. The two parts that thus emerge are divided by Thomas in a parallel fashion. At the beginning of his commentary on Jn 5, Thomas had made a general observation about the way John has written his Gospel: "This is the usual practice in this Gospel: to always join to the teaching of Christ some appropriate visible action so

---

[88] *In Io* 3:1 §423.

[89] "Sed his qui carnaliter generantur tria conferuntur a parentibus carnalibus: scilicet vita, nutrimentum et doctrina sive disciplina; et haec tria a Christo etiam regenerati spiritualiter percipiunt. Primo quidem spiritualem vitam; secundo vero spirituale nutrimentum; tertio spiritualem doctrinam". *In Io* 5:1 §699.

[90] *In Io* 7:1 §1010.

[91] "Habet autem doctrina Christi virtutem illuminativam et vivificativam, quia verba eius spiritus et vita sunt". *In Io* 8:1 §1118.

that what is invisible can be made known through the visible".[92] That observation gives the substructure for Jn 8-11. The two parts that Thomas recognises in these chapters are subdivided in parallel fashion: Jn 8-9 show the illuminative power of Christ's teaching, first by words (Jn 8) and then by a miracle (Jn 9). Likewise, Jn 10-11 show the life-giving power of Christ's teaching, first by words (Jn 10) and then by a miracle (Jn 11).

From this structure already it is clear that Thomas will relate the "I am the light of the word" saying in Jn 8:12 to the healing of the man born blind in Jn 9, and in parallel fashion, will relate the words of Jesus as good shepherd and gate for the sheep ("I came that they may have life, and have it abundantly" Jn 10:10) to the raising of Lazarus in Jn 11. The *divisio textus* that Thomas gives shows already at the level of the chapters his unique perspective on the interpretation of John's Gospel.

3. The *Divisio Textus* of John 1

Having presented the general *divisio textus* that Albert, Bonaventure, and Thomas give of John's Gospel, I will now look at the subdivision they give of Jn 1. M.M. Rossi has argued that in the *divisiones textus* in Thomas's biblical commentaries, one finds a biblical prevalence in the great divisions and a logical prevalence in the smaller divisions.[93] If this is true, we should expect, at least in Thomas's commentary, to find more formal divisions of the text the more deeply we go into a given passage. That does not mean that the *divisio textus* becomes less relevant once one gets more into detail in a commentary, however. At all levels of the *divisio,* a commentator makes decisions that carry interpretative weight: the difference Rossi points to is a general observation, a rule of thumb.

I will now present Albert's, Bonaventure's and Thomas's *divisio textus* at the meso-level, that of the single chapter. As in the previous section, I will begin with Albert's (see *figure 9*).[94] We saw earlier that the primary division Albert makes in his commentary falls after Jn 1:5. For him, the first five verses differ from what follows because they speak of the uncreated Word in itself.

---

[92] "[...] secundum consuetudinem huius Evangelii, in quo semper doctrinae Christi adiungitur aliquod visibile factum, pertinens ad illud de quo est doctrina, ut sic ex visibilibus invisibilia innotescant". *In Io* 5:1 §699.

[93] M.M. Rossi, 'La "Divisio Textus" Nei Commenti Scritturistici', p. 543-544.

[94] *Figure 9* is based on the remarks Albert makes regarding the *divisio textus* in *Super Io* 1:1 p. 12; *Super Io* 1:6 p. 104-106; *Super Io* 1:15 p. 174; *In Io* 1:29 p. 64; and *In Io* 1:37 p. 73.

<table>
<tr><td rowspan="3">Jn 1:1-5</td><td colspan="2">De proprietatibus personalibus et essentialibus Verbi increati in se</td></tr>
<tr><td>Jn 1:1-2</td><td>Per quas refertur ad personas divinas</td></tr>
<tr><td>Jn 1:3-5</td><td>Per quas refertur ad creata per ipsum</td></tr>
</table>

<table>
<tr><td rowspan="11">Jn 1:6-21:25</td><td colspan="5">De proprietatibus Verbi in creaturam rationalem ad sanctificandum eam procedentis</td></tr>
<tr><td rowspan="9">1:6-51</td><td colspan="4">Testimonium per alium</td></tr>
<tr><td>1:6-9</td><td colspan="3">Commendatio testis</td></tr>
<tr><td>1:10-14</td><td colspan="3">Necessitas testimonii</td></tr>
<tr><td rowspan="6">1:15-51</td><td colspan="3">Testimonium</td></tr>
<tr><td>1:15-18</td><td colspan="2">Enarratio rei testificanda</td></tr>
<tr><td>1:19-28</td><td colspan="2">Declaratio testimonii</td></tr>
<tr><td rowspan="3">1:29-51</td><td colspan="2">Testificantis intentio</td></tr>
<tr><td>1:29-36</td><td>Testimonia Joannis ad fidem Christi convertentia</td></tr>
<tr><td>1:37-51</td><td>Conversia facta in audientibus</td></tr>
<tr><td>2:1-21:25</td><td colspan="4">Testimonium per seipsum</td></tr>
</table>

Figure 9 *Albert, Divisio Textus of John 1*

Albert chooses to use the category of testimony to structure the rest of the Gospel: Jn 1:6-51 is the testimony of another, the whole of the Gospel from Jn 2 onwards is the testimony by Christ of the Word itself. While the theme of testimony undoubtedly is an essential Johannine theme, at first sight, Albert's choice seems counterintuitive. Is the whole Gospel not full of others testifying about Jesus? One only has to think of the debate about the Scriptures, God the Father and Moses as witnesses in Jn 5:31-40, about the Paraclete and the disciples as witnesses in Jn 15:26-27 or the testimony of the beloved disciple at the end of the Gospel (Jn 21:24). Albert makes a distinction to explain his structure: while the testimony of the Word by himself is more important than that given by others, and therefore comes first, yet in the way we come to the Word the testimony of others comes before the testimony of the Word. Albert refers to Augustine, who, commenting on Jn 5:35 ("He was a burning and shining lamp") wrote: "Just as by the lamp we come to the light, so by John we come to Christ". It is this comment of Augustine that is the reason for Albert's *divisio*. In Jn 1, the testimony of another is central, while in the rest of the Gospel, even when others testify to the Word, the testimony of the Word itself is primary.[95]

The testimony of another is the lens through which Albert reads Jn 1:6-51: other notions take a back seat. The word 'incarnation' for example, is absent from Albert's division of Jn 1. For Albert Jn 1:14 does not stand out as a core verse about the incarnation, but is read within the context of the necessity of the testimony that according to Albert is the object of Jn 1:10-14. Another consequence of this structure is visible in the division Albert gives of Jn 1:15-51. Albert explains that every testimony consists of three things: the faithful report of the testimony, the impeccable declaration and manifestation of the testimony itself, and the witness's intention. This threefold division then becomes the *divisio textus* of Jn 1:15-51: v. 15-18 is the report of the testimony, v. 19-28 is the testimony itself and v. 29-51 the intention of the witness, which is to lead people to faith.[96] We will look at the consequences of this division in more detail when we study the commentary on these verses, but the *divisio* gives hints as to how Albert will present the text to his students. It is to be expected, for example, that in his interpretation v. 16-18 will somehow be seen as part of the 'report' (*enarratio*) of the testimony, and in that sense be subordinated to v. 15.

A final point to make at this moment about Albert's *divisio* regards the interpretation it suggests of v. 29-51. This part of Jn shows, according to Albert, the intention of the witness, which is to bring hearers of his testimony to faith. This becomes clear in a second testimony, v. 29-36 and in the consequences it has in the hearers in v. 37-51. According to the interpretation that Albert gives through his *divisio textus*, the calling of the first disciples has to be read as the consequence of the testimony of John the Baptist: it shows how the intention of his testimony comes true.

We have seen that for Bonaventure the incarnation is the matter of the Gospel of John and that the manifestation of the incarnation is the

---

[95] "Et quamuis testimonium Verbi factum per ipsum Verbum maius sit testimonio facto per alterum, et sic prius uideatur esse: tamen quo ad nos et nostram inductionem ad Verbum, testimonium factum per alterum, prius est testimonio facto per Verbum. Vnde super illud Joh.V: 'Ille erat lucerna etc' dicit Augustinus: Sicut per lucernam uenitur ad lucem, ita per Johannem uenitur ad Christum. Et hoc modo ordinantur partes iste". Albert, *Super Io* 1:6 p. 104-106.

[96] "Et diuiditur in tres partes secundum tria que sunt in omni testimonio. Quorum primum est rei testificande fidelis enarratio. Secundum autem est testimonii perfecta declaratio et manifestatio. Et hoc incipit ibi: 'Et hoc est testimonium Johannis'. Tertium est testificantis intentio, que est audientium ipsum testimonium ad fidem prudens inductio ibi: 'Altera autem die stabat etc'" Albert, *Super Io* 1:15 p. 174.

dominating theme of his *divisio* of the Gospel. A closer look at his division of Jn 1 shows how this works out for this part of the commentary (See *figure 10*).[97]

1:1-5	De verbo in se	
	1:1-2	In comparatione ad dicentem
	1:3-5	In comparatione ad ea quae dicuntur per Verbum

1:6-11:46	Incarnatio					
	1:6-14a	Incarnatio				
		1:6-8	De adventu praecursoris			
		1:9-14a	De adventu Christi			
	1:14b-11:46	Manifestatio incarnationis				
		1:14b-1:18	In generali			
			1:14b	Cognitio Verbi incarnati		
			1:15-18	Cognitionis ratio		
		1:19-11:46	In speciali			
			1:19-1:42	Per Ioannem		
				1:19-28	Testimonium 1: De naturarum duarum veritate	
				1:29-34	Testimonium 2: De baptizandi potestate	
				1:35-42	Testimonium 3: De sanctitate	
			1:43-11:46	Per seipsum		
				1:43-4:54	Conditiones a parte eorum quibus fit manifestatio	
					1:43-2:11	Discipulis

Figure 10 *Bonaventure, Divisio Textus of John 1*

We saw that Bonaventure, like Albert, sets Jn 1:1-5 apart from the rest of the Gospel: that part speaks about the Word in itself. From Jn 1:6

[97] The *divisio textus* presented in *figure 10* is based on the remarks regarding the *divisio* that Bonaventure makes in *In Io* 1:1 n. 1; *In Io* 1:6 n. 17; *In Io* 1:14b n. 35; *In Io* 1:19 n. 44 and *In Io* 1:43 n. 89.

onwards, however, the Gospel speaks of the Word incarnate, and the incarnation is the subject of Jn 1:6-11:46. Jn 1:6-14a speaks about the incarnation itself, and the *divisio textus* of these verses shows how the stress in Bonaventure is almost opposite to that in Albert. For Albert, these verses speak about the witness and the necessity of testimony, for Bonaventure all the stress is on the incarnation. The naming of v. 6-8 is telling: In Albert v. 6-8 is called *commendatio testis*, in Bonaventure *de adventu praecursoris*. John is named in relation to the coming of Christ. The place of v. 9 ("The true light, which enlightens everyone, was coming into the world") in the *divisio* is suggestive as well: in Albert, it is the end of the section that speaks about the witness to the light, in Bonaventure it is the beginning of the section that speaks of the incarnation and that ends with "The Word became flesh and lived among us" in v. 14a.

With v. 14b ("We have seen his glory, the glory as of a Father's only Son, full of grace and truth") a new section begins that continues until Jn 11:46 and that has the manifestation of the incarnation as its object. Bonaventure divides it into two parts: v. 14b-18 speak of this manifestation in general, Jn 1:19-11:46 speaks of it in particular. The subdivision of that first part shows that Bonaventure singles out v. 14b as speaking of the knowledge of the incarnate Word and the verses that follow as focusing on the reason for that knowledge. Again it is the opposite of Albert's structure: for Albert v. 15 is central to the story of the testimony and the verses that follow are subordinated to that. In Bonaventure v. 14b takes central stage and v. 15 that speaks of John the Baptist is fit into that.

For Bonaventure, it is only from v. 19-42 that testimony becomes the central category: he recognises a threefold testimony of John in these verses and structures this part of the chapter accordingly. From Jn 1:43 onwards the manifestation of the incarnate Word by that Word himself becomes central, starting with the different groups to which the Word manifests itself: first the disciples, than other groups.

One of the characteristics of Thomas's *divisio textus* of the Fourth Gospel, compared to those of Albert and Bonaventure, is that he suggests that Jn 1 should be read as a unity, as we saw before. How does this work out when he gives his structure of John 1?[98] Thomas reads Jn 1 as a chapter that as a whole speaks of the divinity of Christ (See *figure 11*). Under this heading, Thomas not only puts the first five verses of Jn 1 but also v. 6-

---

[98] *Figure 11* is based on the remarks regarding the *divisio textus* that Thomas makes in *In Io* 1:1 §23; *In Io* 1:6 §108; *In Io* 1:14b §179; *In Io* 1:16 §200; *In Io* 1:19 §223; *In Io* 1:35 §280 and *In Io* 1:37 §284.

14a, on the incarnation of the Word of God. Thomas's subdivision of v. 6-14a resembles that of Bonaventure: v. 6-8 about the witness are related to the coming of the Word in the flesh.

1:1-51	Divinitas Christi						
	1:1-14a	Divinitas Christi					
		1:1-5	Divinitas Christi				
			1:1-2	Esse Verbi			
			1:3-5	Virtus seu operatio Verbi			
		1:6-14a	Verbi Dei incarnatio				
			1:6-8	De teste Verbi incarnati			
			1:9-14a	De adventu Verbi			
	1:14b-51	Modus quo Christi divinitas nobis innotuit					
		1:14b-15	Duplex modus manifestationis				
			1:14b	Per visum			
			1:15	Per auditum, ex testimonio Ioannis Baptistae			
		1:16-51	Utrumque modum exponit				
			1:16-18	Per visum			
			1:19-51	Per auditum			
				1:19-34	Testimonium ad turbas		
					1:19-28	In Christi absentia, interrogatus	
					1:29-34	In Christi praesentia, spontaneus	
				1:35-51	Testimonium discipulis suis		
					1:35-36	Testimonium	
					1:37-51	Testimonii fructus	
						1:37-42	Ex testimonio Ioannis
						1:43-51	Ex praedicatione Christi

Figure 11 *Thomas, Divisio Textus of John 1*

The unity of Jn 1 in Thomas's interpretation is clear from the words he uses in his *divisio textus* as well. After having spoken about the existence and operation of the Word in v. 1-5, Thomas calls v. 9-14a 'De adventu Verbi' on the coming of the Word. 'Verbum' remains the main category until v. 14a. From v. 14b onwards words like manifestation and testimony become main categories. However, what has to be made known is the 'divinity of Christ', as Thomas's caption of v. 14b-51 reads. What has to be made known is not the incarnation (as it was for Bonaventure), what has to be made known is the divinity. These two are by no means opposites, but the language Thomas chooses is not coincidental. It shows how seriously he takes the remarks he makes in the prologue to this commentary about the circumstances in which this Gospel was written: Thomas believes John wrote his Gospel at the request of the faithful after heresies had arisen that denied the divinity of Christ.[99] It is the divine Word of which the first verses of the Gospel speak, it is the incarnation of this divine Word that is the subject of v. 6-14a, it is this divinity that has to be made known in ways that are shown in v. 14b-51, and it is the effects and works of this divine Word made flesh that will be the subject of Jn 2-21.

In Thomas's reading of v. 14b-51, the manifestation of the incarnate Word is shown to happen in two ways: it happens by sight and from hearing. Thomas reads v. 14b-51 as first mentioned and then explained both ways. Seeing (v. 14b) and hearing (from the testimony of John the Baptist v. 15) are presented, and then developed: seeing in v. 16-18 and hearing in 19-51. From this, it is to be expected that seeing ("we have seen his glory" v. 14b; "No one has ever seen God" v. 18) will become an important theme for Thomas in this part of the commentary, more so than it is expected to be for Albert and Bonaventure.[100] Thomas structures the testimony of John the Baptist, presented in v. 15 and developed in v. 16-51 in ways that resemble Albert's and Bonaventure's *divisiones*: like Bonaventure, Thomas recognises three testimonies, although he uses more formal categories to present them. There are two testimonies addressed to the people, and a third one addressed to John's own disciples. Of the two testimonies to the people, the first is given in the absence of Christ and in reaction to questions (v. 19-28), the second is given in Christ's presence, and spontaneous (v. 29-34). Like Albert, Thomas reads the calling of the disciples in v. 37-51 as a fruit of the testimony of John the Baptist.

This presentation of the *divisiones textus* at the macro-level of the whole of the Gospel and the meso-level of Jn 1 has shown differences in the way

[99] *In Io* Prol., §10.

[100] Pierre-Yves Maillard has shown how seeing God is an important theme throughout the whole of Thomas's commentary on John: P.-Y. Maillard, *La vision de Dieu chez Thomas d'Aquin: Une lecture de l'In Ioannem à la lumière de ses sources Augustiniennes*, Paris, Vrin, 2001.

Albert, Bonaventure and Thomas structure the text that suggest different interpretations of the Gospel and its first chapter. Albert's *divisio* indicates a reading that is oriented towards the passion narrative, in which the notion of sanctification, so central to Albert's structure, will come to fruition. His *divisio* of Jn 1 focuses on the testimony of John the Baptist: his witness brings us to Christ, whose own testimony will be central from Jn 2 onwards. For Bonaventure, the incarnation is the lens through which he reads the Fourth Gospel: it is the incarnation that is central in the first part of Jn 1 and the manifestation of it that becomes the issue from the second half of Jn 1 onwards, first in more general and then in specific terms. In line with his remarks about the origin of the Gospel as written in response to people who denied the divinity of Christ, Thomas finally takes more than the other two commentators the divinity to be the object of John's Gospel. The whole of Jn 1 speaks of this divinity, showing first the divinity itself and then the way it is made known to us, through seeing and hearing. According to Thomas, from Jn 2 onwards, the Evangelist will show his readers the effects and works of this divine Word made flesh.

CHAPTER 2
THE DIVINE WORD

However different the *divisiones textus* of Albert, Bonaventure and Thomas may be, we have seen that all three commentators read Jn 1:1-5 as a unity. It is this unity on which we will concentrate in this chapter.

Thomas subdivides these five verses into two parts when he writes: "Because there are two items to be considered in each thing, namely, its existence and its operation or power, first he treats the existence of the Word as to his divine nature; secondly of his power or operation, from 'All things were made through Him'".[1] The first two verses speak of what the Word is; the next three of what the Word does.[2] Although Albert and Bonaventure use different categories at this point in their commentaries, the *divisio* they make here is not substantially different. Albert writes that v. 1-2 speak about the personal and essential properties of the Word concerning the divine persons, while v. 3-5 speak of these properties concerning creation.[3] Bonaventure takes his distinction from the implications of *verbum*:

> Now since 'Word' refers to efficacious power, as Augustine says, and indicates the speaker and that which is said by the Word, the first part has two sections. The first section concerns the Word in relation to the speaker. The second focuses on those things which are spoken by the Word: 'All things were made through Him'.[4]

---

[1] "Quia vero in unaquaque re sunt consideranda duo, scilicet esse et operatio, sive virtus ipsius, ideo primo agit de esse verbi quantum ad naturam divinam; secundo de virtute, seu operatione ipsius, ibi 'omnia per ipsum facta sunt'". *In Io* 1:1 §23.

[2] Martin Sabathé has rightly remarked that 'what the Word does' here refers to what the Word does with regard to creation. Operations in God (knowing, loving, rejoicing) are not directly meant here. Sabathé gives two reasons for this absence: first, Thomas is structuring the Gospel here, not writing a systematic treatise; secondly, the *processiones* in God will be explained throughout the commentary via the *missiones* of the divine persons. This last point could be made stronger when it is considered in the context of the soteriological character of Thomas's commentary as a whole. I will return to this point later. Cf. M. Sabathé, *La Trinité rédemptrice dans le commentaire de l'évangile de Saint Jean par Thomas d'Aquin*, Paris, Librairie Philosophique J. Vrin, 2011, p. 98-99.

[3] Albert, *Super Io* 1:1 p. 12.

[4] "Et quia Verbum dicit operativam potentiam, ut dicit Augustinus, et habet respectum ad dicentem, et ad id quod per verbum dicitur; ideo prima pars habet duas. In prima determinatur de Verbo in comparatione ad dicentem; in secunda in comparatione ad

The first two verses of the Gospel consist of four phrases or *clausulae*: on this, too, Albert, Bonaventure and Thomas concur. Albert reads them as four propositions that show four properties of the eternal Word:[5] its inseparability of the intellect of the Father in the first, "In the beginning was the Word;" its distinction from the Father in "And the Word was with God;" its unity with the intellect of the Father in "And the Word was God;" and its coequality and coeternity with the first intellect in "He was in the beginning with God". Albert succinctly adds: "Thus every heretical deformity is repressed".[6] Bonaventure's characterisation of the four *clausulae* with which the Gospel opens is very similar to that of Albert's. He reads them as a description of four conditions of the incarnate (sic) Word: unity in essence, difference in person, equality in majesty and coeternity in duration. Like Albert, Bonaventure adds a remark that these force out four errors.[7]

Thomas's classification of the four *clausulae* differs from that of Albert and Bonaventure. According to Thomas, the fourth evangelist, speaking about the existence of the Word as to his divine nature, first shows when the Word was (*quando*), secondly where he was (*ubi*), thirdly what he was (*quid*) and finally in what way he was (*quomodo*). The first two of these questions, Thomas specifies, pertain to the inquiry "whether something exists" (*an sit*); the second two pertain to the inquiry "what something is" (*quid sit*).[8] I will come back later to these Aristotelian categories because there is a question with these that Thomas addresses a bit later in the commentary. I also will return later to the difference between Thomas's characterisation of these four *clausulae* on the one hand and that of Albert and Bonaventure on the other hand. When we now turn to Thomas's exposition of the text of Jn, the implications for and effects on his reading that his *divisio textus* has, as distinguished from and sometimes concurring with those of Albert and Bonaventure, will become clear.

---

ea quae dicuntur per Verbum,: 'Omnia per ipsum facta sunt'". Bonaventure, *In Io* 1:1 n. 1.

[5] "In priori harum partium quatuor continentur propositiones quatuor Verbi eterni proprietates ostendentes". Albert, *Super Io* 1:1 p. 14.

[6] "Et sic omnis confutatur heretica prauitas". Albert, *Super Io* 1:1 p. 14.

[7] "In prima parte ponuntur quatuor clausulae, in quibus describitur Verbum incarnatum quantum ad quatuor conditiones, quae sunt: in essentia unitas, in persona alietas, in maiestate aequalitas, in duratione coaeternitas. Et per has conditiones eliduntur quatuor errores". Bonaventure, *In Io* 1:1 n. 1.

[8] *In Io* 1:1 §23.

1. Four *Clausulae*: the Commentary on Jn 1:1-2

The *divisio textus* as a hermeneutical instrument aims to understand how parts of Scripture (chapters within a book, verses within a chapter, words within a single verse) hang together in the order in which they are given. The exposition follows the order of the text. Even if a *divisio textus* is provided on the level of words within a verse or clause, the exposition will treat the words in the order in which they are used in the biblical text. Regarding this, the beginning of Thomas's analysis of the first *clausula* of the Fourth Gospel is exceptional. Thomas writes:

> With respect to the first of these four, we must examine the meaning of the statement "In the beginning was the Word". And here, three things present themselves for careful study according to the three parts of this statement. First it is necessary to investigate the name "Word"; secondly, the phrase "in the beginning;" thirdly, the meaning of the Word "was in the beginning".[9]

In his discussion of the first clause of John Thomas treats 'Word' first, and only then will he speak about the interpretation of 'In the beginning'. This is exceptional in medieval commentaries on John. Both Albert and Bonaventure discuss the words of this verse in the order in which they are given, as the *Glossa* had done before them. This reversal in word order is exceptional in Thomas as well, although not for this specific text: in the *Catena Aurea* on Jn 1:1, Thomas gives the patristic interpretations of 'Word' before those on 'In the beginning', just as he does here in the commentary. Neither in the *Catena* nor here an explicit reason is given for this reversal of the order of the words that Scripture offers, but it will become clear later.

Verbum

Thomas's interpretation of the word *Verbum* in Jn 1:1 consists of three steps.[10] Thomas begins with an analysis of *verbum* that leads to a first

---

[9] "Circa primum autem videndum est quid sit hoc quod dicitur 'in principio erat verbum'. Ubi tria diligenter inquirenda concurrunt, secundum tres dictiones huius orationis. Et primo quid sit hoc quod dicitur 'verbum'; secundo quid sit hoc quod dicitur 'in principio'; tertio quid sit hoc quod dicitur 'verbum erat in principio'". *In Io* 1:1 §24.

[10] Thomas's understanding of what a word is, has developed considerably over the course of his career and reached a conclusion in his discussion of it in the *ScG*. Since *In Io* was written after *ScG* and does not differ from that work in its understanding of what a word is, there is no need to discuss the development prior to *ScG* here. Cf. H.J.M.J. Goris, 'Theology and Theory of the Word in Aquinas: Understanding

theological conclusion: the sense *verbum* has in Jn 1. Then he discusses the distinction between the Word of God and human words, which leads to further theological conclusions about the Word. Finally, Thomas discusses four questions about *verbum* that each have their origin in patristic commentaries on John and bring further clarifications.

In order to understand what a 'word' is, one has to study how our language works. Thomas begins his analysis of *verbum* with a remark from Aristotle's *Peri Hermeneias*: "vocal sounds are signs of the affections that exist in our soul".[11] Our words do not refer to external objects in the first place, but they are signs of concepts in our intellect.[12] Therefore it is fitting that both what is within our soul and the exterior vocal sound are called a "word". Augustine had written in *De Trinitate* that "the word which sounds externally, is a sign of the word which lies hid within, to which the name of 'word' more truly appertains", and Thomas quotes this in his *Catena Aurea* on Jn 1:1.[13] In his commentary on John, Thomas does not enter the discussion whether the name 'word' is said more truly of external or internal words, but gives a twofold order. In the order of existence, the interior word comes first and causes the vocal expression. In the order of knowledge, we have to look at the meaning of the exterior word to understand the meaning of the interior word that caused it.

Thomas starts with a reflection on the exterior word. This word needs to be distinguished from three things in our intellect. It needs to be distinguished from the intellect itself, from the act of understanding, and from that through which the intellect comes to understanding, what Thomas here calls the *species rei intellectae*, and elsewhere the *species*

Augustine by Innovating Aristotle', in: M. Dauphinais, B. David, M. Levering (eds.), *Aquinas the Augustinian*, Washington, D.C., The Catholic University of America Press, 2007, p. 62-78; cf. G. Emery, *The Trinitarian Theology of St Thomas Aquinas*, Oxford, Oxford University Press, 2007, p. 180-183.

[11] "Ea quae sunt in voce, sunt signa earum, quae sunt in anima, passionum". Aristotle, *Peri Hermeneias* I, 16a3.

[12] Aquinas tacitly reads Aristotle's "affections that exist in the soul" as "conceptions of the intellect". He does not give arguments for this interpretation in this commentary, but he does so in the commentary on *Peri Hermeneias*. The argument there is that Aristotle is not speaking about vocal sounds in general, but about those that are significant by human institution: "Et uerum est quod huiusmodi passiones significant naturaliter quaedam uoces hominum, ut gemitus infirmorum, et alia similia, ut dicitur in I Politice. Set nunc est sermo de uocibus significatiuis ex institutione humana. Et ideo oportet passiones anime hic intelligere intellectus conceptiones, quas nomina et uerba et orationes significant, secundum sententiam Aristotilis". *In Peryerm I,* lect. 2, lines 92-100.

[13] Augustine, *De Trinitate* Bk 3, Ch 3.20. Cf. *Catena Aurea in Io* 1:1.

intelligibilis. Thomas compares it to the *species sensibilis*: just like the eye achieves sight through the species of colour, so the intellect reaches understanding through the *species intelligibilis*. Thomas equates it with the *forma* of a thing: what in metaphysical terms the *forma* of a thing is, is what in Thomas's theory of understanding is its *species intelligibilis*, that through which we reach understanding.

Thomas uses the example of the word 'stone' to clarify the three things from which the external word needs to be distinguished: that word neither refers to our intellect itself, nor to the act of understanding, nor to that from the stone which makes it intelligible for us, its *species intelligibilis*: none of these are what is signified by the exterior vocal word 'stone'. An interior word, that which we express through our spoken words, is what the one understanding forms when understanding: a concept of the known thing which we form in our mind and which proceeds within our intellect. A word is the fruit of that process. We form words in two ways, according to the two operations of the intellect: either we grasp the essence of a thing, when we form a definition, or we unite and separate it from other concepts and build sentences. An exterior word does not signify something by which the intellect understands, but the understanding itself that the intellect has reached; the definition of 'stone' or the judgment 'it is a stone'. In what is expressed and formed, the intellect sees the nature of the thing understood. "Thus we have the meaning of the name 'word'".[14] As Gilles Emery remarks: "The word is thus relative through and through. It is relative to the mind which forms it and to the known thing which is manifested to the mind which conceives it. It is through the word that we 'unite' ourselves to the known reality".[15]

A word is something that always proceeds from an intellect existing in act. And a word is always a notion (*ratio*) and likeness of the thing understood. This leads Thomas to the next point. When what an intellect understands is something other than itself, the likeness it forms is of the thing understood, not of the one understanding: a conception one has of a stone is the likeness of the stone, not of the intellect. But when the intellect understands itself, it is a likeness and notion of the intellect. Two things here are important for Trinitarian theology: that the word is something that proceeds from an intelligence in act and that therefore there is a relationship of origin between the inner word and the intelligence makes it possible to understand how 'word' can be used

[14] "Sic ergo habemus significationem huius nominis quod est verbum" *In Io* 1:1 §25 (text corrected by L. Reid).
[15] G. Emery, *The Trinitarian Theology of St Thomas Aquinas*, p. 184.

analogically to signify a divine person, the Son.[16] Secondly, that the intellect when it understands itself, is a likeness and notion of the intellect, makes Augustine's likeness of the Trinity in the soul possible: that analogy is about the mind as it understands itself, not as it understands other things.

One final point needs to be made before Thomas can reach a first conclusion about the word that John begins his gospel with. It belongs to understanding that the intellect in understanding forms something. That which the intellect in understanding forms is called a word. Therefore, in every being which understands there must be a word. There are three kinds of intellectual natures: human, angelic and divine. About which is the evangelist speaking? Angels and human beings both exist before their words do. But John states: "In the beginning was the word". Therefore, Thomas concludes, the word of which John speaks here is the Word of God.[17]

After this first conclusion has been reached, Thomas, in a second step, discusses the distinction between the Word of God and our human words. He notes three differences: the first two are derived from Augustine's discussion of the Word in book 15 of his *De Trinitate*, the third from John of Damascus's *De fide orthodoxa*. Firstly, putting aside the first principles, which are known at once, we usually arrive at a word by a process of reasoning. We think and argue, and only when we conceive a notion of a thing completely, we have a word for it. That cannot be true of the Word of God because that Word is always in act, never in potency. Suggesting a thinking process in God would imply change in God.[18] Secondly, we need many imperfect words to express all we know. But it is not like that with God. Because he understands himself through his essence, in one act, in God there is one perfect Word.[19] Thirdly, the word that my intellect forms is not me; it does not exist on its own, nor is it of the essence of my soul, but it exists as an accident in it. But in God, there is no difference between being and understanding. The Word in God, therefore, cannot be an accident but belongs to God's nature. Our words

---

[16] P. Klimczak, *Christus Magister: Le Christ maître dans les commentaires évangéliques de Saint Thomas d'Aquin*, Fribourg, Academic Press Fribourg, 2013, p. 35.

[17] *In Io* 1:1 §25. That the word about which John speaks cannot be a human or an angelic word because humans and angels predate their words, and therefore must be the Word of God, is taken from Basil's homilies on John; Thomas quotes it in the *Catena Aurea in Io* 1:1.

[18] *In Io* 1:1 §26. Cf. *Catena Aurea in Io* 1:1.

[19] *In Io* 1:1 §27. Cf. *Catena Aurea in Io* 1:1.

are concepts in our minds, but the Word in God is a substantial Word, a hypostasis.[20]

This reflection brings Thomas to a theological conclusion which he formulates very succinctly:

> From the above it is to be held that the Word, properly speaking, is always understood as a Person in the divinity, since it implies only something expressed, by the one understanding; also, that in the Divinity the Word is the likeness of that from which it issues; and that it is co-eternal with that from which it issues, since it was not first formable before being formed, but was always in act; and that it is equal to the Father since it is perfect and expressive of the whole being of the Father; and that it is co-essential and consubstantial with the Father since it subsists in his nature.[21]

This brief conclusion reads like a summary of the council of Nicea, based on Thomas's theological understanding of 'Word' when it is used for God: the Word is a person in God, which, because it is something expressed, implies a procession from the one understanding. Therefore it cannot be used essentially, but only personally.[22] The Word is like the person who utters it, and because there is no potency in God, only act, the Word is co-eternal from Him from whom it issues. Since it is the one perfect Word that expresses the Father wholly, it is equal to the Father. Since it shares the divine nature with the Father, it is co-essential and consubstantial with the Father.

Thomas adds one more conclusion: "It is also clear that since in every nature that which issues forth and has a likeness and the nature of that from which it issues is called a son, and since this Word issues forth in a likeness to the nature from which it issues, it is called a 'Son', and its production is called a 'generation'".[23] The implications of the theology of

---

[20] *In Io* 1:1 §28.

[21] "Ex praemissis ergo tenendum est quod verbum, proprie loquendo, semper personaliter accipitur in divinis, cum non importet nisi quid expressum ab intelligente. Item quod verbum in divinis sit similitudo eius a quo procedit; et quod sit coaeternum ei a quo procedit, cum non prius fuerit formabile quam formatum, sed semper in actu; et quod sit aequale patri, cum sit perfectum, et totius esse patris expressivum; et quod sit coessentiale et consubstantiale patri, cum sit subsistens in natura eius". *In Io* 1:1 §29 (text corrected by L. Reid).

[22] That was the point on which Thomas's thinking had developed into the mature understanding first expressed in the *ScG*: cf. H. Goris, 'Theology and Theory of the Word in Aquinas: Understanding Augustine by Innovating Aristotle'.

[23] "Patet etiam quod cum in qualibet natura illud quod procedit, habens similitudinem et naturam eius a quo procedit, vocetur filius, et hoc verbum procedat in similitudine naturae eius a quo procedit, dicitur filius, et productio eius dicitur generatio". *In Io* 1:1 §29 (text corrected by L. Reid).

the Word that Thomas has developed thus far give substance to the appropriateness and content of 'Son'. That the Word of God is the Son of God is based on two characteristics 'Word' and 'Son' have in common: both issue forth from something else, and both have a likeness to that from which they issue.

In his discussion of Thomas's commentary on Jn 1:1, Gilles Emery asks whether Thomas has fallen for the temptation to prove the existence of the Word of God. In the *Summa Theologiae*, Thomas argued that that is not possible because reason does not exist univocally in God and in us.[24] Thomas does not make that point in the commentary, but there can be no question of proving an article from the creed philosophically here. The biblical commentary starts with the revealed word of God and, "using an analogy which gets to grips with the content of the confession of faith, one has disclosed how we can get to grips with the generation of the Word in God".[25]

In a third and final step, Thomas discusses four questions about the understanding of the word. All four questions have a patristic source, and all can be found in the *Catena Aurea*. The first question, stemming from Chrysostom's homilies in John, asks why the evangelist omits the Father and begins at once with the Son. Thomas hands down the double answer Chrysostom gives to this question. One reason is that the Father was known in the Old Testament, albeit not as Father but as God, but the Son was not known. With a meaningful aside, Thomas adds: "And so in the New Testament, which is concerned with our knowledge of the Word, he did begin with the Word or Son".[26] The other reason is that the Son brings us to a knowledge of the Father. Since the evangelist wants to bring us to knowledge of the Father, it is fitting that he should begin with the Son.[27]

The second question also stems from Chrysostom. Why does John say: "In the beginning was the Word" and not "In the beginning was the Son?" Again, two reasons are given. The first is that speaking of the generation of the Son might be misunderstood as a material generation and as change in God. To exclude that possibility, "Word" is used instead. The second reason is that John wishes to show that the Word has come to manifest the Father. "But since the idea of manifesting is implied better in the name 'Word' than in the name 'Son', he preferred to use the name

[24] *STh* I q. 32 a. 1 ad 2.

[25] G. Emery, *The Trinitarian Theology of St Thomas Aquinas*, p. 185.

[26] "et ideo in novo testamento, in quo agitur de cognitione verbi, incepit a verbo, sive filio". In Io 1:1 §30 (text corrected by L. Reid).

[27] *In Io* 1:1 §30. Cf. *Catena Aurea in Io* 1:1.

'Word'".[28] Here, revelation, or, in Thomas's word, 'manifestation', is shown to be central in Thomas's understanding of the beginning of the Gospel. It is because of Revelation that 'Word' is the name used in these verses, and this 'Word' is fundamental to the understanding of 'Son'.[29]

The third question, taken from Augustine, is about the translation. Why is the Greek word *Logos* translated as *verbum* and not as *ratio*, which would have been possible as well? Thomas gives Augustine's answer that both *verbum* and *ratio* signify a concept of the mind. *Ratio*, however, implies merely that, whereas *verbum* also implies a reference to something exterior. Since the evangelist not only wants to signify the Son's existence in the Father but also the operative power of the Son, by whom all things were made, 'Word' is the better translation.[30] With this remark, with its reference to the Nicene creed ("by Whom all things are made") that "securely grounds the argument in the tradition of revelation".[31] Thomas already points forward to the commentary on Jn 1:3-5, which will discuss the relation of the eternal Word to creation.

The final question, taken from Origen's commentary on John, notices that Scripture often speaks of 'the Word of God' and asks why the text here just has 'the Word'. Origen's reply is that just as truth is one, and wisdom is one, so the Word must be one as well. By just speaking of 'the Word', the evangelist is more clearly speaking of the Word elevated above all other (human and angelic) words. Thomas adds that just as it is by participating in the divine Wisdom that wise persons are wise, so it is by participating in the one absolute Word that people who have a word are called speakers. Thomas ends with an implicit quote from Chrysostom that in Greek the article is added to the Word *Logos* to stress the separation and elevation of this Word.[32]

The four small *questiones* are patristic, but the choice to include these questions and include them at this point of the commentary is Thomas's. In his commentary on John, Albert only has the question of

---

[28] "Unde cum ratio manifestationis magis importetur in nomine verbi quam in nomine filii, ideo magis est usus nomine verbi". *In Io* 1:1 §31. Cf. *Catena Aurea in Io* 1:1.

[29] Cf. C. Berchtold, *Manifestatio Veritatis: Zum Offenbarungsbegriff bei Thomas von Aquin*, Münster, Lit Verlag, 2000, p. 162: "Wo es also um die "ratio manifestationis" geht, um Offenbarung als einen Sachgrund der Inkarnation, ist Thomas entschlossen, den Begriff des Wortes dem Sohnesbegriff vorzuziehen".

[30] *In Io* 1:1 §32. Cf. *Catena Aurea in Io* 1:1.

[31] D.B. Burrell, 'Creation in St. Thomas Aquinas's *Super Evangelium S. Joannis Lectura*', in: M. Dauphinais, M. Levering (eds.), *Reading John with St. Thomas Aquinas: Theological Exegesis and Speculative Theology*, Washington D.C., Catholic University of America Press, 2005, p. 115-126, here p. 121.

[32] *In Io* 1:1 §33. Cf. *Catena Aurea in Io* 1:2. The reference to Chrysostom is from his *Homilies on John*, 2, cf. *Catena Aurea in Io* 1:1.

why the evangelist starts with the Word and not with the Son.[33] Bonaventure discusses the same question. However, he adds a question of whether the analogy of the procession of the Word with the procession from the Son from the Father does not imply that the Word is later than God, just as a son is posterior to his father.[34] Thomas discusses this in his description of the differences between God's Word and human words, as we saw.

Thomas profits from his *Catena Aurea*, in which these four questions are all included. That is not the only reason why these four questions are included here, however. Origen discusses why the Gospel here just speaks of 'the Word' and not of 'the Word of God' in his commentary on Jn 1:2, and in accordance with that, Thomas gives it in the *Catena Aurea* at the same verse. In the commentary on John, however, Thomas includes it in his discussion of *verbum* at the beginning of the commentary.

It is worth noticing that there is a common focus in the four questions Thomas discusses, and that focus is the relation of the Word to us. John begins with the Son because it is through the Son that we are brought to knowledge of the Father. John speaks of the Word because he teaches how the Word manifests the Father. The Greek word *Logos* is translated as *verbum* because, contrary to *ratio*, *verbum* implies a reference to something exterior of the speaker. The evangelist finally, points to the Word absolutely because it is in participating in this absolute Word that we have language.

In their commentaries on "in the beginning was the Word", both Albert and Bonaventure state that this *clausula* teaches us the unity in essence of the Word and God.[35] This is not absent from Thomas's commentary either, as we have seen: Thomas's brief 'theology of the Word' with which he starts his commentary allows him to teach his students how to speak well about the Word of God. In Thomas's commentary, the theological understanding of the first *clausula* does not stop there, however. Thomas's analysis also allows him to show from the beginning that the Word is related to us to whom it is spoken. As Graziano Perillo has remarked, based on this notion of Word, Thomas can conclude

---

[33] Albert, *Super Io* 1:1 p. 18. Albert here only gives the first answer of Chrysostom, that speaking of the Son might lead to the misunderstanding of a carnal generation. He also refers to Chrysostom's remarks about the article in Greek. A more elaborate discussion of 'verbum' follows in Albert's commentary on "Et Deus erat verbum:" Albert, *Super Io* 1:1 p. 44-48.

[34] Bonaventure, *In Io* 1:1 n. 6 and n. 8.

[35] "Per quam ostenditur Verbi ad intellectum paternum inseperabilitas". Albert, *Super Io* 1:1 p. 14. "Prima igitur conditio est in essentia unitas". Bonaventure, *In Io* 1:1 n. 2.

that God is not only the one who understands himself but the one who speaks.[36]

In the beginning was the Word

In his commentary on John, Origen lists several meanings that 'beginning' can have and discusses which of those help understand the first verse of John's Gospel.[37] Thomas quotes this text at length in the *Catena Aurea*. In the commentary, he starts his analysis of *principium* with Origen's list, but here he restructures it into a list of four meanings. First, there is a beginning in quantity, a principle of numbers and lengths. Secondly, there is a beginning in time. Thirdly, there is a beginning in learning, both according to the nature of learning itself and to our learning. Thomas refers here to Hebr 5:12, as Origen had done as well: "For though by this time you ought to be teachers, you need someone to teach you again the basic elements of the oracles of God".[38] The distinction between the nature of learning and our learning is from Origen, and Thomas quotes the Christological explanation of it as well: "As to nature, in Christian doctrine the beginning and principle of our wisdom is Christ, inasmuch as he is the Wisdom and Word of God, i.e., in His divinity. But as to ourselves, the beginning is Christ himself inasmuch as the Word has become flesh, i.e., by his incarnation".[39] Finally, there is an order in the production of something, either a beginning on the part of the thing generated, like the foundation of a house, or a beginning on the one generating, and here Thomas sees three principles: one of intention, the goal, one of reason, the idea in the mind of the maker, and the execution, which Thomas calls the operative power.[40]

From this, Thomas draws three explanations for "In the beginning", all three with patristic origins. The first two are derived from the fourth sense of *principium*. From Origen, Thomas receives the

[36] "Per queste ragioni, sulla base della testimonianza della rivelazione, Dio non è da comprendere unicamente come *intelligere* che intende se stesso, dimensione di processione intelletuale del divino che può essere spiegata con il solo ricorso alla *species intelligibilis*, ma come il dicente". G. Perillo, *Teologia del Verbum: La lectura super Ioannis Evangelium di Tommaso d'Aquino*, Napoli, Luciano Editore, 2003, p. 87 (original stress).

[37] Origen, *Commentary on John*, Bk. 1, Ch 16-20, §90-124.

[38] Note that while Thomas only quotes the beginning of the verse here ("deberetis esse magistri propter tempus"), the point is hidden in the implied second half.

[39] "Et hoc modo, secundum naturam quidem, in disciplina Christiana initium et principium sapientiae nostrae est Christus, inquantum est sapientia et verbum Dei, idest secundum divinitatem. Quoad nos vero principium est ipse Christus, inquantum 'verbum caro factum est', idest secundum eius incarnationem". *In Io* 1:1 §34.

[40] *In Io* 1:1 §34. Cf. *Catena Aurea in Io* 1:1.

interpretation that *principium* can be understood to stand for the person of the Son. The verse then reads "In the Son was the Word:" the Word himself is the *principium*, the principle of all creation.[41]

Secondly, *principium* can stand for the Father who, as Thomas writes, "is the principle not only of creatures but of every divine process". Thomas explains this Trinitarian interpretation with a reference to Jn 14:10: "I am in the Father, and the Father is in me". The Son is consubstantial with the Father: both have the same essence.[42] Finally, *principium* can mean a beginning of duration. In this case, the sense is that the Word was before all things, and the phrase shows the eternity of the Word.[43] Thomas does not choose between these three interpretations. All three show something about the Word and are helpful. Thomas concludes: "And thus by the first explanation the causality of the Word is asserted; according to the second, the consubstantiality of the Word with the Father; and by the third, the coeternity of the Word".[44] There is a clear difference in the way this verse is treated by Bonaventure, Albert and Thomas. Both Bonaventure and Albert start their discussion of the *clausula* by stating its meaning, and both read it as stating the unity of the Word with God, as we saw before. Thomas starts by mapping out the possible meanings of a word and from there shows different interpretations of the *clausula*. He does not choose between them, but gives them as parallel interpretations.

It can be understood now as well why Thomas begins his commentary with his interpretation of *verbum*, and only after that gives the three interpretations of *In principium*. All three interpretations presuppose that the word of which the evangelist speaks is the Word of God. Furthermore, because he has shown before that *verbum* implies a double relation, both to the speaker and the ones spoken to, he is now able to give an interpretation that relates the Word to creation, of which it is the *principium*, the principle, and one that relates it to the Father, with whom the Word shares his essence.

Thomas makes two brief remarks about the fact that the text says that the word 'was' ("*erat*"). First, there is a remark regarding the past imperfect tense of the verb. Thomas remarks that John reserves the past imperfect sense ("*erat*") to mention eternal things and uses the past

---

[41] *In Io* 1:1 §35. Thomas refers here to Jn 8:25: "I am the *principium* who also speaks to you".

[42] *In Io* 1:1 §36.

[43] *In Io* 1:1 §37.

[44] "Sic igitur per primam expositionem, asseritur verbi causalitas; secundum autem secundam, verbi consubstantialitas ad patrem; per tertiam, verbi coaeternitas". *In Io* 1:1 §38 (text corrected by L. Reid).

perfect sense ("*fuit*") to refer to temporal things in the past. Ex 3:14, however, "I am who I am", uses the present tense to speak about God's eternity. Is that not better? Thomas makes a distinction: considered from the nature of time, from our human perspective in time, the past imperfect tense is better because it indicates that something has existed and still exists, while the present tense does not describe the past and continued existence of something. The present tense, however, better designates that something is in act, which God always is.[45] The second brief remark about the verb states that *esse* here is a substantive verb, a verb that does not indicate a temporal change but the existence of something.[46]

Before going on to the next *clausula*, Thomas returns one last time to the question of how the Word can be co-eternal to the Father. Since the Father begets it, is it not subsequent to Him? Thomas mentions three erroneous ways of understanding the generation of the divine Word: the procession of the Word is a conception in the intellect, and God does not exist before God understands, for, in that case, God would understand in potency before God would understand in act. Secondly, the Word should not be understood to be unformed before it is formed. Thirdly, if the Father's existence is understood as prior to that of the Word, the procession of the Word is an act of the will of the Father, instead of a natural generation. It would mean that the Word is created and thus lead to Arianism. Instead, speaking of natural generation shows that the processions in God are radically different from the process of creation.

Thomas gives what he calls an analogy to a limited degree (*aliqualis similitudo*) of coeternity, taken from Augustine and already present in the *Catena Aurea*.[47] There is no fire without the brightness of it. If we imagine an eternal fire, the brightness would have to be co-eternal with it. As Augustine mentioned and Thomas quotes, the defect in the analogy is that fire and brightness are not of the same nature. That is why we call the Word 'Son', a likeness that does stress the identity in nature. Thomas concludes that we need many likenesses to attain knowledge of divine things. Different likenesses clarify different things. Thomas inserts a quotation from a sermon of Theodotus, bishop of Ancyra, that he had read in the acts of the council of Ephesus:

---

[45] *In Io* 1:1 §39.

[46] *In Io* 1:1 §40. Thomas refers to the *Glossa* in his remark. In the *Catena Aurea*, a remark to the same extent is included from Origen's commentary on John.

[47] *Catena Aurea in Io* 1:1. The relatively long text in the *Catena Aurea* is an abridged version of Augustine, *Sermo* 117.

> And so we give the Son various names to express His perfection in different ways, which cannot be expressed by one name. We call him "Son" to show that he is of the same nature as the Father; we call him "image" to show that he is like the Father in any way; we call him "brightness" to show that he is coeternal, and he is called the "Word" to show that he is begotten in an immaterial manner.[48]

The importance of a preposition

In his commentary on the second *clausula* "And the Word was with God", Thomas concentrates on the two words that did not appear in the first sentence: 'God' and 'with'. About the word 'God' (*Deus*), Thomas makes a single, brief remark: in contrast to the word 'deity' (*deitas*), which signifies the divinity in the abstract and absolutely and therefore cannot stand for one of the divine persons, the word 'God' can. In this *clausula*, the word 'God' must stand for the Father, Thomas argues, because the preposition 'with' signifies a distinction of 'the Word' and 'God'. This distinction has to be a distinction in person. It cannot be a distinction in nature because the Father and the Son have the same nature.[49]

Thomas gives a more elaborate analysis of the word 'with' (*apud*) in three steps. First, the word in itself is analysed. Thomas remarks that the preposition 'with' signifies a certain union of the thing signified by its grammatical antecedent to the thing signified by its grammatical object. In that sense, it is like the word 'in'. However, the words differ: Thomas calls the union that the preposition 'in' signifies 'a certain intrinsic union' and the union that the preposition 'with' signifies 'in a certain way an extrinsic union'. The comparison with 'in' is not randomly chosen but is relevant for Trinitarian theology: we say both that the Son is in the Father and that the Son is with the Father. 'The Son is in the Father', the intrinsic union, refers to the consubstantiality of the Son and the Father, 'the Son

---

[48] "Nominamus ergo filium diversis nominibus, ad exprimendum diversimode perfectionem eius, quae uno nomine non potest exprimi. Ut enim ostendatur connaturalis patri, dicitur filius; ut ostendatur omnino similis, dicitur imago; ut ostendatur coaeternus, dicitur splendor; ut ostendatur immaterialiter genitus, dicitur verbum". *In Io* 1:1 §42 (text corrected by L. Reid). Cf. H.J.M. Schoot, *Christ the 'Name' of God: Thomas Aquinas on Naming Christ*, Leuven, Peeters, 1993, p. 176 nt.8; G. Emery, *The Trinitarian Theology of St Thomas Aquinas*, p. 194. It is worth noting that while in the *Summa Theologiae* the diversity of the names 'Word', 'Son', 'Splendor' and 'Image' is mentioned in the context of a discussion of the *proprietates* of the Son, Thomas does not enter into that discussion at this place in the commentary, but restricts himself to the remark that we need different names to come to knowledge of the Son: Cf. *STh* I q. 34 a. 2 ad 3.

[49] *In Io* 1:1 §44.

is with the Father', the extrinsic union, refers to the distinction in persons, the only distinction possible because the Son is distinguished from the Father by origin alone.[50] The word 'with' therefore principally signifies a distinction, and secondly, a certain union.[51]

Thomas introduces the second step by stating that the word *apud* signifies four things. It implies the subsistence of its antecedent because it is only used for things that subsist of themselves: we do not say that a colour is with a body, but we do say that a man is with a man and a stone with a stonc. Secondly, it implies authority in its grammatical object, because in Thomas's Latin, it is not properly said that a king is with a soldier, but only that the soldier is with the king. The third and fourth meaning are those given above: *apud* signifies a distinction because we do not say that a person is with himself, and it signifies a certain union and fellowship.

Returning for a moment to the three meanings of *principium* in the first clause of the Gospel, Thomas states that if one leaves out the interpretation of *principium* as signifying the Son, the other two (*principium* as beginning and as signifying the Father) each can be misunderstood in two heretical ways. The four ways in which *apud* can be understood gain their theological importance here: each one of these four corrects one of the misunderstandings.[52]

After analysing the word *apud* and the different things it can mean, the third step Thomas takes is to discuss these four objections to the first clause and explain which interpretation of *apud* helps to reply to the objection. Each of these four answers leads to an interpretation of "the Word was with God" that Thomas found in his sources. The first two objections refer to the interpretation of *principium* as 'beginning'. Firstly there is the objection that if 'in the beginning' means 'before all things', implying that before all things, there was nothing, where then was the Word? This is a question posed by people who can only imagine things as existing in some time and place, Thomas remarks. When *apud* is read as signifying a certain union, this objection can be replied by stating that the Word was 'with God' in the sense that Basil interprets it in his

[50] Thomas expresses some hesitaton about the use of the phrase 'extrinsic union', since the word 'extrinsic' cannot properly be used *in divinis*.

[51] "Hec vero praepositio 'apud' consubstantialitatem quidem designat inquantum coniunctionem aliquam importat, sed distinctionem personarum principalius inquantum coniunctionem quodammodo extrinsecam importat". *In Io* 1:1 §45 (text corrected by L. Reid).

[52] *In Io* 1:1 §46.

commentary: "not in some place since he is unsurroundable, but he is with the Father, who is not enclosed by any place".[53]

The other objection against this interpretation of *principium* is directed towards the idea of procession in God. If the Word was before all things, it cannot have proceeded from something else because that something else would have had to have been prior to the Word. In his reply to this, Thomas uses the interpretation of *apud* as authority, and refers to the interpretation of Hilary, who wrote: "although the Word has no beginning of duration, still he does not lack an author, for he was with God as his author".[54]

The third and fourth objections arise when *principium* is interpreted as signifying the Father. The third concludes from the reading that the Son was in the Father, that the Son, therefore, cannot be subsistent, since something that is in something else does not subsist in itself, as a hypostasis. Here Thomas refers to the signification of *apud* as implying the subsistence of its grammatical precedent and refers to the interpretation of Chrysostom: "he was 'with God', as subsisting, and a divine hypostasis".[55]

The final objection concludes from the reading 'the Son was in the Father' that there is no distinction between Father and Son. Against this, the word *apud*, interpreted as indicating a distinction, makes it possible to read the second clause as a refutation of this objection. Thomas refers here to Alcuin and Bede, who wrote: "he was with the Father by a consubstantiality of nature, while still being 'with' God the Father through a distinction in person".[56] Thomas concludes: "And so, with "and the Word was with God" you have the union of the Word with the Father in nature, according to Basil; their distinction in person, according to Alcuin and Bede; the subsistence of the Word in the divine

---

[53] "Non in aliquo loco, cum incircumscriptibile sit, sed apud patrem, qui etiam neque loco neque circumscriptione aliqua continetur". *In Io* 1:1 §47 (text corrected by L. Reid). The reference is to Basil, *Homily* 16.4.

[54] "Licet verbum careat initio durationis, non tamen caret auctore: erat enim apud Deum, ut apud auctorem". *In Io* 1:1 §48 (text corrected by L. Reid). The reference is to Hilary, *De Trinitate*, bk. 2 §14.

[55] "Erat *apud Deum*, ut subsistens, et hypostasis". *In Io* 1:1 §49 (text corrected by L. Reid). The reference is to Chrysostom, *In Io Homilia* 4.1.

[56] "sic erat in patre per consubstantialitatem naturae, quod tamen est apud Deum scilicet Paterm per distinctionem personae". *In Io* 1:1 §50 (text corrected by L. Reid). The reference is to Alcuin, *Commentary in Io* 1, and Bede, *In S. Ioannis Evangelium expositio*, 1. In the beginning of his commentary on John, Alcuin is heavily relying on Bede's. Cf. M.M. Gorman, 'Rewriting Augustine: Alcuin's Commentary on the Gospel of John', in: *Revue Bénédictine* 119 (2009), p. 36-85.

nature, according to Chrysostom; and the authorship of the Father in relation to the Word, according to Hilary".[57]

A few remarks are in place here. First, In the prologue to his commentary, Thomas had written that John wrote his Gospel in reaction to heresies that denied the divinity of Christ.[58] Against this background, Thomas reads the first clauses of the Gospel as if they are a series of arguments of one side in a debate. The debate opens with the first clause of the Gospel, "In the beginning was the Word". Thomas reads the second clause of the Gospel, "the Word was with God" as if heretical objections had been made against the first clause that have not been recorded in the Gospel. The second clause is read as a reply to these supposed heretical objections. Therefore, we have the arguments of one side of the debate, the side of John the Evangelist. That is the *ordo disciplinae* that is proper to this part of the Gospel. That order is put there intentionally by the evangelist: each new clause replies to heretical objections that might be made against the clause before it.

Furthermore, Thomas's analysis of the word *apud* leads him to four interpretations of the clause, all derived from patristic sources, that he juxtaposes without choosing between them. In this, he differs from Bonaventure and Albert. According to Bonaventure, 'the Word was with God' describes one quality of the Word of God and only that quality, which is the dissimilarity in person between the Father and the Son.[59] Albert comments that the preposition *apud* can signify three things: it shows the diversity between what precedes it and what follows it, it shows a nearness between the two, and it signifies the authority of the grammatical object (Albert uses the same example of the king and the soldier that we found in Thomas). Albert, however, stresses the importance of *apud* as signifying a distinction, beginning his commentary on this clause with a gloss from Augustine that the Word was with God *ut alius apud alium*, and ending it with stating that this clause refutes the heresy of Sabellius, "who denied that there is a distinction of persons in God".[60] Even though he gives three different readings of *apud*, for Albert

---

[57] "Sic ergo per hanc clausulam 'et verbum erat apud Deum', habes coniunctionem verbi ad patrem in natura, secundum Basilium; distinctionem in persona, secundum Alcuinum et Bedam; subsistentiam verbi in natura divina, secundum Chrysostomum; auctoritatem patris ad verbum, secundum Hilarium". *In Io* 1:1 §51 (text corrected by L. Reid).

[58] *In Io* Prol., §10.

[59] Bonaventure, *In Io* 1:1 n. 3.

[60] Albert, *Super Io* 1:1 p. 28-38. Thomas uses the phrase "ut alius apud alium" when he summarises how the first four clauses refute the different heresies: *In Io* 1:2 §64.

"the Word was with God" ultimately has a single meaning, which is to state the distinction between the Father and the Son.[61] In this, he agrees with Bonaventure.

Regarding the use of his sources, Thomas here does not choose between different interpretations he finds in his sources. The different interpretations can be directed against different heresies. That Thomas does not choose between them is therefore not caused by reverence for the authorities that he cites (we will see examples later of places in the commentary where Thomas does state a preference for one patristic interpretation over another), but by his presupposition that the Gospel is written for the refutation of heresies. The four interpretations are juxtaposed because they all contribute to the discussion with heretical understandings of God. That same goal, finally, governs the analysis Thomas makes of the preposition 'with'. The extended analysis of the different things *apud* can signify not only shows Thomas's customary attention to language *in divinis,* but here it has a concrete goal: it prepares the way for and leads up to the four different interpretations Thomas chooses from his sources as useful arguments against heresy.

The order of teaching

We saw before that Thomas recognises an order in the first two clauses of the Gospel: the second clause, "and the Word was with God", responds to possible objections to the first clause "In the beginning was the Word". In his commentary on the third clause, "and the Word was God", Thomas explicitly discusses the order of the text. He writes that this third clause "follows most appropriately considering the order of teaching".[62] That statement can be questioned, as Thomas acknowledges, because it is only after having said both when (In the beginning) and where (with God) the Word was, that this third clause states what the Word is: God.[63]

The context for the question is Aristotelian. Aristotle begins book 2 of his *Posterior Analytics* by distinguishing four scientific questions, to which all questions can be reduced. The precise meaning and the relations

[61] Cf. the *divisio textus*, in which Albert writes: "'Et verbum erat apud Deum', per quam ostenditur Verbi secundum quam procedit a paterno intellectu, distinguens proprietas". Albert, *Super Io* 1:1 p. 14.

[62] "quae quidem secundum ordinem doctrinae congruentissime sequitur". *In Io* 1:1 §53.

[63] Thomas remarks that he takes "Word" to be the subject of the clause, and "God" the predicate: *In Io* 1:1 §53. Cf. §59, where Thomas argues that if 'God' were used here as a subject, the Greek text would have used the article. That Thomas's position is not self-evident is clear from the commentary of Albert, who defends that both readings are possible and both are true. Albert, *Super Io* 1:1 p. 38-40.

between these questions is a complicated matter. Aristotle formulates the questions as follows: whether there is X (*an sit*), what X is (*quid sit*), whether X is Y (*quia* or *quale sit*), and why X is Y (*quare* or *propter quid sit*).[64] He puts the first and third questions on a par. According to Bernard Lonergan, "the first and third questions are empirical questions; they ask about matters of fact; they can be answered by an appeal to observation or experiment".[65] The second and fourth questions also are parallel: presupposing that the question "What is X" can be reformulated as "What makes X to be X", both these questions ask for a cause.[66]

This is the background for Thomas's question of whether the order of the first clauses in the Gospel of John is appropriate. The understanding seems to be that both the question when the Word was and where the Word was, can be reformulated in terms of Aristotle's third question whether X is Y: "Was the Word in the beginning?" and "Was the Word with God?" are questions of this type. The third clause in John, "The Word was God", seems to answer the second Aristotelian question, "What is X?" Hence the objection: "But since one should first inquire what a thing is before investigating where and when it is, it seems that John violated this order by discussing these latter first".[67]

Thomas, expanding on a remark by Origen that he cites in the *Catena Aurea*, remarks that the Word of God is with man and with God in different ways. The Word is with man as perfecting him because it is through the Word of God that man becomes wise and good. Thomas refers to Wisdom 7:27: "She makes them friends of God and prophets".[68] But with God, it is the other way around: God is not perfected and enlightened by his Word. Instead, the Word receives his divinity from Him-who-speaks-the-Word. To clarify that the Word was with God by origin, it is necessary first to show that the Word was in and with the Father from whom the Word receives his divine nature, before showing that the Word was God. When in the *Summa Theologiae* Thomas

---

[64] Aristotle, *Posterior Analytics* II,2.

[65] B.J.F. Lonergan, *Verbum: Word and Idea in Aquinas*, Collected Works of Bernard Lonergan, 2, Toronto, University of Toronto Press, 1997, p. 26.

[66] Ibid., 26. For an account of how Islamic philosophers interpreted these questions and brought them to the attention of medieval Christian thinkers, cf. H.J.M.J. Goris, *Free Creatures of an Eternal God: Thomas Aquinas on God's Infallible Foreknowledge and Irresistible Will*, Leuven, Peeters, 1996, p. 142-147.

[67] "Sed cum prius quaerendum sit de re quid est, quam ubi et quando sit, videtur quod Ioannes hunc ordinem pervertat, insinuans primo de verbo ubi et quando sit". *In Io* 1:1 §54.

[68] Origen, in his commentary, only refers to God's Word coming to prophets. Because of Wis 7:27, Aquinas here broadens the perspective to all people who become wise and good because of the Word. Cf. *Catena Aurea in Io* 1:1.

discusses the Trinity of persons in God, he begins with considering processions in God, "because the divine Persons are distinguished from each other according to the relations of origin".[69] At this place in the commentary, it becomes clear that for Thomas, this *ordo doctrinae* has a biblical foundation in the fourth Gospel's first clauses. Because the relations of origin are the only way to distinguish the persons in God and therefore to speak about the Word of God, the usual Aristotelian way of proceeding must give way to the Johannine order that first shows when and where the Word was, and only after that states what the Word was: God.

Thomas reads the second clause, "the Word was with God" as responding to possible (heretical) objections against the first clause, as was said before. That way of reading is repeated in the commentary on the third clause. Just as in the commentary on the earlier *clausulae*, Thomas here relies heavily on the sources he had assembled in the *Catena Aurea*. First, Thomas returns to the differences between the divine Word and human words. Earlier, Thomas mentioned three differences: our word is in potency before it is in act because it is part of human reasoning; our word is imperfect, we need many words to express our knowledge, and thirdly, our word is not of the same nature as we are.[70] Here Thomas adds a fourth difference. Our words, understood as the exterior words, the vocal sounds with which we express our thoughts, pass away. According to Thomas, the second clause did already help here: our words are 'in' us when they are interior words, and our statements are in motion and pass away when we speak them. But God's Word is 'with' God, as subsistent. To make the point even clearer, the evangelist adds the nature and being of the Word: "the Word was God".[71]

It is worth looking a bit more closely at the terminology Thomas uses here. He states that we generally understand a word to be a manifestation of thoughts (*manifestationem cogitationum*). The word *manifestatio* in Thomas usually has connotations of 'revelation'.[72] It was shown before how central 'manifestation' is to Thomas's understanding

---

[69] *STh* I, q. 27 proe.
[70] *In Io* 1:1 §26-28.
[71] *In Io* 1:1 §55.
[72] C. Berchtold, *Manifestatio Veritatis,* p. 154-157 Cf. E.M. Sweeney, *Divine Revelation in the Commentary of St. Thomas Aquinas on St. John's Gospel*, Unpublished doctoral dissertation, University of Navarra, 1981, p. 66-114. Note that neither in the sources to which Thomas refers here, Hilary's *De Trinitate* and Augustine's *Tract. in Io*, nor in the *Glossa* or *Catena Aurea*, the word *manifestatio* is used at this place.

of the beginning of the Gospel: according to Chrysostom, it is the reason why John begins his Gospel with "In the beginning was the Word", and not with "In the beginning was the Son". Here Thomas expands on that notion and takes away a possible misunderstanding. The Word that reveals, does not pass away, is not in motion. In our understanding of God's revelation, all connotations of time and movement must be understood with reference to us, not to God. Thomas keeps the two things in balance. On the one hand, there is his reading of John that considers the Word "as having come to manifest the Father".[73] On the other hand, the Word is from all eternity. All references to time and change must therefore be kept at bay.

For a second question, Thomas returns to the second clause, "and the Word was with God". Thomas implicitly quotes a remark by the eleventh-century Bulgarian bishop and biblical commentator Theophylact of Ohrid that he earlier inserted in the *Catena Aurea.*[74] Theophylact remarked that from the use of the 'with' in the second clause, it is clear that there is a distinction between the Father and the Son. The third *clausula*, 'the Word was God', is added to clarify that this is not a distinction in nature.

Thomas ends his commentary on this third clause with two remarks about the ways language is used in Scripture. First, implicitly quoting Hilary's *De Trinitate*, Thomas remarks that in Scripture, the word 'God 'is used in different ways. Sometimes it is used for a creature, but then it is always used with a qualification. Ex 7:1 is an example, when JHWH says to Moses: "I have appointed you the god of Pharao". Another example is Ps 82:7: "You are called gods". However, "being given as god and being called god is not the same thing as being God".[75] That the Word is called God without qualification here shows that he is God by his essence, not by participation.

Finally, Thomas discusses why the Greek text of this clause is 'the Word was God' and not 'the God', with an article prefixed to it. Origen had concluded from the absence of this article that the Word "although he was Word by essence, was not God by essence, but is called God by

[73] "Evangelista tractaturus erat de Verbo inquantum venerat ad manifestandum Patrem". *In Io* 1:1 §31.

[74] Theophylact was unknown in the West until Thomas quoted him in the *Catena Aurea*. That Thomas knew his work is an example of Thomas's exceptional knowledge of the Greek fathers. Cf. J.-P. Torrell, *Saint Thomas Aquinas: The Person and His Work*, Washington D.C., Catholic University of America Press, 1996, p. 139.

[75] "Aliud est dari et dici Deum, aliud esse Deum". *In Io* 1:1 §57 (text corrected by L. Reid).

participation; while the Father alone is God by essence. And so he held that the Son is inferior to the Father".[76] Thomas's language is strong, here: Origen "disgracefully misunderstood" (*turpiter erravit*) this verse and "blasphemed" (*blasphemavit*). The antidote comes from Chrysostom, who gives two arguments. If speaking about 'the God', with the article, implied the Father's superiority with respect to the Son, Scripture would only use 'the God' when speaking about the Father. Chrysostom refers to several places in the New Testament where 'the God' with the article has the Son as referent. Secondly, Chrysostom argued that since the evangelist had already spoken about 'the God' twice with the article, it would have been superfluous to do it a third time. Thomas is not convinced by this second argument and gives another reason that he calls 'better' (*melius*). Returning to his interpretation that 'God' here is used as a predicate, Thomas remarks that names used as predicate customarily go without the article because the article indicates separation.[77]

An epilogue

In the commentary on the final clause on the existence of the Word, "He was in the beginning with God" we recognise a by now familiar pattern: Thomas reads it as a correction to possible misunderstandings that the previous clause could have given rise to. Thomas gives two potential misunderstandings. In the *Catena Aurea*, he had quoted Theophylact as saying that according to the pagans, there are different gods that rebel against each other. In the commentary, Thomas gives the examples of Jupiter fighting with Saturn and puts it on a par with the Manicheans "who have contrary principles of nature". In his commentary, Hilary also remarked that 'the Word was God' could have been misinterpreted as going against God's unity. Against that error, Thomas reads this fourth clause as confirming the unity of the Word with God, with whom he was from the beginning. Thomas adds that the union consists of the sharing of one nature by the three persons and by the bond of love between the Father and the Son, referring to the Holy Spirit.[78]

The other misreading is a double misreading from the Arians. According to Thomas, Arius did accept "In the beginning was the Word"

---

[76] "quod verbum non esset Deus per essentiam, licet sit essentialiter Verbum; sed dicitur per participationem Deus: solus vero Pater est Deus per suam essentiam. Et sic ponebat filium patre minorem". *In Io* 1:1 §58.

[77] *In Io* 1:1 §59. Note that the *Catena Aurea* only has Chrysostom's reply, without mentioning Origen's name or interpretation: *Catena Aurea in Io* 1:1. In the commentary Thomas apparently wants to hand on the whole discussion, with Origen's interpretation and with the addition of his own argument for the absence of the clause.

[78] *In Io* 1:2 §60.

but understood 'beginning' only to be a beginning of creatures, thereby denying the coeternity of the Word with the Father. Against this, Thomas quotes Chrysostom's remark that this verse shows that the Father was never without the Word because he was in the beginning, i.e. whenever God existed, with God.[79] The second Arian misreading is to understand the Word as a lesser God. According to Thomas, there are two attributes that Arius attributed solely to God the Father: eternity and omnipotence. This time quoted silently, Chrysostom shows that the Gospel attributes both of these to the Word: the eternity in this verse, "He was in the beginning with God", and the omnipotence in the next: "Through him all things came into being".[80]

Origen called this fourth clause "in a certain sense an epilogue" (*quemdam epilogum premissorum*), a characterisation that Thomas calls "rather beautiful" (*satis pulchre exponens*).[81] Thomas gives his own conclusion, starting with the rather startling remark that "if one considers these four propositions well, he will find that they clearly destroy all the errors of the heretics and of the philosophers".[82] Thomas links the four clauses to four heresies: the first clause, "In the beginning was the Word" refutes the heresy that Christ was a mere man, who took his beginning from the virgin Mary and did not exist from eternity (Thomas mentions Ebion and Cerinthus, Photinus and Paul of Samosata as heretics who defended this); the second clause, "the Word was with God" refutes the heresy of Sabellius, who did not distinguish the Trinity of persons in God; the third clause "the Word was God" refutes Eunomius's heresy that the Son is entirely unlike the Father; the fourth clause, finally, "He was in the beginning with God", refutes Arius, who said that the Son is less than the Father.[83]

That the four clauses are read as refutations of four heresies from the patristic time, is not original to Thomas: both Albert and Bonaventure do the same in their commentaries, as we saw before. Thomas, however, differs from these contemporaries in two ways. First of all, in Thomas's commentary this list of four is a summary, in line with Origen's "very

[79] *In Io* 1:2 §61.
[80] *In Io* 1:2 §62. The two references to Chrysostom's *Homilies on John* are present as a single text in the *Catena Aurea in Io* 1:2.
[81] *In Io* 1:2 §63. Cf. *Catena Aurea in Io* 1:2. The reference is to Origen, *Commentary on John* bk. 2 n. 67-68, where the word 'epilogue' is not mentioned, but the idea that this clause sums up the earlier three is.
[82] "Si quis ergo recte consideret has quatuor propositiones, inveniet evidenter per eas destrui omnes haereticorum et philosophorum errores". *In Io* 1:2 §64.
[83] *In Io* 1:2 §64.

beautiful" characterisation of the fourth clause. Up until this moment, as we have seen, Thomas gives several interpretations of each of the clauses, based on the different patristic commentaries he uses and directed against different heresies. Thomas uses all of these and quotes them side by side. Only here, in the end, he summarises. Both Bonaventure and Albert, on the other hand, direct each of the clauses against one heresy only.

The second difference between Albert and Bonaventure on the one hand and Thomas on the other consists of the list of heresies. Bonaventure's and Albert's interpretations are the same. According to both, the first clause, "In the beginning was the Word", is directed against the pagans who thought that the Father and the Son are different gods.[84] The main point of the first clause for them is the unity of God. Albert and Bonaventure read the second clause as directed against Sabellianism: the word 'with', read as indicating a distinction, is key to this reading.[85] Thomas's two contemporaries both see the third clause as a refutation of Arianism. "The Word was God" shows the equality and unity of the Son with the Father.[86] The fourth clause is read by both as directed against the Photinians and Ebionites, who taught that Christ received his beginning from the virgin Mary.[87] Whether or not the parallel list of heresies in Albert and Bonaventure is a coincidence is not certain. I have not been able to find a text that could have functioned as a source they both used.[88] When at the end of this chapter the different characteristics of Thomas's commentary on Jn 1:1-5 will be brought together, I will present a hypothesis as to why Thomas differs from Albert and Bonaventure in this respect.

Thomas does not only read the four clauses as refutations of heresies but also states that they exclude the errors of philosophers. He mentions four philosophical positions to which the evangelist reacts. Against natural philosophers who maintain that the world came to be by chance (Thomas mentions the name of Democritus), the first clause

---

[84] Albert, *Super Io* 1:1 p. 22. Bonaventure, *In Io* 1:1 n. 2. Both Albert and Bonaventure refer to Augustine's *De agone Christiano* c.15 n. 17, where this criticism can be found, albeit without a reference to Jn 1.

[85] Albert, *Super Io* 1:1 p. 34. Bonaventure, *In Io* 1:1 n. 3.

[86] Albert, *Super Io* 1:1 p. 48. Bonaventure, *In Io* 1:1 n. 4.

[87] Albert, *Super Io* 1:2 p. 52-54. Bonaventure, *In Io* 1:2 n. 5.

[88] Both refer to Augustine's *De agone Christiano*, Bonaventure even several times in his brief commentary on Jn 1:1-2. In *De agone*, Augustine gives a list of heresies that is to be avoided in Ch 14-32 (after already having argued against the Manicheans in ch. 4) that could have been used by Abert and Bonaventure. Against this hypothesis however, it must be said first, that *De Agone* does not link the heresies it discusses to the four clauses in Jn 1:1-2, and secondly neither Albert nor Bonaventure use this text as their only source.

confirms that things derive their beginning from the Word. Against Plato's conviction that the ideas in which material things participate exist independently, apart from God, Thomas refers to the second clause. Against another Platonist thesis that the ideas and likenesses of all things exist in a certain mind that exists as less than God, Thomas directs the third clause. The fourth clause, finally, is directed against Aristotle's conviction that the world is eternal. Against that thesis, the final clause, read as "only" the Word was in the beginning with God, is contrasted.[89]

A few remarks need to be made here. First of all, both with the four heretical positions refuted by the four clauses, and with these four philosophical theses, Thomas explicitly says that it is John the evangelist who contrasts these opinions. In both cases, the words read like a refrain: *"Contra hoc est quod Evangelista dicit ... addit Evangelista ... addit Evangelista ... contra hoc est quod Evangelista dicit*". Surprising as this may be to our ears, it is undeniable that Thomas sees John the Evangelist as deliberately refuting errors from ancient Greek philosophers.

Secondly, these four 'refutations', whatever their philosophical value may be, are the counterpart of the four ways Thomas mentioned in his prologue to the commentary. There Thomas described four ways in which ancient philosophers came to knowledge of God. [90] The evangelist's contemplation was described as being high, full and perfect. Thomas stated that these three characteristics belong to different sciences and that the Gospel of John contains what these sciences have in a divided way.[91] Thomas's prologue gives the hermeneutical lens through which he reads the Gospel. The parallel, pronounced in the prologue, that this Gospel both contains what the natural sciences have in a divided way and was written to refute the heresies that had come up after the other Gospels had been written, is reflected in the parallel that is given here at the conclusion of the first four clauses, that these refute both the errors of the heretics and the philosophers.

In this interpretation, thirdly, Thomas differs remarkably from Albert and Bonaventure. Apart from the quotation from Augustine that the first clause of the Gospel is directed against pagan polytheism, Bonaventure does not discuss philosophers and their theses in this part of the commentary and hardly at all in the rest of it. Albert asks why John, who could have proved the things he is stating in these clauses by reason alone, did not do so. Albert refers to Chrysostom for the three reasons he gives. Firstly, human reasoning often is fallacious and void, which might

[89] *In Io* 1:2 §65.
[90] *In Io* prol., §2-6.
[91] *In Io* prol., §9.

hinder faith; secondly, if divine truth were to be proved by human reasoning, the assent given to the first truth would not be because of itself, which would be absurd. Thirdly, he would not be able to use arguments from similitudes or conformities since these only follow an already established faith and have no value before it.[92] While Albert will sometimes notice similarities and differences between the Gospel and ancient philosophy, these remarks are relatively rare and piecemeal.[93] Of these three theologians, Thomas is the only one who reads the fourth Gospel as containing and surpassing all philosophical knowledge and interprets the first four clauses as parallel refutations of both patristic heresies and philosophical errors.

After this conclusion, almost as an afterthought, Thomas adds a synoptic comparison that is mainly a quotation from the *Glossa* to which Thomas seems to have added biblical references. John begins his Gospel nobler than the other evangelists. While they announce Christ's birth in time, John tells how he is from eternity; while they show him immediately appearing among people, John shows how he always was with the Father; while they show that he is human, John writes that he is God.[94] It is a confirmation and expansion on what we already saw as the main distinction that Thomas, following Augustine, sees between the synoptic gospels and John's: that while the other Gospels are principally about the humanity of Christ, John is about Christ's divinity.[95]

2. The Creator Word: The Commentary on Jn 1:3-4a

After the four clauses with which the Gospel of John begins and which we know as v. 1-2, in Thomas's view, something new begins with verse 3: "After the Evangelist has told of the existence and nature of the Divine Word, so far as it can be told by man, he moves on to show his power and operation".[96] The distinction is not original; in the *Catena Aurea,* Alcuin is quoted as giving the same *divisio,* and both Albert and Bonaventure make comparable *divisiones*, albeit with other words, as we saw before.

[92] Albert, *Super Io* 1:1 p. 36.
[93] As an example, cf. Albert's remarks that one can read in the books of the ancient philosophers that the Word is in the intellect of the Father and that all things are made through the Word, but not that the Word became flesh: Albert, *In Io* Prol. p. 44-45.
[94] *In Io* 1:2 §66.
[95] Cf. *In Io* prol., §10.
[96] "Postquam Evangelista esse et naturam divini verbi, quantum dici potest ab homine, procedit ad eius virtutem seu operationem insinuandam". *In Io* 1:3 §68 (text corrected by L. Reid).

In their subdivisions of v. 3-5, however, our three commentators do differ. Bonaventure sees in v. 3-5 four qualities of the Word: it is the sufficient, unfailing and foreknowing principle of creation that bestows understanding on others.[97] Albert subdivides v. 3-5 into two parts: v. 3-4a describe the principle of being of all things, and v. 4b-5 the principle of knowledge of all things.[98] He even feels the need to give an explanation for this orderly way of proceeding: John was speaking with people who were wise and perfect and nourished in philosophy, and against heretics that were full of irony and would have destroyed the teaching unless it was treated strong enough.[99] Thomas divides these verses by stating that v. 3-4a show Christ's power with respect to the whole of creation, and v. 4b-5 show Christ's power with respect to man.[100] He does not further subdivide the three clauses that make up for v. 3-4a for now because he will discuss different patristic commentators who distinguished these verses in different ways, as was mentioned before.

Thomas starts the commentary on the first clause, "All things were made through him", with the juxtaposition of three patristic explanations that were all already present in the *Catena Aurea*. Chrysostom reads this clause as having an anti-Arian point: if all things were made through the Word, the Word must be equal to the Father.[101] Hilary makes the point that if all things were made through the Word, then that must include time as well. The Word is, therefore, co-eternal with the Father.[102] Augustine concludes that if all things are made through the Word, the Word itself cannot be said to have been made. The Word of which the evangelist speaks here cannot be a creature and must therefore be of the same substance with the Father, that being the only substance that is not made. In this interpretation, the verse points towards the consubstantiality of the Word.[103] And so, Thomas concludes, "in saying "All things were made

---

[97] Bonaventure, *In Io* 1:3 n. 9.

[98] Our division in verses and punctuation of v. 3-4, goes against the punctuation that is generally accepted in medieval commentaries, where v. 3-4 is usually read as: "Omnia per ipsum facta sunt. Et sine ipso factum est nihil. Quod factum est in ipso vita erat. Et vita erat lux hominem". I will come back to this because Thomas discusses this punctuation.

[99] "Causa autem quare sic artificiose procedit Johannes iam in parte dicta est: quia sapientibus et perfectis loquebatur et in philosophia enutritis et contra hereticos, qui erant cauillosi et destruxissent doctrinam, nisi ualde sufficienter esset tradita". Albert, *Super Io* 1:3 p. 60.

[100] *In Io* 1:3 §68.

[101] *In Io* 1:3 §69. Cf. *Catena Aurea in Io* 1:3.

[102] *In Io* 1:3 §70. Cf. *Catena Aurea in Io* 1:3.

[103] *In Io* 1:3 §71. Cf. *Catena Aurea in Io* 1:3.

through him", you have, according to Chrysostom, the equality of the Word with the Father; the coeternity of the Word with the Father, according to Hilary; and the consubstantiality of the Word with the Father, according to Augustine".[104]

After the patristic readings, three erroneous readings are mentioned. Thomas says that Valentinus misread this clause to mean that the Word caused the Father to create the world. In the *Catena Aurea*, Origen is quoted as saying that the wording of the clause would have been inversed if that were the case. Thomas repeats that same remark in the commentary.[105] Origen himself, however, wrote in his commentary that the Holy Spirit has to be included among the things that were created through the Word.[106] Thomas remarks that this would lead to the heretical conclusion that the Spirit is a creature. That "all things" were created through the Word should therefore not be read absolutely, as if to include not only the Holy Spirit but also the Father, but that it should be read with regard to creatures only.[107] The third erroneous interpretation, again by Origen, is to read 'through' in "through him all things were made" as implying inferiority.[108] In the *Catena Aurea*, Thomas included a remark from Chrysostom in which he refers to several places in Scripture where *per* does not signify inferiority in its grammatical object.[109] In the commentary, Thomas only mentions 1 Cor 1:9 as an example, and notes that there are more: the conclusion that the use of the word *per* implies inferiority is therefore not correct.[110]

This wrong interpretation and its refutation by Chrysostom leads Thomas to his own interpretation, which he presents as a discussion of the word *per*. What does it mean to say that all things have been made 'through' the Word? For Thomas, 'Word' is not only a name that describes the relation of the Son to the Father who speaks the Word, from whom the Word proceeds, but also implies a relation to creatures. The analysis of *per* explains this. Thomas discusses three interpretations of the word *per*, that lead to three interpretations of the text. The first is erroneous. The other two are correct but in different ways. Thomas starts by noting that the word *per*, used in the context of an operation, refers to

---

[104] "Sic ergo habes verbi aequalitatem ad patrem, secundum Chrysostomum; coaeternitatem secundum Hilarium, et consubstantialitatem, secundum Augustinum per hoc quod dicit 'omnia per ipsum facta sunt'". *In Io* 1:3 §72.
[105] *In Io* 1:3 §73. Cf. *Catena Aurea in Io* 1:3.
[106] Origen, *Commentary on John*, bk. 2 n. 75.
[107] *In Io* 1:3 §74.
[108] Origen, *Commentary on John*, bk. 2 n. 72.
[109] *Catena Aurea in Io* 1:3
[110] *In Io* 1:3 §75.

a kind of causality. This operation can be regarded in two ways. In one way, we can concentrate on the one acting, the one who causes the operation. In the other way, we can concentrate on the operation with regard to the thing produced.

When it refers to the cause of an operation, the word *per* can mean 'on the authority of' in the sense of an efficient cause. Thomas uses his standard example of the bailiff acting on the authority of the king: the bailiff does not act on his own authority but receives the authority to act from the king as an efficient cause.[111] This first meaning of the word *per* cannot be right for the verse under consideration. The verse would read, "All things were made (by the Father) on the authority (*per*) of the Word", as if the Word causes the Father to act. The Father, however, being the source of all things, both in creation and in the Trinity, does nothing on the authority of the Son but does all things on his own authority.

In a second sense, *per* can signify a formal causality, that which makes something what it is. Thomas gives the standard example of heat being the formal cause of the heating that a fire does: it is through heat that a fire makes things hot. Understood in this sense, the Father operates through his wisdom. God's wisdom belongs to God's essence: God is Wisdom. To help us understand God as Father, Son and Holy Spirit better, however, words like 'wisdom' are appropriated to one of the divine persons. According to Thomas, appropriation is a kind of analogical argument aimed at deepening our understanding of the persons in the Trinity. An essential attribute like wisdom is proper to God's nature, not to only one of the persons in God: God is wisdom. By appropriating it to one of the persons, however, we may be able to understand the persons better.[112]

God's wisdom is appropriated to the Son, the Word of God, which is "the concept of God's wisdom".[113] In the commentary on Jn 1:3, Thomas explains that appropriation is a fitting way to understand the way Scripture speaks. The apostle Paul writes about "Christ crucified, a stumbling block to Jews and foolishness to gentiles, but to those who are called, both Jews and Greeks, Christ the power of God and the wisdom of God" (1 Cor 1:23-24). Thomas concludes that by appropriation we say

---

[111] I translate *per* in this case with 'on the authority of' and not with 'through' because the word 'through' does not have the meaning of an efficient cause in this sense in English: the policeman who gives me a parking ticket does not do that 'through' Her Majesty the Queen, but 'on her authority'.

[112] This understanding of appropriation is based on G. Emery, *The Trinitarian Theology of St Thomas Aquinas*, p. 326-337.

[113] "conceptio sapientiae" *STh* I q. 47 a. 1c.

that the Father does all things through the Son, i.e. through his wisdom,[114] and adds that according to Augustine, the phrase "from whom all things" is appropriated to the Father, the phrase "through whom all things" to the Son and "in whom all things" to the Holy Spirit.[115]

The word *per* can not only be read with regard to the one operating but also with regard to the cause of the operation as terminated in the thing produced. Thomas gives the example of a carpenter making a bench through, by means of, a hatchet. The hatchet does not cause the carpenter to make the bench but is the means through which the carpenter makes it. Thomas makes two remarks about this reading. One is a cautionary remark about interpreting the Word as instrument of the Father. When something is moved by something to a certain effect, it is like an instrument, Thomas concedes, but it is better not to speak about the Word as the Father's instrument because the language of instrumentality suggests inferiority and therefore subordinationism. In God, however, the power of the Father and the power of the Word is numerically the same, and thus the Word that operates through the power received from the Father is equal, not inferior, to the Father.

The other remark Thomas makes about this reading of *per* is brief but has important consequences. Thomas writes: "But if the "through" denotes causality from the standpoint of the thing produced, then the statement, "The Father does all things through the Son", is not appropriation but proper to the Word, because the fact that he is a cause of creatures is had from someone else, namely the Father, from whom he has being".[116] From the standpoint of the creatures being produced,

---

[114] "Per istum modum appropriationis dicimus quod pater omnia operatur per filium, idest per sapientiam suam". *In Io* 1:3 §76 (text corrected by L. Reid). That the Father acts through his Son is a point that is developed more extensively in the commentary on John than in the *Summa Theologiae*, as G. Emery has observed: G. Emery, 'Biblical Exegesis and the Speculative Doctrine of the Trinity in St. Thomas Aquinas's Commentary on St. John', in: M. Dauphinais, M. Levering (eds.), *Reading John with St. Thomas Aquinas*, Washington D.C., Catholic University of America Press, 2005, p. 23-61, here p. 39 nt. 46.

[115] Augustine, *De Trinitate*, bk. 6 n. 12. Augustine begins book 6 with a discussion of 1 Cor 1:24.

[116] "Si vero ly per denotet causalitatem ex parte operati, tunc hoc quod dicimus "patrem omnia per filium facere" non est appropriatum verbo, sed proprium eius, quia hoc quod est causa creaturarum, habet ab alio, scilicet a patre, a quo habet esse". *In Io* 1:3 §76 (text corrected by L. Reid). The English translation by Fabian Larcher and James Weisheipl adds the word 'mere' ("not 'mere' appropriation but proper to the Word"), which seems unfortunate. The point Thomas is making is not that what we say properly of one of the persons in the Trinity is somehow 'more' than what we appropriate to one of the persons. The contrary is true: understanding the personal

looking back as it were, when we say that we are created through the Word, we say something about where the Word's causality in creating us is from, which is from the Father. "'Through' designates the Word's causility with respect to creatures", as Dominic Legge put it.[117] In other words, when we say that the Word receives its being from the Father, we are speaking not in terms of appropriation, but we say something *proprie* about the Son because we say something about the eternal processions in God.

The importance of this lies in the relation between God, Father, Son and Holy Spirit and creation. 'Word' is proper to the Son in the first place because it signifies a real relation with the Father who speaks it.[118] As we saw in the beginning of this chapter, for Thomas, it also implies a relation to creation: that was the reason why, according to Thomas, John begins his Gospel speaking about the Word, not the Son. In the words of Emery: "The Word represents everything that the Father knows, it expresses all the creatures that pre-exist in the understanding of the Father. For this reason, the Word is not only the Word of the Father but also the Word of all things (*verbum omnium rerum*): since God does not act by a necessity of nature but by his wisdom, the Father accomplishes all things by his Word. By begetting his Word, the Father engendered the One by whom he produces creatures in being".[119] As Thomas writes in the *Summa Theologiae*: "God the Father made the creature through his Word, which is his Son; and through his Love, which is the Holy Spirit".[120] Because creation is the work of the Triune God, it is Trinitarian in form. Key to this understanding are the processions in God: "God's activity in the world is rooted in the intra-divine activity of the processions".[121] For this

---

properties more deeply strengthens the appropriations which are based on them. The point of Thomas's remark 'not appropriation but proper' is rather to be understood as referring back to the previous interpretation of *per* as a formal cause, and clarifies that different interpretations of the *per* in Jn 1:3 are based on different ways of speaking about the Triune God.

[117] D. Legge, *The Trinitarian Christology of St Thomas Aquinas*, Oxford, Oxford University Press, 2017, p. 65.

[118] G. Emery, 'Trinity and Creation', in: R. van Nieuwenhove, J. Wawrykow (eds.), *The Theology of Thomas Aquinas*, Notre Dame, University of Notre Dame Press, 2005, p. 58-76, here p. 64.

[119] Ibid., 64-65. "Verbum rerum omnium" is a reference to *ScG* IV,13: "Cum vero Deus, intelligendo seipsum, omnia alia intelligat, ut dictum est, oportet quod Verbum in Deo conceptum ex eo quod seipsum intelligit, sit etiam Verbum omnium rerum".

[120] "Unde et Deus Pater operatus est creaturam per suum Verbum, quod est Filius; et per suum Amorem, qui est Spiritus Sanctus". *STh* I q. 45 a. 6c.

[121] G. Emery, 'Trinity and Creation', p. 61.

reason, Thomas writes that John the Evangelist "wrote with utmost exactitude" (*propriissime fuisse locutum*) when he wrote that "All things were made through the Son". Thomas returns to his example of the artisan who has the concept of the cabinet he is to make in his mind before he makes it. Whenever someone makes something, he must preconceive it in his mind. Analogously, we can speak about God who creates all things through the conception of his intellect. However, that conception is his eternally conceived wisdom, the Word of God and Son of God who proceeds from the Father from eternity.[122] Starting from the commentary on the *Sentences*, it is an insight that repeatedly appears in Thomas's works: "The eternal processions are the cause and the rationale of the making of creatures".[123] It is that same insight that is the key to Thomas's understanding of John 1:3, an understanding he uniquely develops via his analysis of the word *per*.[124]

It is this understanding of the Word as God's eternal plan for creation that is the foundation for Thomas's claim that knowledge of God as Father, Son and Holy Spirit is necessary for a deep understanding of God as Creator. As he writes in a beautiful reading of Gn 1:1-4:

> It [knowledge of the divine persons, SM] was necessary for the right idea of creation. When we say that God made all things by His Word, we exclude the error of those who say that God produced things by necessity. When we say that in Him there is a procession of love, we show that God produced creatures not because He needed them, nor because of any other extrinsic reason, but on account of the love of His own goodness. So Moses, after having said, 'In the beginning God created heaven and earth', added, 'God said, Let there be light', to manifest the divine Word; and then said, 'God saw the light that it was good', to show the divine love. The same is also found in the other works of creation.[125]

---

[122] *In Io* 1:3 §77.

[123] "Processiones personarum aeternae, sunt causa et ratio totius productionis creaturarum" *1 Sent.* d. 14 q. 1 a. 1c, quoted in G. Emery, *The Trinitarian Theology of St Thomas Aquinas*, p. 343. For other places in Aquinas's work where this idea is expressed, cf. G. Emery, 'Trinity and Creation', p. 59, nt. 9-11.

[124] Uniquely, also in the sense that there is nothing similar in the commentaries by Albert and Bonaventure. According to Emery, the insight is not present in other works of Bonaventure or Albert either, but is particular and characteristic of Aquinas. G. Emery, 'Trinity and Creation', p. 59-60; cf. G. Emery, *La Trinité créatrice: Trinité et création dans les commentaires aux Sentences de Thomas d'Aquin et de ses précurseurs Albert le Grand et Bonaventure*, Paris, Vrin, 1995.

[125] "Uno modo, ad recte sentiendum de creatione rerum. Per hoc enim quod dicimus Deum omnia fecisse verbo suo, excluditur error ponentium Deum produxisse res ex necessitate naturae. Per hoc autem quod ponimus in eo processionem amoris, ostenditur quod Deus non propter aliquam indigentiam creaturas produxit, neque

Thomas ends his commentary on the clause “All things were made through him” with a reference to John Chrysostom, who reads this clause as a summary of the creation narrative. While Moses enumerates individually all the things God creates, John transcends and embraces them in this one phrase. Thomas quotes with agreement the reason Chrysostom gives for this difference between the author of Genesis and the author of the fourth Gospel: “The reason is that Moses wished to teach the emanation of creatures from God; hence he enumerated them. But John, hastening toward loftier things, intends in this book to lead us specifically to a knowledge of the Creator himself”.[126] It is a fitting reminder from Thomas to his students of where we are: reading the Gospel that speaks primarily of the divine Word, the creator Word.

The nature of nothing

Thomas’s commentary on the next clause, “and without him nothing was made” reads like a developed *quaestio*. Thomas starts with a remark by Augustine that he already included in the *Catena Aurea*: that some have misunderstood the ‘nothing’ of which the Gospel here speaks in an affirmative sense as if there exists a thing called ‘nothing’ that was made without the Word. That would make this clause restrictive in relation to the prior one as if to say: all things were made through the Word, except for one thing, the ‘nothing’.[127]

As a reader of the commentary will expect by now, Thomas proceeds by listing the erroneous exegeses that have been given of the clause he is commenting on. This time, however, he states that the three errors all came from the misunderstanding Augustine mentioned. The first heresy is taken from Origen’s commentary on John, in which Origen takes issue with a reading of Heracleon, whom he supposes to be a disciple of Valentinus. Heracleon had defended that there were ages before the Word that were therefore not created by the Word.[128] In both the *Catena Aurea*

---

propter aliquam aliam causam extrinsecam; sed propter amorem suae bonitatis. Unde et Moyses, postquam dixerat, in principio creavit Deus caelum et terram, subdit, dixit Deus, fiat lux, ad manifestationem divini verbi; et postea dixit, vidit Deus lucem, quod esset bona, ad ostendendum approbationem divini amoris; et similiter in aliis operibus. *STh* I q. 32 a. 1 ad 3.

[126] “Cuius ratio est quia Moyses tradere volebat emanationem creaturarum a Deo, et ideo eas enumerat; Ioannes vero ad altiorem festinans materiam, in hoc libro intendit nos inducere specialiter in cognitionem ipsius creatoris”. *In Io* 1:3 §78 (text corrected by L. Reid). Cf. *Catena Aurea in Io* 1:3.

[127] *In Io* 1:3 §79. Cf. *Catena Aurea in Io* 1:3.

[128] Origen, *Commentary on John*, bk. 2, n. 100.

and Thomas's commentary, Origen is quoted as saying that this position was Valentinus's. The second heresy takes the 'nothing' to mean corruptible things that have a source different from the Word. It is the Manichean interpretation, and it is no surprise that the Dominican friar Thomas stresses his opposition against this heresy here: preaching against the dualist convictions of the Cathars, whom Thomas usually calls 'Manicheans' is the reason why the Order of Preachers was founded.[129] No author is given for the third error, which is to interpret 'nothing' as the devil, but in the *Catena Aurea* there is a remark by Origen who denies that with 'nothing' the devil could be meant because while his being the devil is not caused by God, nevertheless as created by God he is not nothing.[130] In the commentary, Thomas does not mention this but instead refers to an interpretation of Job 18:15 ("May the companions of him who is not, dwell in his house"), in which "he who is not" is read as a reference to the devil, as the cause for this reading of 'nothing' in Jn 1:3 as referring to the devil.[131] These three errors have as a common cause that they all take 'nothing' in some positive sense, whereas Thomas states that 'nothing' here is meant in a negative sense only: "all things were made through the Word in such a way that there is nothing participating in being that was not made through Him".[132]

The suggestion to read 'nothing' in a purely negative way leads to an objection: does that not make the clause redundant, just a duplication of "all things were made through him", the clause that went before? Thomas replies that "according to many expositors, this clause was added in for a number of reasons".[133] What follows are five patristic explanations of the clause, all of them also present in the *Catena Aurea*. But the formulation Thomas uses is telling. It suggests that he reads the patristic commentaries in a cumulative way: the different interpretations they give are supposed to stand side by side. Thomas will sometimes choose between different

[129] It is the only heretical interpretation that Albert and Bonaventure also discuss. Albert, *Super Io* 1:3 p. 76-78. Bonaventure, *In Io* 1:3 n. 10.

[130] *Catena Aurea in Io* 1:3.

[131] Aquinas does not discuss this reading in his commentary of Job. This is unsurprising, as the commentary of Job is not an academic work, but the fruit of Aquinas's teaching his Dominican brothers in Orvieto.

[132] "Ut sit sensus: ita facta sunt omnia per verbum, quod nihil est participans esse, quod non sit factum per ipsum". *In Io* 1:3 §83. The text that L. Reid suggests here seems questionable to me since it does not explain the text but merely repeats it: "Ut dicatur: Sine ipso factum est nihil, id est ita dico quod omnia per ipsum facta sunt quod nihil est factum sine ipso".

[133] "Ad quod dicendum quod secundum multos multipliciter introducitur hec particula" (text corrected by L. Reid).

interpretations, usually with the words "but better is…" (*sed melius*), but that is not the case here: Thomas explicitly interprets the different commentaries here as parallel reasons for the presence of this verse. What are these reasons?

From Chrysostom, Thomas uses the argument that parallel with Genesis 1, where only visible creatures are mentioned, the clause "all things were made through him" could be misunderstood to mean only visible things. The clause "and without him nothing was made" makes clear that invisible things are created by the Word, too. Thomas refers to Col 1:16 ("in him all things in heaven and on earth were created, things visible and invisible") as a parallel text.

Chrysostom also gives a second possible interpretation of the preceding clause that is too narrow. "All things were made through him" could be read as referring to Christ's miracles that the Gospels speak of. To bring out the total causality of the Word, the evangelist adds: "And without him nothing was made". A third reason, taken from Hilary, returns to the implications of the preposition 'with' that Thomas discussed earlier. "All things were made through him" could be misread in a way that excludes the Father from all causality. "Without him nothing was made" suggests another person, the Father, working with the Word.

Thomas finds an exposition that he calls "rather beautiful" (*satis pulchra*) in the homily *Vox spiritualis aquilae*, of which Thomas writes that it is "attributed to Origen" (*attribuitur Origeni*).[134] In that sermon, it is explained that "without" (*sine*) is a translation of the Greek *choris*, which means "outside of".[135] Thomas interprets this 'outside of' in the sense of conservation, and refers to Hebr 1:3 "He sustains all things by His powerful Word". Explained in this way, the clause "All things were made through him" speaks about the activity of the Word in the creation of all things, "and outside of him nothing was made" speaks about the Word preserving them in their existence.

---

[134] The sermon is in fact from John Scotus Eriugena. As H. Dondaine first remarked, the phrase "attribuitur Origeni" might suggest that Thomas doubted whether the sermon actually was Origen's. Another reason to suspect this, not given by Dondaine, could be that Thomas sometimes refers to the sermon by mentioning its *incipit* only without naming Origen: *In Io* 1:3 §90; *In Io* 1:5 §102. On the other hand Thomas just as often calls the sermon Origen's without qualification: *In Io* 1:9 §130; *In Io* 1:11 §158. In the *Catena Aurea*, when Thomas refers to this sermon, he always gives the name of Origen. Cf. H.-F. Dondaine, 'S. Thomas et Scot Érigène', *Revue des Sciences Philosophiques et Théologiques* 35 (1951), p. 31-33.; Jean Scot, *Homélie Sur Le Prologue de Jean,* SC 151, p. 140-141.

[135] The word 'Thoris' that the Marietti gives, is of course a mistake, as was recognised by L. Reid as well: *In Io* 1:3 §86.

The final reason Thomas gives why this clause was added, based on both Origen and Augustine, interprets 'nothing' as indicating sin. Thomas returns to the image of the artisan he used before and refers to 1 Cor 8:4: "We know that an idol is nothing in the world" to explain that an idol is not made by the Word in so far as it is sinful and bad, even though the *forma* of an idol, in so far as it is a certain *forma*, is made by the Word.[136]

Thomas can now come to a conclusion of this developed question. After arguing that 'nothing' in the clause cannot be interpreted in any positive sense but must be read as a purely negative statement, the objection that if understood this way, the clause adds nothing to the previous one has been answered by giving five reasons why it does contribute. Taking the first two reasons, both from Chrysostom, together, Thomas concludes: "So then, this clause is added to show the universal causality of the Word, according to Chrysostom; his association with the Father in operating, according to Hilary; the power of the Word in the preserving of things, according to Origen; and finally, the purity of his causality, because he is so the cause of good as not to be the cause of sin, according to Augustine".[137]

Divisio textus interrupted?

The syntax of Jn 1:3-4 is notoriously difficult. The Vulgate text reads: "*et sine ipso factum est nihil quod factum est in ipso vita erat*". Where should the interpunction be? From patristic times onwards, commentators of the fourth Gospel interpreted the way the words hang together in these verses differently, thereby giving distinct interpretations of the text. To give three patristic examples: Origen reads "Without him nothing was made. What was made in him, was life". Augustine reads "Without him nothing was made. What was made, in him was life". Augustine explains his reading as a reaction to a heretical reading that he ascribes to the Manichaeans, and that suggests that "what was made in him, was life"

---

[136] "Ideo per Verbum quod est ars plena rationum viventium non fit aliquid ordinatum nec aliquod malum seu peccatum, quod dicitur non ens, secundum illud apostoli "Scimus quod ydolum nihil est in mundo". Unde ydolum non est factum per Verbum in quantum est peccatum et malum, quamvis forma ydoli inquantum est forma quedam fit per verbum". *In Io* 1:3 §87. I follow the corrections by L. Reid, whose text here differs rather substantially from that of the Marietti.

[137] "Sic ergo ista particula additur ad ostendendum ipsius verbi universalem causalitatem secundum Chrysostomum, societatem ad patrem operando, secundum Hilarium et virtutem verbi in conservando, secundum Origenem. Item puritatem causalitatis: quia sic est causa bonorum, quod non est causa peccati, secundum Augustinum". *In Io* 1:3 §88 (text corrected by L. Reid).

implies that there is life in all things, including inanimate things like wood and stones. To counter that reading, Augustine suggests making a short pause after "what was made" and then to go on with "in him was life". Chrysostom reads "Without him nothing was made that was made. In him was life". Like Augustine, Chrysostom explains his reading as a reaction to a heretical interpretation, albeit a different one. He argues against a reading that interprets 'Life' as standing for the Holy Spirit and that concludes from the reading "What was made in Him, was Life" that the Holy Spirit is created. To refute this interpretation, Chrysostom suggests reading it as one sentence that ends at "was made" and begins the next sentence with "In Him was life".[138]

Medieval commentators are aware of the difficult syntax of these verses. Bonaventure mentions Chrysostom's reading but reads it as directed against the heresy that Augustine had mentioned. Bonaventure mentions other interpretations than the examples I mentioned but chooses Augustine's reading because he "expresses the matter most elegantly of all" (*elegantius omnibus*). In Bonaventure's reading, the verse expresses the quality of the Word as foreknowing principle of creation. He cites Augustine's metaphor that all things are in the Word like a chest of drawers in the mind of a cabinet maker.[139] Albert follows the same Augustinian interpretation, explaining that things like a chest of drawers do not live in so far as they are wood, but do live in so far as they are in the mind of the cabinet maker: "And so something lives in the mind, which does not live in matter".[140] At the end of his exposition, Albert briefly mentions other readings. He does not choose between them but

[138] Origen, *Commentary in Io* bk. 2, n. 128, cf. 131; Augustine, *Tract. in Io* 1:16; Chrysostom, *Homilies on John* 5,1-2. According to Raymond Brown, Eusebius, Cyril of Alexandria and most of the Latin Fathers agree with Augustine, while Hilary, Ambrose and the older Greek fathers agree with Origen. Brown does not mention Chrysostom by name, but argues against his reading: R. Brown, *The Gospel According to John I-XII*, p. 6-7. The differences continue in our times: F.J. Moloney, *The Gospel of John*, p. 35-36, prefers Origen's interpretation, M.M. Thompson, *John: A Commentary*, p. 27 follows Chrysostom, while C.S. Keener, *The Gospel of John: A Commentary*, p. 382 does not choose. For a study that takes this textual problem as a key to understanding Jn 1:1-5 (and defends Origen's reading) cf. E.L. Miller, *Salvation-History in the Prologue of John: The Significance of John 1: 3/4*, Leiden, Brill, 1989.

[139] Bonaventure, *In Io* 1:4 n. 11. The discussion about the right reading is treated as a question in n. 15.

[140] "Et sic uiuit in mente, quod non uiuit in materia". Albert, *Super Io* 1:3 p. 84.

simply ends with: “This is what it means according to different commentators”.[141]

Thomas starts by giving the heretical ‘Manichaean’ reading that Augustine mentioned. After stating that this explanation is false, Thomas continues to say: “There are nevertheless, a number of ways to explain it without error”.[142] Thomas gives fives explanations, one from the sermon “*Vox spiritualis*” that he used earlier, the others from Augustine, Origen, Hilary and Chrysostom. All these explanations are taken directly from the *Catena Aurea*. I will focus on the commentaries by Origen, Hilary and Chrysostom, as they seem to be the most interesting ones. From Origen, Thomas gets a rule for speaking about change when speaking about the Word. Origen remarks that some things are said of the Word as such and Thomas adds the examples: that he is God, omnipotent, and the like. Some things are said of the Word in relation to ourselves. Origen here gives the examples of ‘shepherd’, ‘way’, ‘door’ and ‘rod’, the last example based on Is 11:1: “A shoot shall come out from the stock of Jesse, and a branch shall grow out of his roots”. Thomas gives the examples of ‘saviour’ and ‘redeemer’ instead. Thirdly, some things are said in both ways. Origen mentions ‘wisdom’, and Thomas adds ‘justice’ as an example of this third way. The point of this distinction is that while it is impossible to say of the Son absolutely that in some respect he was made (the Son is not made God or omnipotent), we can use the word ‘made’ for both the two other groups of words. Thomas here adds a reference to 1 Cor 1:30 to what he has read in Origen, which clarifies why he has changed the examples Origen uses. 1 Cor 1:30 contains words from both the second and the third group, exactly the words Thomas has used as examples: “God made Him our wisdom, our justice, our sanctification and redemption”. While sanctification and redemption are words from the second category, words that are said of the Word in relation to ourselves, wisdom and justice are words from the mixed category: the Word always was justice and wisdom, but it can be said that he was made justice and wisdom for us. Going back to Jn 1:3-4, Origen regards ‘life’ as a word of this mixed category as well, and reads the verse as saying “The Son who is life in himself, was made life for us because He gave us life”. In his

[141] “Hoc est ergo quod intendit secundum diuersos expositores”. Albert, *Super Io* 1:3 p. 88.
[142] “Potest tamen sine errore multipliciter exponi”. *In Io* 1:3 §90.

rendering of Origen's interpretation, Thomas adds a reference to 1 Cor 15:22: "Just as in Adam all die, so in Christ all will come to life".[143]

We have seen before that Thomas interrupted his *divisio textus* of Jn 1:3-4a because the three clauses that it consists of are distinguished in different ways given by the commentators.[144] After having given three different readings of this verse that used the same punctuation (*Vox Spiritualis*, Augustine and Origen), Thomas now gives the interpretations of two commentators who punctuate differently.[145] Hilary reads "without him nothing was made, that was made in him", and then reads "he was life". Hilary explains that there might be a question of whether there are things made by him that were not made without him but were neither made through him. The verse explains that all things were made in him and through him. Thomas explains Hilary's commentary with the example of a father having a young son. In that situation, the father will do many things while having the son, but not doing them through the son: while the son is present as the son of the father, he does not participate in all things the father does. To take this objection away, the evangelist added "He was life", taken as perfect life. Because the Word is perfect life, there never was imperfection in him: we cannot understand the Son as someone who is growing up. Therefore, nothing was made without him that was not also made in him, i.e. through him.[146]

The final interpretation Thomas gives is that of Chrysostom, who reads "and without him nothing was made that was made", and then "in him was life" as a separate sentence to contradict a heretical reading that reads "what was made in him, was life", interprets 'life' here as standing for the Holy Spirit and concludes from that that the Spirit is created.[147] According to Chrysostom, the sentence "In him was life" was added for a double reason: to show that the Word's work in creation did not stop

[143] *In Io* 1:3 §92. Cf. the commentary of Origen in *Catena Aurea in Io* 1:3 and the original in Origen, *Commentary In Io* bk II, n. 124-132. Elsewhere, I have interpretated *In Io* 1:3 §92 with regard to transcendence and immanence: S. Mangnus, 'Understanding God's Word: Thomas Aquinas' Explanation of John 1,1-5', in: H. Goris, H. Rikhof, H. Schoot (eds.), *Divine Transcendence and Immanence in the Work of Thomas Aquinas*, Leuven, Peeters, 2009, p. 283-297, here p. 292-294.

[144] *In Io* 1:3 §68.

[145] The difference is clear in the introduction to the five commentaries to which Aquinas refers here: "Illa homilia Vox spiriualis exponitur;" "Augustinus [...] legit;" "Origenes [...] legit;" "Hilarius [...] punctat;" "Chrysostomus autem aliud modum legendi habet, et punctat sic" *In Io* 1:3 §90-94.

[146] *In Io* 1:3 §93. Cf. Hilary, *De Trinitate* bk II, 19-20.

[147] Albert identifies these heretics as Nestorius and Eutyches. Albert, *Super Io* 1:3 p. 72.

once the world was created but is indefectible also with respect to things yet to be created. A Christological reading of "With you is the fountain of life" (Ps 35:10) is the reason for this interpretation: the Word is this fountain that does not dry up. The second reason is to show that things are not only created, but also governed by the Word. Here, Thomas adds a quotation from Hebr 4:12 to Chrysostom's interpretation: "The Word of God is living".

After having thus given Chrysostom's interpretation, Thomas adds a remark about the status of this interpretation:

> Chrysostom is held in such esteem by the Greeks in his explanations that they admit no other explanation where he expounded anything in Holy Scripture than his. For this reason, in all the Greek works this passage is not found to be punctuated differently from the way it is arranged here, namely, "And without him was made nothing that was made".[148]

This is a strong claim. Thomas does not mention other Greek commentators here, and he seems to presuppose that for orthodox theologians among the expositions that lose their authority once the interpretation of Chrysostom has been given, other Greek-writing commentaries would have to be included, like the one of Origen that Thomas has just mentioned.

The remark gives special weight to the use of Chrysostom in the commentary. Chrysostom is after Augustine the second most-quoted authority in Thomas's commentary on John.[149] If this remark has to be taken at face value (and there is no reason why it should not be), the implication is that for Thomas Chrysostom's commentary stands for the Greek fathers. This would shed new light as well on the famous anecdote, reported by William of Tocco and used in Thomas's canonization process at Naples, in which Thomas is said to have remarked that he would rather have the commentary by Chrysostom on Matthew than possess the entire city of Paris. Torrell argues that "the clearest meaning" of this anecdote

---

[148] "Et quia apud Graecos Chrysostomus est tantae auctoritatis in suis expositionibus, quod ubi ipse aliquid exposuit in sacra Scriptura, nullam aliam expositionem admittant nisi suam. Inde est quod in omnibus libris Graecis non invenitur aliter punctatum quam sicut hic positum est scilicet: 'sine ipso factum est nihil quod factum est'". *In Io* 1:3 §94 (text corrected by L. Reid).

[149] Augustine is mentioned 426 times explicitly in the commentary, Chrysostom 259 times, and Origen 91 times. P.-Y. Maillard gives these numbers as well, but mistakenly gives the number of mentions Chrysostom gets as 251: P.-Y. Maillard, *La vision de Dieu chez Thomas d'Aquin: Une lecture de l'In Ioannem á la lumière de ses sources Augustiniennes*, Paris, Librairie Philosophique J. Vrin, 2001, p. 27.

is Thomas's intellectual curiosity for sources.[150] I see no reason to argue with this interpretation, but the remark Thomas makes at this place in the commentary on John suggests that the choice of the text in the anecdote is significant. Thomas would happily give up Paris not just for any book but for a biblical commentary by the Greek commentator *par excellence*, the commentator that represents Greek theology. Seen in that light, the anecdote could very well be interpreted as highlighting both Thomas's passion for Scripture and his ecumenical interest.

Because of the esteem the 'Greeks' have for Chrysostom, his punctuation of Jn 1:3-4 is found in all Greek works, Thomas states. Thomas does not choose between the three different punctuations he presents through the sources he refers to. Instead, he juxtaposes the different commentaries, shows the diversity, and shows that the different readings of v. 3-4 they give are answers to different questions. What Thomas does is not just juxtaposition, however. He goes one step further: the different interpretations stand side by side, and so do the different interpunctions of the text with them. To do this, Thomas has to interrupt his *divisio textus*. Or so it seems on first sight.

There might be another explanation, however. It is exactly as a commentator who is so attentive to the *divisio textus*, that Thomas pays attention to the coherence between the structure of the text and its interpretation. This coherence happens to be the difficulty with Jn 1:3-4. As we saw, Thomas writes:

> [The evangelist] uses three clauses; and we will not distinguish these at present because they will be distinguished in different ways according to the different explanations given by the saints.[151]

More than just an interruption, it is for the sake of the coherence between the structure and the interpretation of the text that Thomas here does not restrict himself to just one *divisio textus*. And the other way round: it is because Thomas is so attentive to the *divisio textus*, that he can stress the coherence between structure and interpretation in the commentary on Jn 1:3-4.

---

[150] J.-P. Torrell, *Saint Thomas Aquinas: The Person and His Work*, p. 140.

[151] "ponit tres clausulas, quas non distinguimus ad praesens, quia secundum diversas expositiones sanctorum sunt diversimode distinguendae". *In Io* 1:3 §68.

3. 'Manifestible' Light: The Commentary on Jn 1:4b-5

With Jn 1:4b-5 ("And that life was the light of men. And the light shines in the darkness, and the darkness did not overcome it".), we come to the end of what in Thomas's *divisio textus* is the first big section of the first chapter of the Gospel, the section that speaks of the divinity of Christ in his being and operation. Having spoken about the power of the Word as creator of all things, Thomas interprets Jn 1:4b-5 as speaking about Christ's power as it is related to humans. With v. 4b, we go from creation in general to the relation to human beings. That is an important step, and I will argue that it is precisely at this point in the commentary that Thomas begins to unwrap the theological meaning of the Word *quoad nos*.

Thomas recognizes three things in these two verses: the introduction of a certain light, the light's irradiation and participation in the light. The theme of light often returns in the fourth Gospel. In his study on symbolism in John Craig Koester calls it "probably its most striking motif".[152] In his commentary, Thomas uses the image of light to refer to a large number of realities. Pierre-Yves Maillard lists them: truth, love, good works, faith, baptism, honesty, and eternal life all have a certain luminous quality about them. Conversely, darkness can refer to notions as varied as sin, ignorance, sadness, fear, persecution or unbelief.[153]

According to Thomas, Jn 1:4b-5 may be explained in two ways: these two verses may be explained "according to the influx of natural knowledge and according to participation in grace".[154] This distinction is not to be read as a separation. As Serge-Thomas Bonino writes: "Saint Thomas distinguishes only to unite better, and avoids a division of the movement of the Spirit. The communication of the Truth only finds concrete achievement in the order of grace".[155] As far as the distinction goes, Thomas finds it useful to read Jn 1:4b-5 in two parallel ways. This twofold way of interpreting 'light' will return in Thomas's commentary on Jn 1:9

---

[152] C.R. Koester, *Symbolism in the Fourth Gospel: Meaning, Mystery, Community*, Second Edition, Minneapolis, Fortress Press, 2003, p. 141.

[153] P.-Y. Maillard, *La vision de Dieu chez Thomas d'Aquin,* p. 89-90. References there. For a Christological interpretation of 'light' in Aquinas, cf. D.L. Whidden, *Christ the Light: The Theology of Light and Illumination in Thomas Aquinas*, Minneapolis, Fortress Press, 2014.

[154] "Potest autem totum dupliciter exponi. Uno modo secundum influxum cognitionis naturalis; alio modo secundum communicationem gratiae". *In Io* 1:4 §95.

[155] S.-T. Bonino, 'La théologie de la vérité dans la *lectura super Ioannem* de Saint Thomas d'Aquin', *Revue Thomiste* 104 (2004), p. 141-166, here p. 152.

("He was the true light, which enlightens every man coming into this world"), where Thomas writes: "'enlightenment' or 'being enlightened' by the Word is taken in two ways. First, in relation to the light of natural knowledge, as in "The light of your countenance is marked upon us" (Ps 4:7). Secondly, as the light of grace, "Be enlightened, O Jerusalem" (Is 60:1)".[156] In his commentary on v. 4b-5, Thomas will give both explanations side by side, starting with the explanation according to the influx of natural knowledge. In this, Thomas differs from both Albert and Bonaventure. In their commentaries on Jn 1:4b-5, one reads remarks about the light of natural knowledge and the light of grace. Still, neither of these commentators use that distinction to give two complete and parallel interpretations of these verses, as Thomas does.

The word 'light' is used both for things we see with our physical eyes and for things we understand. In the *Summa Theologiae*, Thomas discusses which of these is the proper use of the word: is 'light' said properly of spiritual things, and only secondarily of sensible things, or the other way around? In the *Summa Theologiae*, Thomas distinguishes an original from an extended meaning of the word. In its primary meaning, 'light' refers to the sense of sight. When it is applied to spiritual things, it is used metaphorically. The extended use of the word has become part of common speech, Thomas notes, and in that sense, it is properly applied to spiritual things.[157] In the commentary on John, Thomas makes the distinction differently. The power of light itself belongs to spiritual things in a prior and truer way than to sensible things. However, according to the way we know, light is discovered first in sensible things because we use it first to name sensible light, and only later we use it for intelligible things.[158] Thus, in the commentary on John, Thomas no longer solves the question by making a distinction between a stricter and an extended use of the word 'light' but by making a distinction between the nature of light and our knowledge of it.

Before he gives this distinction in the commentary, however, Thomas qualifies it. After having presented the two different views, he writes:

---

[156] "Illuminatio seu illuminari per verbum, intelligitur dupliciter: scilicet de lumine naturalis cognitionis, de quo dicitur in Ps IV, 7: 'signatum est super nos lumen vultus tui', etc. Item de lumine gratiae, de quo dicitur Is LX, 1: 'illuminare, Ierusalem'". *In Io* 1:9 §128 (text corrected by L. Reid).
[157] *STh* I q. 67 a. 1c.
[158] *In Io* 1:4 §96.

> But this is not a great issue, for in whatever way the name 'light' is used, it implies a manifestation, whether that manifestation concerns intelligible or sensible things. If we compare sensible and intelligible manifestation, then, according to the nature of things, light is found first in spiritual things.[159]

From the *Summa Theologiae* to the commentary, Thomas has discovered a word that includes both meanings of light: manifestation. Whatever we want to say about whichever kind of light, either sensible or spiritual, the first thing to say about light is that it implies a manifestation.[160] In other words: manifestation is the point of speaking about light. This is a first important step Thomas takes in this part of the commentary: whenever we think of 'light' theologically and biblically, the first thing that should come to mind is not the distinction between intelligible and sensible light, but 'manifestation'. 'Light' means revelation.[161]

For the second step, Thomas starts with an explanation of 'life' by stating that there are several grades of life. He writes:

> To clarify the statement, 'And that life was the light of men', we should remark that there are many grades of life. For some things live, but do so without light, because they have no knowledge; for example, plants. Hence their life is not light. Other things both live and know, but their knowledge, since it is on the sense level, is concerned only with individual and material things, as is the case with the brutes. So they have both life and a certain light. But they do not have the light of men, who live, and know, not only truths, but also the very nature of truth itself. Such are rational creatures, to whom not only this or that is made manifest, but truth itself, which is *manifestabilis* and is manifestive to all.[162]

---

[159] "Sed in hoc non est magna vis facienda: nam de quocumque nomen lucis dicatur ad manifestationem refertur, sive illa manifestatio sit in intelligibilibus, sive in sensibilibus. Si ergo comparentur manifestatio intelligibilis et sensibilis, secundum naturam prius invenitur lux in spiritualibus" *In Io* 1:4 §96.

[160] This description of the difference between Thomas's view in the *prima pars* of the *Summa Theologiae* and the commentary on John as a development, implies that the generally accepted view that Thomas wrote the *Prima pars* before the commentary on John is true. For the dating of the *Prima pars* as written in Rome (1265-1268), see J.-P. Torrell, *Saint Thomas Aquinas: The Person and His Work*, p. 145-146. As we have seen, the commentary on John can be dated with reasonable certainty to Thomas's second period of teaching in Paris, probably in the years 1270-1272.

[161] By saying 'light means revelation', I focus on God's giving of the light. David Whidden makes the same point from our human perspective when he writes: "illumination properly understood is knowledge of truth as it is ordered to God". D. Whidden, *Christ the Light*, p. 207.

[162] "Ad evidentiam autem eius quod dicitur 'et vita erat lux hominum', sciendum est quod multiplex est gradus vitae. Quaedam namque vivunt, sed absque luce, quia

The distinction between 'grades of life' can be found in other works of Thomas as well.[163] Carlo Leget has shown that it is related to three interrelated meanings of the word 'life' that can be traced back to Aristotle. First, 'life' can refer to the existence of a being that can move itself in a certain manner. Secondly, it can refer to a specific act of a living substance that is characteristic of its mode of being; in this sense, the acts of the intellect and will of a human being can be called their 'life' because they are the characteristically human modes of self-movement. Thirdly, 'life' can refer to the chief occupation or direction of a human being: Leget mentions living an honourable life or a contemplative life as examples of this. 'Self-movement' is what links these three meanings of life, and because the human mode of being is an intelligent mode of being, the three meanings might even be said to imply one another. Leget writes:

> The life (in the third meaning) we lead follows from our free, deliberate choices ('life' in the second meaning) that follow from our mode of being ('life' in the first meaning).[164]

Thomas recognizes the three grades of life in the verse he is commenting on: "And so the Evangelist, speaking of the Word, not only says that he is life but also "light", lest anyone suppose he means life without knowledge. And he says that he is the "light of men", lest anyone suppose he meant only sensible knowledge, such as exists in the brutes".[165] But he does go one step further by stating that 'having the light of men' means not only knowing truths but also the nature of truth itself. This truth, Thomas says, is *manifestabilis et manifestativa omnium*. Christoph Berchtold has rightly drawn attention to the importance of the word

---

nullam cognitionem habent, sicut sunt plantae: unde vita earum non est lux. Quaedam vero vivunt et cognoscunt; sed tamen eorum cognitio, cum sit sensus tantum, non est nisi particularium et materialium, sicut est in brutis: et ideo haec et vitam habent sed non lucem hominem, quedam vero et vivunt et cognoscunt non solum ipsa vera, sed ipsius veritatis rationem, sicut sunt creaturae rationales, quibus non solum manifestatur hoc vel illud, sed ipsa veritas quae manifestabilis est et manifestativa omnium". *In Io* 1:4 §97 (text corrected by L. Reid). Commenting on Jn 5:24 ("Amen, amen, I say to you, that whoever hears my voice and believes in him who sent me, possesses eternal life") Aquinas makes a distinction in four grades of life: plants, animals that only sense, 'perfect animals' and those who understand: *In Io* 5:24 §771.

[163] Cf. *STh* I, q. 18 and *ScG* I, 97-99.

[164] C. Leget, 'The Concept of "Life" in the Commentary on St. John', in: M. Dauphinais, M. Levering (eds.), *Reading John with St. Thomas Aquinas*, p. 153-72, here p. 154-156.

[165] "Et ideo Evangelista loquens de verbo dicit non solum esse vitam, sed etiam esse lucem, ne intelligas vitam sine agnitione; 'hominum' autem ne tantum cognitionem sensibilem suspiceris, qualis est in brutis". *In Io* 1:4 §97.

manifestare in Thomas's thinking about revelation.[166] Berchtold also notices that *manifestabilis* is a *hapax legomenon* in Thomas's works.[167] However, there is more to be said about this word than the sheer fact that it is a *hapax legomenon* because there is an important parallel with another extraordinary word in Thomas's theological thinking about revelation, which is the word *revelabilium*. Thomas uses that word only twice in his works, both times in the plural *revelabilia* in article 3 of the very first question of the *Summa Theologiae*.[168] The grammatical parallel *-ilis* and *-ilium* is no coincidence but points to a theological parallel. To explain this, a look at this fundamental article in the *Summa* is necessary.[169]

In article 3 of the *Summa Theologiae*'s first question, Thomas discusses the unity of *sacra doctrina*. Both God and creatures are treated in *sacra doctrina*, but since the Creator and creatures cannot be grouped in one class, it seems that *sacra doctrina* is not one science (obj. 1). Furthermore, *sacra doctrina* treats very different things, from angels to bodily creatures to human morality. These subjects belong to different philosophical sciences, and therefore seem to obstruct the unity of *sacra doctrina* (obj. 2). Thomas answers that it is not the objects in themselves in their material aspects but the formality under which they are studied that determines the unity of a faculty or a habit. Just like Scripture considers things under the formal aspect of being divinely revealed, the unity of *sacra doctrina* is determined by the fact that it studies all things as *revelabilia*.[170] What can at one level be studied in differentiated ways by different sciences, can at a higher level be studied under a "more universal" (*universalior*, a

---

[166] C. Berchtold, *Manifestatio Veritatis*. Cf. M. Sabathé, *La Trinité rédemptrice,* p. 367-385. In the French translation of the commentary however, the references to 'manifestation' disappear at this point: "Telles sont les créatures douées d'intelligence, qui non seulement connaissent telle ou telle réalité [vraie], mais sont capables de connaître la vérité elle-même, par laquelle elles peuvent connaître toutes les réalités". Thomas d'Aquin, *Commentaire sur l'Évangile de Saint Jean: Préface par M.-D. Philippe, traduction et notes sous sa direction*, Paris, Les Éditions du Cerf, 2002, p. 92.

[167] C. Berchtold, *Manifestatio Veritatis*, p. 164 nt.406. Berchtold also remarks that Thomas uses the adjective *manifestativus* from the commentary on the *Sentences* onwards, albeit not very often: 39 times.

[168] *STh* I q. 1 a. 3c and ad 2.

[169] My reading of *STh* I q. 1 a. 3 is mainly based on M. Corbin, *Le chemin de la Théologie chez Thomas d'Aquin*, Paris, Beauchesne, 1974, and E.F. Rogers, *Thomas Aquinas and Karl Barth: Sacred Doctrine and the Natural Knowledge of God,* Notre Dame, University of Notre Dame Press, 1995.

[170] *STh* I q. 1 a. 3c.

remarkable comparative) formal aspect: what is studied by different sciences is studied by the single science that is *sacra doctrina* under the formal aspect of being *revelabilia*.[171]

Notice that Thomas does not say that *sacra doctrina* studies things in so far as they are revealed (*revelata*). As Eugene Rogers has remarked, that would make two domains, one of the world revealed in the Bible and one of the world we know through our own experience. Rogers writes:

> [*Revelabilia*] remind us that all things whatsoever [*omnia quaecumque*] are revealable; that is, they place *omnia quaecumque* under God's providence; all things whatsoever, and not just the revealed ones, form part of the great salvation history of which the Bible narrates the important parts; all things whatsoever might, in principle, show up in these pages. Our world and the world of the Bible are again one unitary world, and they are one on God's terms, one under providence.[172]

That things are *revelabilia* means more than just that they can be or could have been revealed. Rogers makes the comparison with *visibilia*: *visibilia* does not just mean visible, that things can be seen. It says something about the form of these things: they remain *visibilia* even if there is no one to see them.[173] Likewise, *revelabilia* are not just things that could have been revealed, whether they are or not; calling things *revelabilia* is to say something about their *forma*.

> They possess an intrinsic under-God-ness, they enjoy natural citizenship in the world that revelation depicts, they already belong to and compromise that world, quite apart from whether scripture comes to mention them or not. They are revealable as God-created and God-ordered.[174]

One way of making the move from *intelligibilia*, the formal rationale under which Aristotelian metaphysics studies things, to *sacra doctrina* as the science that studies *omnia quaecumque* as *revelabilia* is that God is precisely not intelligible to us in this life but has chosen to become revealable. Rogers again:

---

[171] *STh* I q.1 a. 3 ad 2.

[172] E. Rogers, *Thomas Aquinas and Karl Barth*, p. 37. Cf. M. Corbin: "Bref ce qui prouve l'unité de la science théologique et de son contenu prodigieusement divers, ce n'est point que ce contenu soit révélé, puisque seuls les *aliqua* de l'Ecriture le sont, mais qu'il soit *éclairable* par ces *aliqua* et tout entier placé sous le cône de lumière de la Révélation". M. Corbin, *La Chemin de la Théologie*, p. 736 (original stress).

[173] E. Rogers, *Thomas Aquinas and Karl Barth*, p. 29.

[174] Ibid., p. 49.

> Sacred doctrine never denies, rather affirms the intelligibility of things. But the very first article of Question 1, when it asks whether a discipline exists beyond (*praeter*) and not among (*inter*) philosophical disciplines, leaves the consideration of *res* as *intelligibilia* behind. It replaces metaphysics with or subsumes it under another genre, in which *omnia res quaecumque* are *revelabilia*.[175]

It is this *universalior* formal aspect of *revelabilia* that makes it possible that things that are studied in different philosophical sciences are studied in the one science that is *sacra doctrina*.

I return to the commentary on John. In comparison with the animals, who have a certain light because they can know individual and material things on a sense level, what is proper to the light of men is that they cannot just know certain truths about individual things, but the nature of truth itself. I will have more to say about how Thomas speaks about truth in this commentary in the next chapter. What is important here is to see what Thomas says about this nature of truth, which is that it is *manifestabilis et manifestativa omnium*. The parallel with a. 3 in the *Summa Theologiae* is clear. Just as Thomas argues in the *Summa* that the unity of *sacra doctrina* is determined by the formal rationale under which all things (*omnia quaecumque*) are studied as *revelabilia*, falling under divine providence, so truth itself, the uncreated Word, is *manifestabilis* to human beings. The *forma* of truth is that it can be made manifest by God because it belongs to God, that it is for God to reveal truth itself, and that this truth itself is the Word, the 'light of men'. This truth itself that exceeds all human cognition (as Thomas often stresses in the commentary) is *manifestabilis*.[176]

It is in the light of this remark by Thomas that truth itself, the Word, is *manifestabilis*, that it belongs to the form of truth that it can be revealed to us, that the strong claim Thomas makes about the relationship of the sciences to this Gospel in the prologue to his commentary is to be understood. Starting from Is 6:1, Thomas described the contemplation of John the evangelist as perfect, full and high, and made a parallel between those characteristics and three sciences: moral science, natural science and metaphysics. Because John's contemplation was perfect, full and high, Thomas concluded that "the Gospel of John contains all together

175 Ibid., p. 49.

176 Cf. *In Io* prol. §2 and §6; *In Io* 1:18 §213; *In Io* 7:29 §1063: "Veritas enim divina excedit omnem cognitionem nostram" (text corrected by L. Reid).

what the above sciences have in a divided way, and so it is most perfect".[177]

Thomas makes a noteworthy remark at the end of the commentary that is less well known than the remark in the prologue and that parallels it. Jn 19:20 mentions that the inscription put on the cross was written in three languages: in Hebrew, in Latin, and in Greek. Augustine comments that these languages stand out above others: Hebrew because the Jews glory in God's law; Greek because of the wisdom of the people; and Latin because at the time, the Romans ruled over almost all peoples.[178] This becomes the standard explanation, included in the *Glossa ordinaria* and many medieval commentaries.[179]

Thomas includes it both in the *Catena Aurea* and in the commentary. In the commentary, however, he adds another interpretation that I have not been able to find in his sources, nor in Albert or Bonaventure's commentaries. Thomas writes: "Or, the use of Hebrew signified that Christ was to rule over theological philosophy because the knowledge of divine matters was entrusted to the Jews. The Greek signified that Christ was to rule over natural and physical philosophy, for the Greeks were engaged in speculation about nature. Latin signified that Christ was to rule over practical philosophy because moral speculation was especially flourishing among the Romans. And so, all thought is brought into captivity and obedience to Christ, as we see in 2 Corinthians (10:5)".[180] This quotation from 2 Corinthians is a favourite of Thomas; he uses it more often when he discusses the relationship of natural, philosophical knowledge to faith, like in the first question of the *prima pars* of the *Summa Theologiae*.[181] Here it leads to a new interpretation of the significance of the three languages in which the title above the cross

---

[177] "Sed Evangelium Ioannis, que divisim scientiae praedictae habent, totum simul continet, et ideo est perfectissimum". *In Io* Prol., §9 (text corrected by L. Reid).

[178] "Hae quippe tres linguae ibi prae caeteris eminebant: Hebraea propter Iudaeos in Dei lege gloriantes; Graeca propter gentium sapientes; Latina propter Romanos multis ac pene iam tunc omnibus gentibus imperantes". Augustine, *Tract. in Io* 117.4

[179] *Glossa Ordinaria In Io* 19:20; Albert, *In Io* 19:20 p. 656. Bonaventure does not mention the gloss in his commentary.

[180] "Vel per Hebraeam significabatur quod Christus dominari debebat theologicae philosophiae, quae significatur per Hebraeam, quia Iudaeis est tradita divinarum rerum cognitio; per Graecam vero philosophiae naturali et physice: nam Graeci erga naturalium speculationem insudaverunt; per Latinam vero philosophiae practicae, quia apud Romanos maxime viguit scientia moralis: ut sic in captivitatem redigantur omnem intellectum in obsequium Christi, ut dicitur II Cor. X, 5". *In Io* 19:20 §2422 (text corrected by L. Reid).

[181] *STh* I q. 1 a. 8 ad 2; Cf. *De Trin* I q. 2 a. 3c.

is written: with and after Augustine, the languages point to the universality of the cross, but in the interpretation Thomas adds, the languages do not only speak of the universality of the cross but also signify the relation of the sciences to theology, in the way it does in the other places where Thomas refers to 2 Cor 10:5.

What Thomas does by referring to this verse in his interpretation of the three languages above the cross parallels the interpretation of the relationship of the sciences to the Gospel of John in Thomas's prologue to the commentary. John the Evangelist's threefold contemplation of which Thomas speaks in the prologue is the contemplation of Christ, as Thomas writes at the very beginning of the prologue.[182] When Thomas concludes that because this contemplation of John was perfect, full and high, it contains what the sciences have in a divided way, it is the same christocentric orientation of all the sciences that is made because of 2 Cor 10:5 in the comment on the languages above the cross. Both at the very beginning and towards the end of the commentary, Thomas stresses this christocentric orientation of all human knowledge.[183] The reason for this christocentric orientation is that the form of God's truth is such that it can be made known to us, rational creatures. The Word, the life of men, is *manifestabilis*.

Thus far, we have seen Thomas taking two steps in his commentary on v. 4b: the first was to explain the language of light in the Gospel as manifestation. The second step was to use the grades of life to state that what is at stake is not whether something is or is not revealed, but that it belongs to the *forma* of the truth that it can be revealed: it is *manifestabilis.* A question that Thomas inserts introduces the third step. The question is why the evangelist speaks of 'the light of men' since the Word is also the light of angels. Origen had answered this question in his commentary by stating that the text should not be read exclusively, just like the biblical expression "the God of Abraham and the God of Isaac and the God of Jacob" in Ex 3:6 should not be interpreted to mean that God is the God of these three patriarchs only. 'Men' here stands for all

---

[182] "In verbis autem propositis describitur contemplatio Ioannis tripliciter, secundum quod tripliciter domini Iesu divinitatem contemplatus est". *In Io* Prol., §1 (text corrected by L. Reid).

[183] Otto Hermann Pesch was the first to draw attention to the programmatic character of the remarks in Thomas's prologue to the commentary: O.H. Pesch, *Theologie der Rechtfertigung bei Martin Luther und Thomas von Aquin: Versuch eines Systematisch-Theologischen Dialogs*, Mainz, Matthias-Grünewald Verlag, 1967, p. 583, nt.10. Cf. E. Rogers, *Thomas Aquinas and Karl Barth*, p. 51.

spiritual beings, according to Origen.[184] Thomas had included this answer in the *Catena Aurea* and includes it in the commentary as well. Parallel to this answer, however, he gives a second answer, taken from the homilies of John Chrysostom: "Chrysostom says that the Evangelist intended in this Gospel to give us a knowledge of the Word precisely as directed to the salvation of men and therefore directs his aim more to men than to angels".[185] Thomas includes this remark in his commentary without further comment, and by doing so, shows his agreement. After all, it is a proper choice of a medieval *magister* which references from patristic commentaries to include and which not to include. Both Bonaventure and Albert had Chrysostom's homilies on John at their disposal, and both make ample use of them for their own commentaries. Still, neither of these two theologians quotes this text from Chrysostom. That, of course, does not mean that they would disagree with Chrysostom's remark: drawing that conclusion would be an *argumentum ex silentio*. What it does show, however, is that it is relevant that Thomas does quote this remark from Chrysostom. The first thing that has to be said is that he must have found it important enough to hand it on to his students. Because it is such a programmatic statement, however, it carries more weight. We saw that in his *divisio textus* on Jn 3, Thomas calls our reformation by grace the Evangelist's "principal subject".[186] That remark subsequently becomes the foundation for Thomas's reading of the whole of Jn 3-11: Jn 3-4 speak about the reformation by grace, Jn 5-11 about the benefits God gives to those who are spiritually reborn. Therefore, when Thomas in his commentary on 'the light of men' in Jn 1:4b uses the quote by Chrysostom to give a soteriological direction to the way the fourth Gospel speaks about the Word, Thomas is not just handing on a patristic reading of a particular verse to his students. Instead, he is making a statement about how the Gospel, and therefore, this commentary, should be read: the Fourth Gospel is about our salvation, and what it teaches about the divine Word is oriented towards that salvation.

---

[184] Origen, *Comm. In Io* bk. II, n. 140-148.

[185] "Chrysostomus enim dicit quod Evangelista intendebat in isto Evangelio tradere nobis cognitionem de verbo, secundum quod ad salutem hominum ordinatur; et ideo magis refert suam intentionem ad homines quam ad angelos". *In Io* 1:4 §98 (text corrected by L. Reid).

[186] "Supra ostendit Evangelista virtutem Christi quantum ad immutationem naturae; hic vero ostendit eam quantum ad reformationem gratiae, de qua principaliter intendit". *In Io* 3:1 §423 (text corrected by L. Reid).

Light and darkness

After having given the Gospel's expression 'the light of men' a soteriological direction, Thomas makes two more remarks about light and darkness that should be mentioned here. First, in the verse 'that life was the light of men', 'light' is related to 'life'. Thomas suggests this can be done in two ways. The 'light of men' can be an object that only human beings (and angels) can see because only human beings are *capax Dei*, capable of the vision of God. While other animals may know certain truths, only human beings can know the nature of truth (*ratio veritatis*), which is meant by saying that it is *manifestabilis* as we saw before. It is because truth is inherently *manifestabilis*, that all our knowledge is christocentric in its orientation. Truth can be known because the world is created truthfully by God, and that truth is Christ. To recognize that is to know the *ratio veritatis*, which only rational creatures can do.

The second way 'life' as the light of men can be understood is by way of participation. According to Thomas's biological knowledge, for eyes to see light, they must participate in an inner light that makes it possible for them to see external light: "The eyes know external light as an object, but if they are to see it, they must participate in an inner light by which the eyes are adapted and disposed for seeing the external light".[187] By analogy, we can only see the Word, recognize the light by participating in it. I will have more to say about this participation in the next chapter. It is important to note here that Thomas shows how this participation is only something human beings do. Our participation is in the superior part of our soul, that is to say, in our capability to understand things, the capability which sets us apart from other animals.[188] Thomas calls it here 'the intellectual light'. It is through understanding it that we participate in the Word. Thomas quotes Ps 4:7, "The light of your countenance, O Lord, is marked upon us", and paraphrases it by saying that it is the light "of your Son, who is your face, by whom you are manifested".[189] We participate in the light that Christ is not because of

---

[187] "Oculus enim lucem exteriorem cognoscit tamquam obiectum, sed oportet ad hoc quod eam videat, quod participet aliquam lucem interiorem, per quam aptetur et disponatur oculus ad lucem exteriorem videndam". *In Io* 1:4 §101.

[188] Calling the intellect 'the highest part or power of the soul' is another way of naming the different grades of life. Plants only have a vegetative soul; the soul of an animal has both a nutritive and a sensory power; the soul of a human being has a nutritive, sensory and rational power. See *STh* I q. 77 a. 4. Cf. R. Pasnau, *Thomas Aquinas on Human Nature: A Philosophical Study of Summa Theologiae, Ia 75-89*, Cambridge, Cambridge University Press, 2002, p. 143-145.

[189] "lux intellectiva, de qua dicitur in Ps IV, 7: 'Signatum est super nos lumen vultus tui', idest filii tui, qui est facies tua, qua manifestaris". *In Io* 1:4 §101.

some activity of our own, but because the Son reveals the Father to us. It is this manifestation by Christ that makes our participation in the light possible.

The second remark on light and darkness comes in the commentary on v. 5, "And the light shines in the darkness, and the darkness did not overcome it". Thomas gives two explanations side by side, according to two meanings 'darkness' can have in the realm of nature. First, darkness can refer to us as creatures. Thomas compares what the 'light of men' does to human beings to what the sun does to the air: Air is receptive to the light of the sun, but it is not light in itself. Just so, Thomas says, the life which is the light of men shines in our souls and in our minds. The words "The darkness did not overcome it" (*Tenebrae eam non comprehenderunt*), therefore shows us as creatures: "For to overcome (*comprehendere*) something, is to enclose and understand its boundaries". [190] Enclosing and understanding the boundaries of the Creator, however, is impossible for creatures. In this interpretation, for Thomas, 'darkness' does not have negative connotations. Light and darkness are used to signify the unique distinction between Creator and creatures, a distinction that differs from all the distinctions we know because all the distinctions we know are distinctions between creatures. In a phrase that Henk Schoot coined: "God differs differently".[191] The word *comprehendere* refers to this 'Christian distinction', as Robert Sokolowski called it; Thomas refers to Jer 32:19, which uses the word *incomprehensibilis*: "Great in counsel, incomprehensible in thought".[192]

Scripture gives Thomas the other meaning of 'darkness' as well. Eccl 2:13 reads, "And I saw that wisdom excels folly as much as light excels darkness". Darkness in Jn 1:5 can thus be understood as a natural lack of wisdom, as both Origen and Augustine had done before Thomas: "Someone is without wisdom, therefore, because he lacks the light of divine wisdom".[193] Human wisdom is a participation in divine wisdom, in the divine light, and when people are not or not yet wise, they can be

---

[190] "Illud enim dicitur comprehendi, cuius fines concluduntur et conspiciuntur". *In Io* 1:5 §102.

[191] H. Schoot, *Christ the 'Name' of God*, p. 144, 198.

[192] "Magnus consilio et incomprehensibilis cogitatu". R. Sokolowski coined the phrase 'the Christian distinction' to explain the Christian (maybe one should say 'Abrahamic'?) distinction between Creator and creation: R. Sokolowski, *The God of Faith and Reason*: *Foundations of Christian Theology*, Washington D.C., Catholic University of America Press, 1995.

[193] "Ex eo ergo aliquis insipiens est quod privatur lumine sapientiae divinae". *In Io* 1:5 §103.

said to be darkness. Remember that Thomas here is not speaking of any culpable lack of wisdom: the *divisio textus* has made it clear that Thomas means to speak about our natural capacities or lack thereof. Nor is the darkness the fault of the light, as Thomas is quick to point out. The light radiates upon all, but the foolish are not able to apprehend it, to participate in it.[194] Darkness thus understood is never the final word to be said about any human being, Thomas adds. No person is entirely devoid of divine light because whatever truth someone may know is a participation in the divine light. A quotation that is dear to Thomas confirms the point: "Every truth, no matter by whom it is spoken, comes from the Holy Spirit".[195]

The light of grace

Parallel to the commentary on Jn 1:4b-5 according to nature, Thomas gives a second reading of these verses, according to grace. The reason for this reading, Thomas asserts, is Christological: that "that life was the light of men" can be understood according to the influx of grace, is so because we are illuminated by Christ.[196] The 'soteriological turn' that we saw beginning with the quotation from Chrysostom is intensified here: this part of the commentary in a way is the preparation for what follows when

---

194 P.-Y. Maillard rightly mentions that the point that when people are in darkness it is not because of a defect in the light, is a recurring theme in the commentary. He refers to *In Io* 1:7 §121; *In Io* 1:10 §139; *In Io* 3:32 §536; *In Io* 6:37 §920-937 *In Io* 17:9 §2207, and *In Io* 20:23 §2544. In all these texts however, Thomas speaks of a culpable darkness: people do not receive that light that is Christ because they actively obstruct it. That is not what Thomas is talking about in this part of the commentary on Jn 1:5: here he speaks of the natural lack of wisdom. Cf. P.-Y. Maillard, *La vision de Dieu chez Thomas d'Aquin*, p. 96 nt.1.

195 "Omne verum, a quocumque dicatur, a spiritu sancto est". *In Io* 1:5 §103. Thomas refers to this text three more times in the commentary. Cf. *In Io* 7:16 §1037, where it is used to read "My doctrine is not mine" as related to Christ's humanity; *In Io* 8:44, where the verse under comment ("When he [the devil, SM] lies, he speaks according to his own nature") leads Thomas to discuss whether the devil can speak the truth; and *In Io* 14:17 §1916, where Thomas explains why Scripture calls the Holy Spirit 'the Spirit of truth'. In the last two of these references, Thomas ascribes the quotation to Ambrose, as he does in other writings as well. We now know that it is in fact from an anonymous contemporary of Ambrose who was called 'Ambrosiaster' by Erasmus. See the article Serge-Thomas Bonino wrote on Thomas's use of this quotation: S.-T. Bonino, '"Toute Vérité, quel que soit celui qui la dit, vient de l'Esprit-Saint": Autour d'une citation de l'*Ambrosiaster* dans le corpus thomasien', *Revue Thomiste* 106 (2006), p. 101-47. Cf. J.-P. Torrell, *Saint Thomas Aquinas: Spiritual Master*, Washington D.C., Catholic University of America Press, 2003, p. 293-297.

196 "Alio modo ab illo loco 'et vita erat lux hominum', exponitur secundum influxum gratiae, quia irradiamur per Christum". *In Io* 1:4 §104 (text corrected by L. Reid).

Thomas starts discussing the incarnation in the commentary on Jn 1:6-14. Thomas introduces his reading with a remark that has the grammar of a *divisio textus*:

> Above the evangelist had considered the creation of things through the Word, here he considers the restoration of the rational creature through Christ, saying, "And that life", of the Word, "was the light of men".[197]

What does the 'above' (*supra*) that Thomas uses here refer to? The only explanation that makes sense in the context is that it refers to verses in the Gospel leading up to this verse. That means that the reading that Thomas is about to give here is a complete alternative to the reading according to nature that he has just given. The reading according to nature structures Jn 1:3-5 as speaking about the power of the Word with respect to the whole of creation first (v. 3-4a), and then about the creative power of the Word with respect to human beings (v. 4b-5). In this second interpretation, the distinction is not creation as a whole first, and then human beings, but creation first (v. 3-4a) and then restoration (v. 4b-5).

Paweł Klimczak has rightly remarked that the notion of light and that of grace here become almost equivalent: it is only He who is light, who can manifest the truth.[198] It is by the influx of grace that Christ enlightens us.[199] Thomas writes:

> It was fitting to join light and life by saying, 'And that life was the light of men', in order to show that these two have come to us through Christ: life, through a participation in grace, 'Grace and truth have come through Jesus Christ' (below 1:17); and light, by a knowledge of truth and wisdom.[200]

In the next chapter, we will have more to say about the soteriological interpretation Thomas gives to 'light' as a name for Christ. What is

---

[197] "Supra egit Evangelista de creatione rerum per verbum, hic vero tractat de restauratione rationalis creaturae facta per Christum dicens: 'et vita', verbi, 'erat lux hominum'". *In Io* 1:4 §104.

[198] Thomas makes this point explicit when he paraphrases Jn 18:37 ("For this I was born, and for this I have come into the world, to bear witness to the truth") as: "Et inquantum manifesto me veritatem, intantum regnum mihi paro. Hoc enim non potest fieri nisi per manifestationem veritatis, quam manifestationem non decebat fieri nisi per me, qui sum lux". *In Io* 18:37 §2359.

[199] P. Klimczak, *Christus Magister*, p. 182.

[200] "Congrue etiam coniungit lucem et vitam dicens 'et vita erat lux hominum', ut ostendat ista duo, lucem scilicet et vitam, nobis provenisse per Christum. Vitam quidem per participationem gratiae; infra: 'gratia et veritas per Iesum Christum facta est;' lucem vero per cognitionem veritatis et sapientiae". *In Io* 1:4 §104.

important to notice here is how, in this soteriological reading, 'light' and 'life' become closely linked. As Klimczak comments: "The vivification and the light are two inseparable faces of the gift of salvation that is the result of the incarnation of Christ".[201]

According to Thomas, it is within this context that 'darkness' in "The light shines in the darkness and the darkness did not overcome it" can be read in three different ways. The first way is to read 'darkness' as punishment and sadness. Micah 7:8 ("When I sit in darkness and in suffering the Lord is my delight") leads Thomas to this reading. He ties it to an interpretation of Origen, who reads "The light shines in the darkness" as referring to Christ's coming in the flesh, which "is called a darkness insofar as it has a likeness to sinful flesh". The second way is to read 'darkness' as referring to the devils. Thomas recognizes them in what Eph 6:12 calls "the rulers of the world of this darkness". Read in this way, Thomas interprets "the light shines in the darkness" as meaning: "The Son of God has descended into the world where darkness, i.e. the devils, hold sway".[202] But "the darkness did not overcome it:" "the devils were unable to obscure him by their temptations" interprets Thomas with a reference to the temptations of Christ in the desert.[203] The third way that Thomas interprets Jn 1:5 in this context is to read 'darkness' as sinful error or ignorance. Thomas' reference to Eph 5:8 gives only the first words, "You were at one time darkness", but it is clear from the context that the passage speaks of sin. Commenting on the second half of v. 5, "and the darkness did not overcome it", Thomas makes it explicit that the ignorance he is speaking about here is sinful ignorance:

> For in spite of the number of men darkened by sin, blinded by envy, shadowed over by pride, who have struggled against Christ (as is plain from the Gospel) by upbraiding him, heaping insults and calumnies upon him, and finally killing him, nevertheless they 'did not overcome it', i.e., gain the victory of so obscuring him that his brightness would not shine throughout the whole world.[204]

---

[201] P. Klimczak, *Christus Magister*, p. 256.

[202] "Secundum hoc dicit: 'lux', idest filius Dei, 'in tenebris lucet', idest in mundum descendit, ubi tenebrae, idest daemones, dominabantur". *In Io* 1:5 §106.

[203] "'Et tenebrae', idest daemones, 'eam non comprehenderunt', idest eum obscurare non potuerunt tentando, ut patet Matth. IV". *In Io* 1:5 §106.

[204] "Quia quantumcumque homines peccatis obscurati, invidia excaecati, superbia tenebrosi, contra Christum pugnaverunt, ut patet ex Evangelio, exprobrando scilicet, iniurias et contumelias inferendo, et tandem occidendo, non tamen 'eum comprehenderunt;' idest non vicerunt eum obscurando, quin potius eius claritas per totum mundum fulgeret". *In Io* 1:5 §107 (text corrected by L. Reid).

Later in the commentary, commenting on Jn 7:31 ("Many of the people, however, believed in him"), Thomas remarks that it was especially the leaders of the people who were not receptive to the wisdom of Christ: "He does not say, many 'of the leaders', because the higher their rank, the further away they were [from him]".[205]

In his commentary on this verse, Albert too gives a distinct explanation of the light of grace. In an exposition that is reminiscent of the parable of the sower in Mc 4 (and the parallels in Mt 13 and Lk 8), Albert discusses three kinds of heavenly bodies and their reaction to sunlight: some only receive light to show their own darkness and unsightliness; others only receive light to show their beauty on the outside; a third group receives the light in their depths, like precious stones, and they start to give light themselves. The comparison will be clear: some people do not receive the light of grace in any other sense than that it shows their darkness; other people are touched by the light, but it seems to stay on the outside; they have a certain virtue, but not true virtue. In a final group, the light of grace has become internalized so that they become a light for others.[206]

The reason I mention this interpretation of Albert is not just to show that even when they use the same framework (in this case, the framework of interpreting 'darkness' and 'light' in Jn 1:4b-5 in terms of sin and grace), medieval commentators can have very different ways of interpreting a biblical text. What is remarkable in Thomas's interpretation is that when he reads Jn 1:4b-5 in terms of sin and grace, each of the three interpretations he gives of 'darkness' points forward to the incarnation. In Thomas's reading of Jn 1:3-5, 'light' is a soteriological term. In the next chapter, we will see that this interpretation will be deepened when Thomas comments on the verses from Jn 1 that speak about the incarnation.

4. Conclusion

Thomas's commentary on these first verses of the fourth Gospel is a profound theology of the Word that is unique within Thomas's writings. While it has the characteristics almost to be a complete treatise on 'the

---

205 "Non dicit de principibus: quia quanto maiores erant, tanto magis erant elongati". *In Io* 7:31 §1070. Klimczak reads this comment in the context of the remarks Thomas makes about the darkness in Jn 1:5 in §103, but that is not correct, since Thomas is speaking about a natural lack of knowledge there, as we have seen. Cf. P. Klimczak, *Christus Magister*, p. 326-37.

206 Albert, *Super Io* 1:5 p. 96-98.

Word of God', it never stops to be what it is in the first place: biblical commentary, biblical theology. This theology of the Word centres around the relation of the Son of God in relation to the Father. In our speech of God, the relationship of origin as it is presented through the analogy of the Word as understood and spoken by the Father provides understanding both of the distinction between the Father and the Son, and their consubstantiality.

The importance of a theology of the Word lies not only in understanding the relation between the Father and the Son, however. Chrysostom's remark that the Gospel begins with 'In the beginning was the Word' and not with 'In the beginning was the Son' because contrary to 'son', which implies a relationship to 'father' only, 'word' implies a relation to both speaker and the person spoken to is fundamental to Thomas's reading of Jn 1:1-5. His patristic sources teach Thomas to discuss the Word *quoad nos*, to understand that from the beginning of his Gospel, John has God's revelation to us in mind. Thomas's theology of the Word binds Christology, trinitarian theology, and a theology of revelation, which is why Gilles Emery rightly states that "the doctrine of the Word is incontestably the heart of Thomas' trinitarian theology".[207]

A point to take away from the *divisio textus* Thomas uses is the trinitarian character of his reading. While he uses a framework for the first clauses that is Aristotelian, he turns the framework inside out when speaking about God. It is because divine persons in God can only be distinguished from each other according to relations of origin, that it is proper for theological thinking about the Word to start with its origin ('when' and 'where' the Word was) before discussing what the Word is. It is as a discussion with heretical interpretations of the Word, a discussion that is structured by the insight from trinitarian theology that the Word should be distinguished from the other persons in God according to the relations of origin, that the *divisio textus* Thomas gives of the first verses of the Gospel shows its theological strength: it is the *ordo disciplinae* according to which the Evangelist presents his theology.

The relationship of the Word to creation is central in Thomas's reading of Jn 1:3-5. It is through the Word and through Love that God creates the world. Creation is therefore trinitarian in form. Thomas's thinking about the divine processions is especially helpful here. The eternal Word proceeds from the Father as spoken. With regard to creation, the Father speaks all things into being through his Word. In God, the Holy Spirit

[207] G. Emery, *The Trinitarian Theology of St Thomas Aquinas*, 179.

proceeds in the form of love. With regard to creation, the Father and the Word love all things through the Holy Spirit. Thus, "the eternal processions are the cause and the rationale of the making of creatures".[208]

In the commentary on Jn 1:4b-5 this relation of the Word to creation is concentrated on the relation of the Word to human beings. Here Thomas starts to unwrap his theology of the Word *quoad nos* through his reflection on what it means that the evangelist calls the Word 'light'. The central category for Thomas here is 'manifestation'. It is because the Word comes forth from the Father and shares the Father's divinity, that it manifests the Father.[209] It belongs to the form of the truth that is the Word that it is *manifestabilis*, that although in itself it exceeds all our human knowledge, it can be made known to us, rational beings. We can know the truth because the world is created truthfully by God, and that Truth is Christ. The truth, therefore, all truth, is christoform, because it falls under the category of *manifestabilia*, it participates in the Word, who is *manifestabilis*.

---

[208] "Processiones personarum aeternae sunt causa et ratio totius productionis creaturarum". *1 Sent*. d. 14 q. 1 a. 1c.

[209] Commenting on Jn 6:44 ("No one can come to me unless the Father, who sent me, draws him") Thomas discusses the question whether it is the Father who draws us to the Son or the other way round. Thomas answers the question by distinguishing the two natures in Christ and showing how both in Christ's humanity and in Christ's divinity, both directions are true: That the Father draws us to Christ and Christ to the Father. It is in this context, speaking explicitly about the divinity of Christ, that Thomas writes: "Inquantum vero Christus, est verbum Dei, et manifestativum Patris". *In Io* 6:44 §936, text corrected by L. Reid.

CHAPTER 3
THE INCARNATION

After discussing the divinity of Christ as the topic of the first five verses of the Gospel of John, Thomas continues his commentary by focussing on Jn 1:6-14, which according to his *divisio textus* speaks of the incarnation of the Word of God. In this chapter, I will follow Thomas in his commentary on Jn 1:6-14 closely in order to understand the cohesion in this part of the commentary and in order to show how the *divisio textus* brings about this cohesion.

This chapter consists of four sections, which follow the *divisio textus* Thomas gives of Jn 1:6-14. In the first section, we will look at the commentary on v. 6-8, which according to Thomas, speaks of the witness to the incarnate Word, the precursor John the Baptist; in the second section, we will consider the commentary on v. 9-10 which in Thomas's view states why the incarnation was necessary; in the third section, we will study the commentary on v. 11-13 which according to Thomas speaks of the benefit we received from the incarnation; and finally, in the fourth section, we will examine the commentary on v. 14, which in Thomas's interpretation presents the way in which the Word came.

1. Participation in the Light: John the Baptist (Jn 1:6-8)

In the previous chapter, we saw how Thomas interprets 'light' as a soteriological term in his commentary on Jn 1:4-5. The next three verses in the Gospel speak about John the Baptist and his relation to the light. Taken together, these verses for Thomas make the connection between the verses that spoke about the Word of God per se and those that speak about the incarnation. That 'light' remains a soteriological category for Thomas in these verses is confirmed by a remark that reads like a summary of Thomas's soteriology in a single sentence: "The salvation of man lies in participating in the light".[1]

Thomas reads v. 6-7 as describing John in four ways. As to his nature, John is a man, not an angel. He received his authority because he

[1] "salus hominis in hoc consistit, quod participet ipsam lucem". *In Io* 1:8 §122.

was sent by God. His name tells us that "in him was grace" (the meaning of the name John that Thomas already used to describe John the Evangelist in his prologue to the commentary), and his office is that he is a witness.[2] These four characteristics are traditional: we find them in the commentary by Bonaventure and with one exception also in that of Albert.[3]

It is the fourth characteristic, that of John's office to bear witness, that Thomas chooses to elaborate on. He describes three groups of witnesses, each a subset of the previous one. God does not create to add anything to himself because God does not need that, but as a manifestation of his goodness. In that sense, each creature is a witness to God as it shows God's goodness. The vastness of creation as a whole is a witness to God's power and omnipotence, and its beauty is a witness to God's wisdom. Thomas refers here to the Scriptural text that he often refers to when he speaks of our natural cognition of God: "His eternal power and divinity are clearly seen, being understood through the things that are made" (Rom 1:20). Within the whole of creation, all holy men and women are witnesses in a particular way because they not only witness to God by their natural existence but also spiritually by their good works. Within the group of these holy people, there is a group of even more special witnesses: those that not only share the gifts God has given them through their good lives but also spread them to others by their teaching and encouragement of others. John the Baptist falls in this last category.[4]

In the Gospel of John, the testimony of Christ is mentioned. Christ is a witness himself. When he is commenting on Jn 3:32 ("He testifies to what he has seen and heard, yet no one accepts his testimony"), Thomas will allocate being a witness to Christ according to his humanity: "Christ, as God, is truth itself; but as man, he is its witness".[5] Christ as witness manifests the truth that he himself is. The keyword 'manifestation' that we saw in the previous chapter reappears at this place

---

[2] *In Io* 1:6, §108. The interpretation of the name of John the Evangelist as "in whom is grace" is in *In Io* Prol., §11.

[3] Bonaventure, *In Io* 1:6 n. 18. Albert, *Super Io* 1:6 p. 106.

[4] *In Io* 1:6 §116. That spreading the good gifts to others by teaching and encouragement is to be preferred to merely doing good works, is a recurrent theme in Thomas's works. One finds a parallel to it in his ordering of the different forms of religious life: "Sicut enim maius est illuminare quam lucere solum, ita maius est contemplata aliis tradere quam solum contemplari". *STh* II-II q. 188 a. 6c.

[5] "Christus enim, inquantum Deus, est ipsa veritas; sed inquantum homo, est testis veritatis". *In Io* 3:32 §533 (text corrected by L. Reid).

in the commentary as an interpretation of what it is that the divine Light does. Thomas writes:

> For as light is not only visible in itself and of itself, but through it all else can be seen, so the Word of God is not only light in himself, but he manifests all things that are made manifest. For since a thing is made manifest and understood through its form, and all forms exist through the Word, who is the art full of living forms, the Word is light not only in himself but also as manifesting all things; 'all that is made manifest, is light' (Eph 5:13). And so it was fitting for the Evangelist to call the Son 'light' because he came as 'a revealing light to the Gentiles' (Lk 2:32). Above, he called the Son of God the Word, by which the Father expresses himself and every creature. Now since he is, properly speaking, the light of men, and the Evangelist is considering him here as coming to accomplish the salvation of men, he fittingly interrupts the use of the name 'Word' when speaking of the Son, and says, 'Light'.[6]

Christ is light, not just in himself, but as light, he manifests all things. According to Thomas, John is speaking here about Christ in relation to the salvation of man. It is because of this soteriological direction that the word 'light' is so appropriate.

In the commentary on Jn 1:7, Thomas makes a comparison between Christ and John the Baptist as witnesses. They both testify but in different ways. John's office as witness is great because one can only testify about something in the measure in which he has shared in it. Bearing witness to divine truth indicates knowledge of that truth. Christ, however, is the perfect witness of the truth; John and other prophets only are witnesses in so far as they have a share of divine truth.

The word Thomas uses for sharing in the light that is Christ is 'participation'. While Christ is light itself, John bears witness insofar as he participates in the light.[7] Later in the Gospel, in Jn 5:35, John the

---

[6] "Nam sicut lumen non solum in seipso et per se visibile est, sed etiam omnia alia per ipsum videri possunt, ita verbum Dei non solum in se lumen est, sed etiam est omnia manifestans quae manifestantur. Cum enim unumquodque manifestaetur per suam formam et cognoscatur, omnes autem formae sint per verbum, quod est ars plena rationum viventium: est ergo lumen, non solum in se, sed etiam omnia manifestans; Eph. V, 13: 'omne quod manifestatur, lumen est' etc. Congrue autem Evangelista filium dicit Dei lumen, quia venit 'lumen ad revelationem gentium', Lc. II, 32. Supra autem dixit filium Dei verbum, quo pater dicit se, et omnem creaturam. Unde cum proprie sit lux hominum, et hic Evangelista de eo agat secundum quod venit ad salutem hominum procurandam, congrue intermittit hoc nomen verbum, cum loquitur de filio, et dicit illud lumen". *In Io* 1:7 §118 (text corrected by L. Reid).

[7] *In Io* 1:7 §117.

Baptist will be called a lamp ("He was a burning and shining lamp, and you were willing to rejoice for a while in his light"). Commenting on that verse, Thomas writes: "Now a lamp differs from a light: for a light radiates light of itself, but a lamp does not give light of itself, but by participating in the light. Now the true light is Christ".[8]

Participation is a word to which Thomas often returns in the commentary when speaking about the relation of creatures to the Creator. This participation can happen in different ways, but the kind of participation Thomas is discussing here is a participation in the light that is Christ. Earlier in the commentary, Thomas stated that participation in the light is in the superior part of our soul: Thomas speaks of an intellectual light.[9] We also saw earlier that participation in the light could be understood both as participation in the natural light and as participation in grace.[10] Speaking of John the Baptist as a witness who participates in the light of Christ, participation is understood as a participation in grace. This participation can happen in two ways, Thomas explains: in an imperfect way, through faith, and in a perfect way in our heavenly homeland, in glory. This eschatological remark shows that 'participation' is not a static description for Thomas but is related to the ultimate human destination. Human participation in God awaits fulfilment in glory; in this life, it is a participation through faith. Through his testimony, John the Baptist brings people to faith, by which they participate in the Light.[11]

Already in this life, however, participation supposes a certain likeness, Thomas writes: "because John participated in the true light, it was fitting that he would bear witness to the light; for fire is better exhibited by something afire than by anything else, and colour by

---

[8] "Differt enim lucerna a luce: nam lux est quae per seipsam lucet; lucerna vero quae non per se lucet, sed per participationem lucis. Lux autem vera Christus est". *In Io* 5:35 §812 (text corrected by L. Reid).

[9] *In Io* 1:4 §101.

[10] A treatment of participation both as regarding creation and as regarding grace can be found in R. te Velde, *Aquinas on God: The 'Divine Science' of the Summa Theologiae*, Aldershot, Ashgate Publishing, 2006, p. 139-142 and 160-165 respectively.

[11] *In Io* 1:7 §120. On participation as an eschatological notion, cf. C. Leget, 'Eschatology', in: R. van Nieuwenhove, J. Wawrykow (eds.), *The Theology of Thomas Aquinas*, Notre Dame, University of Notre Dame Press, 2005, p. 365-85, here p. 370. P.-Y. Maillard has shown how pervasive the succession from faith to vision is in Thomas's commentary on John: there is hardly a chapter that does not mention it, and this gives the commentary a distinctive eschatological colour. Cf. P.-Y. Maillard, *La vision de Dieu chez Thomas d'Aquin: Une lecture de l'In Ioannem à la lumière de ses sources Augustiniennes*, Paris, Vrin, 2001, p. 129.

something coloured".[12] John's office as witness is great because of his participation in the divine light and because of his likeness to Christ who carried out the office of witness himself.[13]

In between the impressive first five verses of the Gospel of John and v. 9-14, which speak about the incarnation, the verses about John the Baptist can seem to be an interlude that is easily overlooked. From our reading of Thomas's commentary on these verses, it can now be concluded that the importance of these verses for Thomas is twofold.

In the previous chapter, we saw that Thomas starts to unwrap his theology of the Word *quoad nos* through his reflection on what it means that the evangelist calls the Word 'light'. John the Baptist as witness to the light is as it were a case study of this. The fullness of his testimony, as a creature, a holy man, and a teacher, is given to him through grace. Through grace he participates in the divine light. The terminology of participation allows Thomas to keep the distinction between the graced human being and God clear: John the Baptist "was not the Light". On the other hand, the terminology of participation also allows Thomas to explain the relation of John the Baptist to God: it is because of this graced participation that John can be the witness of the divine Light.

Secondly, in his *divisio textus,* Thomas reads Jn 1:6-14a as a whole that speaks about the incarnation, as we saw before. Within this unit, v. 6-8 is presented as speaking about "the witness of the incarnation".[14] By reading those verses in terms of the Baptist's participation in the light as the condition for his ability to be a witness of the incarnation, these verses form the bridge between what went before and what comes after.

2. The Necessity of the Incarnation (Jn 1:9-10)

In his *divisio textus*, Thomas labels the next couple of verses ("He [the Word] was the true light, which enlightens every man coming into this world. He was in the world, and through him the world was made, and the world did not know him", Jn 1:9-10) as showing why it was necessary for the Word to become incarnate. Thomas sees this reason identified in the last clause of these verses: "The world did not know him". The

---

[12] "Et ideo quia Ioannes participabat verum lumen, congruenter testimonium perhibebat de lumine: ignis enim convenientius manifestatur per aliquod ignitum quam per aliquid aliud, et color per coloratum". *In Io* 1:8 §123.
[13] *In Io* 1:7 §117.
[14] *In Io* 1:6 §108.

necessity for the incarnation is the lack of divine knowledge in the world, and Thomas recognizes this in Jesus's response to Pilate: "For this was I born, and I came into the world for this, to testify to the truth" (Jn 18:37). This lack of knowledge, Thomas argues, is not a lack in God or in the Word, but it is a lack in human beings. This then becomes the structural lens through which Thomas reads Jn 1:9-10. As he states in the *divisio textus*: first, the Evangelist shows that the lack of knowledge that is the reason for the incarnation is not a lack in God. Secondly, that it is a lack in human beings.

An analysis of the expression 'true light' serves as an introduction to both points. Thomas notes that in Scripture, 'true' can be contrasted with three different things. These three show different ways in which human beings know God. First, 'true' can be contrasted with false, as saint Paul does in the letter to the Ephesians: "Put an end to lying, and let everyone speak the truth" (Eph 4:25). Thomas applies this to the philosophers who lived before Christ. Quoting Rom 1:21 ("for though they knew God, they did not honour him as God or give thanks to him, but they became futile in their thinking, and their senseless minds were darkened"), he states that the light they prided themselves on having was a false light.

Scripture also contrasts true with 'figurative'. Thomas refers to Jn 1:17 ("The law was given through Moses; grace and truth have come through Jesus Christ") and explains that "the truth of the figures contained in the law was fulfilled by Christ". The teaching of the Jewish law is a figurative light that points forward to the true light, which is the way Thomas reads Hebr 10:1: "The law has a shadow of the good things to come, not the image itself of them". This is not the place to discuss Thomas's understanding of the relation between the old law and the new, or his views on salvation history and the Jewish people.[1] What is relevant here is that, as Paweł Klimczak has mentioned, the notion of *figura* keeps two things together: *figura* is an announcement of a reality that is not yet realized or manifest. There is, therefore, something 'imperfect' to a *figura*. On the other hand, it is important to underline the truthfulness of a *figura*: it contains truth and is a step towards its full manifestation.[15]

---

[1] For a study on the image of the Jews in Thomas's commentary on John, cf. M. Hammele, *Das Bild der Juden im Johannes-Kommentar des Thomas von Aquin: Ein Beitrag zu Bibelhermeneutik und Wissenschaftsgeschichte im 13. Jahrhundert*, Stuttgart, Verlag Katholisches Bibelwerk, 2012.

[15] P. Klimczak, *Christus magister: Le Christ maître dans les commentaires évangéliques de Saint Thomas d'Aquin*, Fribourg, Academic Press Fribourg, 2013, p. 238-241, with examples from Thomas's commentary on John.

Finally, Scripture contrasts 'true' with 'by participation'. Thomas recognizes this in 1 Jn 5:20: "that we may be in his true Son", interpreting it as "who is not his son by participation". Participated light is present in the angels and holy people, who know God by grace. Thomas recognizes this in Job 25:3 "Upon whom does this light not shine?" explaining it as "Whoever shine, shine to the extent that they participate in God's light".[16] This participated light did not just have its place before the coming of Christ (as Thomas says of both the false and the figurative light), but is present in the angels and the saints, both before and after the coming of Christ.[17]

Contrasting 'true' with 'false', 'figurative' and 'participated' leads Thomas to further clarification of his interpretation of the word 'light' when it is used for the Word of God. In the previous chapter, we saw that it has a soteriological meaning, but the supposition of 'light' was not yet made explicit. Here, however, Thomas writes: "But the Word of God was not a false light, nor a figurative light, nor a participated light, but the true light, i.e. light by his essence".[18] "His essence" here means 'divine essence'. That this is so becomes clear from what follows. Thomas reads "he was the true light" as refuting two Christological errors: that Christ derived his beginning from the virgin Mary and that Christ was not true God, but only God by participation.[19] The reason Thomas gives for stating that 'light' refers to divinity is biblical: Thomas refers to 1 Jn 1:5: "God is light, and in Him there is no darkness at all". Speaking about Christ as 'light' therefore means speaking about his divinity. Later in the commentary, when he is commenting on Jn 8:12 ("I am the light of the world"), Thomas reinforces this by linking this verse to the story of the woman caught in adultery that went right before it by saying that Jesus's remark "Nor will I condemn you" is forgiving the woman's sin. Thomas adds: "And so they would not doubt that he could forgive and pardon sins, he saw fit to show the power of his divinity more openly by saying that he is the light which drives away the darkness of

---

[16] *In Io* 1:9 §125.

[17] M. Sabathé, *La Trinité rédemptrice dans le commentaire de l'évangile de Saint Jean par Thomas d'Aquin*, Paris, Vrin, 2011, p. 338-339. Cf. S.-T. Bonino, 'La théologie de la vérité dans *la lectura super Ioannem* de Saint Thomas d'Aquin', *Revue Thomiste* 104 (2004), p. 141-66, here p. 143-145.

[18] "Sed verbum Dei non erat lux falsa, non figuralis, non participata, sed lux vera, idest per essentiam suam". *In Io* 1:9 §125.

[19] *In Io* 1:9 §126.

sin".[20] Forgiving the darkness of sin is what the light does. It can do that because it is God. Thomas's analysis of the expression 'true light', contrasting it with false, figurative and participated light, leads to a rule for speaking about Christ: when Scripture speaks about Christ as 'light' (or when we do), it speaks about his divinity.

A lack not in God...

'Participation' is the bridge that leads Thomas to his next point: that the cause for a lack of divine knowledge in the world is not God. Thomas sees three reasons in Jn 1:9-10 for saying that this lack of knowledge was not caused by God. Firstly, the Word of God is efficient, for "He enlightens every man coming into this world". 'Participation' is key here: all human enlightenment is a participation in what is light by its essence, the Word of God.

At this point, Thomas inserts a *quaestio* in his commentary. Is it true that "He enlightens every man coming into this world?" Are there not many people in darkness, people who do not participate in the light that is Christ? Two distinctions in the way words are used in Scripture help Thomas answer this question here. When "world" is used in Scripture, it can be looked at from its being created, it can be seen from the point of view of its perfection (Thomas refers to 2 Cor 5:19 "God was, in Christ, reconciling the world to himself"), and it can be looked at from the point of view of its perversity (Thomas mentions 1 Jn 5:19 "The whole world lies under the power of the evil one"). "Enlightenment", on the other hand, can be interpreted as regarding nature or as regarding grace.

The difficulty, Thomas argues, does not lie on the level of nature. When 'world' is understood as 'creation', and 'enlighten' is taken to refer to the light of natural reason, there is no problem: through our participation in the true light of natural knowledge, we are enlightened in the sense that we receive natural knowledge.[21] Thomas uses the three possible interpretations of 'world' to give three patristic interpretations of the verse on the level of grace. When it is read with our perfection in view, "every person that comes into the world", read as the spiritual world, the

---

[20] "ideo ne aliqui dubitarent utrum ipse absolvere posset, et peccata dimittere, dignatur apertius divinitatis suae potentiam demonstrare, dicens se esse lucem, qui peccati tenebras pellit". *In Io* 8:12 §1141.

[21] From this, N. Healy rightfully draws the conclusion: "The condition for the possibility of rational debate between people of diverse traditions is thus conceived theologically. Natural reason is not a neutral forum in any secularist sense. It, too, is created and sustained by the Word and it would be misunderstood if that basis were ignored". N.M. Healy, *Thomas Aquinas: Theologian of the Christian Life*, Aldershot, Ashgate, 2003, p. 53.

Church, does this by being enlightened by the light of grace, as Origen had commented. In this sense, the full weight of the verse stands. Chrysostom read 'world' as creation, and commented that the Word does not refuse the enlightenment by grace to anyone (He "wants all men to be saved, and to come to knowledge of the truth", 1 Tim 2:4). If someone is not enlightened, it is because he himself has turned away from the light. Augustine reads 'world' in its perverted sense and gives the restricted reading that every man who comes in this world, in so far as he is enlightened, is enlightened by the Word. From the point of view of the Word, who wishes to give the light of grace to everyone (Chrysostom), and in so far as someone is enlightened (Augustine), this light of grace enlightens everyone. Therefore, Thomas concludes, the efficacy of the divine Word that enlightens everyone shows that it was not a defect in God or in the Word that prevented human beings from knowing God.[22]

The second reason why God is not the reason for the lack of divine knowledge in the world is that God is present in the world. That the true light has not withdrawn from the world, nor is absent in it, Thomas recognizes in the next clause in the Gospel: "He was in the world". How is this presence to be understood? Thomas mentions two ways. Something can be present by existing in a certain place, like the cup of tea I have been sipping from is present next to my computer. The other way something can be present is as a part of a whole. Thomas refers to spiritual substances like angels: they are not in the world as in a place, but they are nevertheless part of it.[23]

In neither of these two ways is the true light present, however, because neither way fits God who as Creator is neither localized nor present as part of a greater whole. God is not one more thing in the universe. With the strong *caveat* "if we can speak this way", Thomas suggests it is instead the other way around: "the entire universe is in a certain sense a part of Him since it participates in a partial way in his goodness".[24]

Thomas, therefore, suggests that the light is present in the world in a third way, as an efficient and preserving cause. This needs to be qualified, however. Whereas other agents cause from without, God acts in all things from within, "because he acts by creating" (*quia agit*

---

[22] *In Io* 1:9 §125-131.

[23] "sicut substantiae spirituales, licet locales non sint in mundo, tamen sunt ut partes". *In Io* 1:9 §133 (text corrected by L. Reid). The Marietti's 'substantiae supernaturales' is a mistake.

[24] "immo quodammodo (ut ita liceat loqui), totum universum est pars eius, bonitatem eius partialiter participans". *In Io* 1:9 §133 (text corrected by L. Reid).

creando). To create is to give being to things. This being, *esse* is the innermost in each thing. God acts from within by giving being. That is how God is present in the world, Thomas explains, by giving *esse*, being to the world.[25]

He adds one more remark. It is significant that the Evangelist uses the word 'was' in "He was in the world:" it shows that He always was in the world, from the beginning of creation, creating and preserving all things. Giving being is not just about the first moment of existence. It also implies preservation, keeping in existence. Creation and conservation belong together because whenever God acts, he acts as Creator. Thomas gives an evocative comparison here that he ascribes to Origen, but in fact comes from John Scotus Erigena: when we stop speaking, there is no longer any sound, there are no more words to be heard. So, in God, if the Father were to stop speaking the Word, creation would immediately cease to be.[26]

This second reason why the defect of divine knowledge in the world was not caused by God is a theology of creation in a nutshell. God, the maker of heaven and earth, is not the deists's watchmaker who is withdrawn from his creatures, nor is he another object in the universe, either as being at a certain place or being part of a larger whole. There is no 'larger whole' of which God can be a part because that would make God one of the creatures. It would blur 'the Christian distinction'.[27] God is present by giving being and by preserving creatures in being. God does this, 'from the inside', intimately, which means that creatures can never be without the Creator, as David Burrell has argued.[28] This ever-present God cannot be the cause of a lack of divine knowledge in the world.

The third reason why the lack of divine knowledge in the world is not due to God is a consequence of the second. Thomas is brief on this point: not

---

[25] *In Io* 1:9 §133.

[26] *In Io* 1:9 §135. Cf. J.-P. Torrell, *Saint Thomas Aquinas: Spiritual Master*, Washington D.C., Catholic University of America Press, 2003, p. 76-77.

[27] R. Sokolowski, *The God of Faith and Reason: Foundations of Christian Theology*, Washington D.C., Catholic University of America Press, 1995.

[28] D.B. Burrell, 'Creation in St. Thomas Aquinas's *Super Evangelium S. Joannis Lectura*', in: M. Dauphinais, M. Levering (eds.), *Reading John with St. Thomas Aquinas: Theological Exegesis and Speculative Theology*, Washington D.C., Catholic University of America Press, 2005), p. 115-26, here p. 126. Cf. also his beautiful D.B. Burrell, 'Providence', in: P. McCosker, D. Turner (eds.), *The Cambridge Companion to the Summa Theologiae*, Cambridge, Cambridge University Press, 2016, p. 156-67, here p. 165-167. For more on the inner connection of providence with creation, cf. H.J.M.J. Goris, *Free Creatures of an Eternal God: Thomas Aquinas on God's Infallible Foreknowledge and Irresistible Will*, Leuven, Peeters, 1996.

only is the Word present in the world, but he is also recognizably so. Because "through him the world was made", his likeness is reflected in creation. The Augustinian image of the work of art manifesting the artisan returns here, just as the reference to Rom 1:20, the standard text for Thomas to refer to when discussing how creation allows us to see the things of the Creator.

Thomas's interpretation of v. 9-10 has given him three reasons why God is not the reason for the lack of divine knowledge in the world. It has done that by discussing three things about the divinity of Christ, the light for the world: he is efficient, because all our natural knowledge is a participation in the light that is Christ and because all who receive grace receive it from Him who is the true light; he is present in the world as the one who acts by creating, by giving being to all creatures and sustaining them by acting in them; and he is knowable because the creation represents the divine Wisdom of the Father.[29]

... but in human beings

The lack of divine knowledge in the world is not caused by God. Thomas finds the reason for the lack of knowledge in the next verse in the Gospel: "The world did not know him". 'World' should be read here as 'human beings', Thomas explains, because the angels know God by their understanding and the elements by obeying him. Human beings do not know him.[30] Thomas returns to the distinction between nature and grace. The lack of divine knowledge can be attributed to human nature. Thomas refers to Job, who says that "Man beholds Him from afar", and therefore "God is great beyond our knowledge" (Job 36:25). Those who did know God were those "for whom the world was not worthy". This implicit quotation from Hebr 11:38, where the author of the letter is singing the praise of the heroes of the Old Testament, shows that Thomas here is primarily thinking of the people of Israel. What eternal knowledge they had, whatever they truly knew about God, they knew insofar as they were not of this world.

The lack of knowledge can also be understood from man's guilt. In that case, 'the world' stands for the inordinate lovers of the world. Thomas follows Augustine and the *Glossa* closely, here: inordinate love of the world draws us away from the love of God. This shows that Thomas is not thinking of merely intellectual knowledge of God but of a

---

[29] *In Io* 1:9 §136.
[30] *In Io* 1:10 §137.

knowledge that is informed by love. As Thomas writes: "Whoever does not love God, cannot know him".[31]

Before he reaches his conclusion about the necessity for the Word to become incarnate, Thomas makes an observation about the style of the Evangelist. Repetition is a well-known feature of Johannine style.[32] Thomas notes the parallels between v. 3-5 and v. 9-10: the former calls the Word "the light of men", here John says that he was "the true light". Earlier John said that "all things were made through him", here he says that through him the world was made. Earlier he said that "without him nothing was made", which according to one explanation means that he conserves all things; here he says "He was in the world", which has the same explanation. Earlier he wrote, "the darkness did not overcome it", here he says "the world did not know him". Why these repetitions? Thomas gives a theological reason that is drawn from his *divisio textus*. The first five verses speak of the divine Word. From v. 6 onwards, John speaks of the Word incarnate. The repetition here, Thomas states, functions "to show that the incarnate Word and that which "was in the beginning with God", and God, are the same".[33] The repetition functions to stress the identity of the divine Word and the Word incarnate. "And so, all he says after "he was the true light", is an explanation of what he had said before".[34]

"From the abovementioned things" (*ex supradictis*), Thomas gathers three reasons why God willed to become incarnate.[35] The first reason is the sinfulness of human nature. Thomas refers back to v. 5: "The light shines in the darkness, and the darkness did not overcome it". Because of its malice, human nature "had been darkened by vices and obscurity of its own ignorance".[36] In order that human beings might receive a knowledge

---

[31] "Qui autem non diligit Deum, non potest eum cognoscere". *In Io* 1:10 §138. This sentence is absent in the English translation by Larcher and Weisheipl. Cf. Augustine, *Tract. in Io* 2,11 and the *Glossa* on Jn 1:10 (both the *Glossa ordinaria* and the *interlinearis*).

[32] E.g. C.S. Keener, *The Gospel of John: A Commentary*, 2 volumes, Grand Rapids, Baker Academic, 2003, p. 48-49.

[33] "ut ostendat idem esse verbum incarnatum, et quod 'erat in principio apud Deum' et Deus". *In Io* 1:10 §140.

[34] "Et ideo totum hoc quod sequitur ab illo loco 'erat lux vera', videtur quaedam explicatio superiorum". *In Io* 1:10 §140.

[35] "Possumus etiam ex praedictis accipere triplicem rationem, quare Deus voluit incarnari". *In Io* 1:10 §141 (text corrected by L. Reid).

[36] "Una est perversitas humanae naturae, quae ex sui malitia iam obtenebrata erat vitiorum et ignorantiae obscuritate". *In Io* 1:10 §141.

of the true light, that darkness may apprehend the light, God came in the flesh. Thomas quotes Isaiah: “The people who walked in darkness saw a great light”.[37]

For the second reason, Thomas refers back to v. 8 about John the Baptist: “He was not the light”. John the Baptist and the prophetic tradition before him were not enough to give knowledge of the light: for that the true light needed to come itself. This second reason is an argument from salvation history. Thomas refers to Hebr 1:1: “In past times, God spoke in many ways and degrees to our fathers through the prophets; in these days he has spoken to us in his Son”.

The third reason is the difference between creatures and the Creator. Thomas quotes v. 10 here: “through him the world was made, and the world did not know him”. Creatures alone are not sufficient to bring us to knowledge of God the Creator. Therefore the Creator came in the flesh so that He could be known through himself.

The three reasons Thomas gives are not on the same level. The first reason is a clear contrast: falsehood must give way to truth, just as darkness must disappear before the light. However, the other two lights are not untrue: both the figurative light and the participated light share in some way in the true light. Of both of these lights, however, Thomas says that they are “insufficient”.[38] They need the true light to lead to loving knowledge of God.

These three reasons for God to become incarnate are not necessarily exhaustive. In the *Summa Theologiae*, for example, Thomas gives ten reasons for the incarnation, structured in two groups of five: five reasons with respect to our furtherance in good, and five with respect to our withdrawal from evil.[39] Here, Thomas writes that the reasons given here can be gathered “from the abovementioned things” (*ex supradictis*). To what does that refer? It does not seem to relate to the arguments Thomas gives to explain that the lack of divine knowledge in the world is not caused by God. Nor do all three reasons Thomas gives here seem to be derived from the explanation of the two ways, according to human nature and human guilt, that the lack of knowledge is caused by human beings: that explanation might provide for two of the three reasons Thomas gives

---

[37] Is 9:2. A parallel thought can be found in Augustine’s second *Tract. in Io*. cf. P.-Y. Maillard, *La Vision De Dieu*, p. 256.

[38] “Secunda propter insufficientiam prophetici testimonii”. […] “Tertia propter creaturarum defectum. Nam creaturae insufficientes erant ad ducendum in cognitionem creatoris;” *In Io* 1:10 §141.

[39] *STh* III q. 1 a. 2c.

here, but not for the explanation that the Old Testament prophets up until and including John the Baptist were not sufficient.

The obvious reason is the three verses from Jn 1:1-10 Thomas quotes in the three reasons: the exposition of these verses provides the three arguments for the incarnation Thomas gives here. That must be true, but there might be an additional explanation of the *ex supradictis*. Thomas began his commentary on v. 9-10 with an explanation of the Word as 'true light', and contrasted the truth of that light with three things, as we saw: it is not a false light, it is not a figurative light, it is not a participated light. These three contrasts with 'the true light' correspond with the three reasons for the incarnation Thomas gives here at the end of his commentary on v. 9-10. The perversity of human nature obscures knowledge, makes one take pride in untruths, in false light. Figurative light is what the prophets of the Old Testament had to offer. Their light, the light of the old law, points forward to the true light, but is not the true light itself: the figurative light alone cannot give sufficient enlightenment of itself. Finally, the natural shortcomings of creatures make them capable of participation in the light, but that in itself is not sufficient for a knowledge of the Creator.

Thomas's interpretation of 'the true light' is the key to understand his interpretation of v. 9-10 as a text in which John the evangelist "shows why it was necessary for the Word to come". The Word of God, the true light of which John speaks here, became human to enlighten the human nature darkened by sin, to give full knowledge of God that had been prefigured in the prophets of the Old Testament, and to be known through himself by those who participate in Him.

3. The Fruit of the Incarnation (Jn 1:11-13)

Having argued that a lack of knowledge of God in the world was the reason why the light became incarnate, Thomas now continues to discuss the fruit of the incarnation, which is the name he gives to v. 11-13 in the *divisio textus*. In the strict sense, this is the topic of v. 12-13; prior to that, Thomas reads v. 11 as making two points about the incarnation.

Two preliminary remarks

"He came unto his own, and his own did not receive him". Who are meant by "his own?" The patristic sources medieval theologians use for their commentaries give two main answers. One answer, usually associated with Augustine, is 'all human beings whom God created'. The other answer, associated with Chrysostom, is 'the Jews'.[40]

Thomas gives both interpretations and distributes them over the two halves of the verse. He interprets "He came unto his own" as referring to creation, the point being that the 'coming' of the light should not be understood as a local motion. incarnation does not mean that the light was in one place (heaven) and now leaves that place to move to another place (earth) where it had not been before: he came "to the things that were his, that he himself made, and where he himself was".[41] Thomas mentions the other interpretation, confirming that Judea was in a special way his own but, quoting Ps 24:1 ("The earth is the Lord's"), he states that the interpretation of 'his own' as 'the world he created' is better (*Sed melius est*). As usual, Thomas does not explain why he thinks this interpretation is better, but it is not unreasonable to presume that Thomas prefers this reading because it better fits the context: according to his reading, the Gospel speaks about the incarnation in general, here, not just in relation to the Jews.

The remark that the coming of the light is not to be understood as a change of place raises the question of how this coming into the world should be understood. Rather than as a change of place, Thomas understands it as a change in the way the light is present. Earlier in the commentary, Thomas had explained that God is in all things by his power, presence and essence. God is everywhere by his power because all things are subject to his power; God is everywhere by his presence because all things are open to his eyes, nothing is invisible for God; and God is everywhere by his essence because his essence is innermost in all things, it is by his creative act that all things receive their being from God.[42] The newness of the incarnation is the way in which God comes present: God already was there by his power, presence and essence; now he comes by

---

[40] I formulate 'associate with' here, because while Chrysostom indeed reads this verse this way, Augustine gives both interpretations in his *Tractatus* on the Gospel. In the *Catena Aurea* Thomas cites Chrysostom, and cites from Augustine only the interpretation that reads 'his own' as all created human beings: *Catena Aurea in Io* 1:11. The same can be seen in Albert's commentary: Albert, *Super Io* 1:11, p. 140. Bonaventure only mentions the interpretation that reads the verse as referring to the Jews: Bonaventure, *In Io* 1:11 n. 26. Cf. Augustine, *Tract. in Io* 2.12 and Chrysostom, *Homilies In Io* 9.1-2.

[41] "in ea quae erant sua, quae ipse fecit, et ubi ipse erat". *In Io* 1:11 §143 (text corrected by L. Reid).

[42] *In Io* 1:10 §134. For a more extensive explanation of the distinction Thomas makes between three ways God can be said to exist in creation (through his power, presence, and essence), cf. J.-P. Torrell, *Thomas Aquinas, Spiritual Master*, p. 69-70.

assuming flesh. Thomas adds: "He was there invisibly, and he came in order to be visible".[43]

To explain this, Thomas gives his standard analogy: a king who visits a city in his kingdom might be said to have come in person where previously he was present only by his power. I am not sure how convincing this example still is in our times since the concept of a sovereign being present 'by his power' might not be understood as a presence at all by many people nowadays. Another analogy could be a party where a guest falls ill, and another guest presenting herself as a doctor begins to help the guest who had fallen ill. Before the first guest fell ill, the doctor was already present at the party, albeit as a guest; now she becomes present as a doctor. Likewise, in the incarnation, God who already is present by his sovereignty, by knowing his creation and by continuously giving it its existence, now becomes present by assuming flesh: it is the unique way in which the divine light, the Word of God "comes to his own" in the incarnation.[44]

For the second half of v. 11 ("…and his own did not receive Him"), Thomas returns to the two possible ways of reading "his own" as either all people or the Jews. This time he prefers the second possibility, to read this clause as referring to the Jews (*Sed melius est*).[45] Thomas gives three reasons why the Jewish people are Christ's own, all three times referring directly to Scripture: they are his own because they were chosen by him to be his special people (Dt 26:18), because he is related to them according to the flesh (Rom 9:3) and because they were enriched by his kindness, being reared and brought up by him as sons, as Is 1:2 says.

---

[43] "Erat invisibiliter, venit ut esset visibiliter". *In Io* 1:11 §144 (text corrected by L. Reid).

[44] Further on in the commentary, when commenting on Jn 15:26 ("When the Advocate comes, whom I will send to you from the Father, the Spirit of truth who comes from the Father…") Thomas makes a parallel remark about the coming of the Holy Spirit: "Note that the Holy Spirit is said to be sent not because the Spirit is changing place, since the Spirit fills the entire universe, as we read in Wisdom (1:7), but because, by grace, the Holy Spirit begins to dwell in a new way in those he makes a temple of God: 'Do you not know that you are God's temple and that God's Spirit dwells in you?' (1 Cor 3:16)" *In Io* 15:26 §2061.

[45] To an English-speaking reader it might be surprising that Thomas would give the two times "his own" appears in this verse two different interpretations: the first time ("he came unto his own") he prefers to read it as referring to 'all human beings', the second time ("his own did not receive him") he reads is as referring to the Jews. Note however, that while in English ("his own") and in the original Greek (τὰ ἴδια / οἱ ἴδιοι) the same word is used twice, Thomas's Latin text has two words that have different roots: "In propria" and "sui".

Three very different reasons: the election of the Jewish people by God, the Jewish background of Jesus and the upbringing, that is to say, the education the Jewish people received from God, constitute the special way in which the Jewish people belong to God the Word, are "his own". Almost in passing, Thomas presents his view on the Jewish people in a nutshell.

These, his own, "did not receive him". Thomas again does not explicitly argue why it is better to read "his own" here as referring to the Jews, just as he did not argue for his reading of "his own" earlier to all people. Two reasons can be gathered from Thomas's exposition of the clause. The first reason is the context of the Gospel of John. Thomas refers to two verses elsewhere in the Gospel that have Jesus say to the Jews that they have not received him (Jn 5:43) and that they have dishonoured him (Jn 8:49).

The second reason is the continuation of the text Thomas is commenting on here: "His own did not receive him, but whoever received him he gave the power to become sons of God". Thomas here stresses the importance of the word 'whoever' (*quotquot*), in two ways: first, it shows that "the deliverance would be more extensive than the promise".[46] For the promise of salvation had been made to the Jews (Thomas refers to Is 33:22: "The Lord is our lawgiver, the Lord is our king; he will save us"), but the deliverance is for whoever believes in Him. It is as an act of Gods mercy, Thomas explains, that the Gentiles are included in the offer of deliverance. Secondly, 'whoever' shows that God's grace is given without distinction to all who receive Christ. The first of these two remarks only works if "his own" is read as referring to the Jews.

The fruit of the incarnation

These remarks out of the way, Thomas discusses the benefit of the incarnation, what he calls "the fruit of the incarnation". He recognizes it in the *clausula* "he gave them power to become sons of God". The benefit of the incarnation is that we are made children of God. It is fitting, Thomas states, that we who are children of God by the fact that we are made to be like the Son, are reformed by the Son. The central point is that "people become sons of God by being made like God".[47] Sonship here for Thomas means likeness, "being like". The Word of God is called "Son of God" because it shares the divine nature with God the Father. Human

[46] "Ut ostendat ampliorem esse factam solutionem, quam fuerit promissio". *In Io* 1:12 §146.

[47] "Homines fiunt filii Dei per assimilationem ad Deum". *In Io* 1:12 §150.

beings do not share the divine nature, but we become children of God by adoption and then are made like God.

Thomas sees this likeness as a threefold likeness that he finds in Scripture. First, we are made like God by the infusion of sanctifying grace, grace as that which makes us lovable to God, that undoes the effects of sin and unites us to God.[48] Thomas here refers to two verses from Scripture that both relate our receiving the Holy Spirit to our being adopted children of God: Rom 8:15 ("You did not receive the spirit of slavery … but the spirit of adoption as sons") and Gal 4:6 ("Because you are sons of God, God sent the Spirit of the Son in your hearts"). Secondly, we are made like God by the perfection of our works. Thomas recognizes this relation between our works and our sonship in Mt 5:44 ("Love your enemies … so that you may be children of your Father"). Thirdly, we are made like God by the attainment of glory. Thomas recognizes this eschatological side to our sonship in Rom 8:23 ("We are waiting for our adoption as sons of God"). Unsurprising for a Dominican brother, Thomas adds the remark that the glory we receive is the glory of both the soul and the body.[49] The threefold likeness Thomas describes here form a way, a lifelong path towards conformity with God that begins with the reception of sanctifying grace, continues with the reception of habitual grace that sustains our daily life and becomes visible in virtuous actions, and finally reaches its fulfilment in God in the eschaton.

Up until this point in the commentary, we have seen how Thomas has been referring to grace several times: he used the distinction between nature and grace to characterize two different interpretations of the light that shines in the darkness (v. 4b-5), and again of the light that shines in the darkness (v. 9); he has spoken of the office of John the Baptist to be a witness of the light in terms of a freely given grace (in the sense of *gratia gratis data*, a grace that is given to someone to enable him to help make others graceful before God), and spoken about our becoming adopted children of God as a lifelong path of sanctifying and habitual grace that leads to our homeland with God. At this point in the commentary, however, Thomas, for the first time, discusses grace somewhat more in-depth by inserting a question that the verse in John raises. Saying that

---

[48] Cf. P. McCosker, 'Grace', in: P. McCosker, D. Turner (eds.), *The Cambridge Companion to the Summa Theologiae*, p. 206-21, here p. 214.

[49] *In Io* 1:12, §150. This remark is 'unsurprising' for a Dominican friar in the sense that the Dominican order was founded to a certain extent in order to debate the Cathars, who held a dualist view of a human being's body and soul.

God's Word gave whoever received him the power to become God's children is not problematic when it is understood as referring to the perfection of our actions or the attainment of glory, the second and third way in which we are made like God: it is through the habitual grace that we have received that we can perform works of perfection and attain glory. There is a problem with the first way, however, the infusion of sanctifying grace. The wording of the verse "he gave them power to become sons of God" suggests that it is in our own power to receive sanctifying grace, which would be (semi-)Pelagian. In Thomas's words: "In that sense, he did not give them the power to become sons of God, but to be sons of God".[52]

Thomas wants to maintain that the reception of grace requires an act of our free will: grace is not forced upon us. In order for us to accept this grace, we need the help (*auxilium*) that moves our free will to receive grace. This *auxilium* itself is grace, not habitual grace but movent grace. Thus, the movement of receiving grace consists of three steps: the grace that is God's help, *auxilium* prepares our free will to receive grace; moved by this *auxilium*, our free will consents to receive grace; finally, the grace to be children of God is infused. Thomas summarizes the whole path:

> Thus, 'he gave them power to become the sons of God', through sanctifying grace, through the perfection of their actions, and through the attainment of glory; and he did this by preparing this grace, moving their wills, and preserving this grace.[53]

In a beautiful passage later in the commentary, Thomas returns to the divine *auxilium* which moves our free will to receive grace. Thomas recognizes it in Jn 6:44: "No one can come to me unless the Father, who sent me, draws him". This drawing by the Father is the divine *auxilium* that makes it possible for us to come to the Son. That raises the question of whether this divine *auxilium* does not force us, whether our will when it is thus moved, is still free. Thomas replies by stating that what this verse says about the Father drawing us does not imply coercion because there are ways of being drawn that do not involve coercion. Someone might draw another person by persuading him with a reason. The Father might

---

[52] "Et sic non dedit eis potestatem filios fieri Dei, sed filios Dei esse". *In Io* 1:12 §152 (text corrected by L. Reid).

[53] "Sic ergo dedit eis potestatem filios Dei fieri, per gratiam gratum facientem, per operum perfectionem, per gloriae adeptionem, et haec praeparando, movendo et conservando gratiam". *In Io* 1:12 §156. On the divine *auxilium*, cf. J. Wawrykow, 'Grace', in: R. van Nieuwenhove, J. Wawrykow (eds.), *The Theology of Thomas Aquinas*, p. 192-221, here p. 194-199.

do this either by an interior revelation or by a miracle. Or one person might draw another by attraction or by captivating him. And in this way, the Father draws people to the Son either because captivated by the greatness of the Father, whose Son he is, or by a wonderful joy and love of the truth, which is the very Son of God himself. Finally, the Father draws many to the Son by moving a person's heart to believe.[54] The divine *auxilium*, therefore, does not coerce; instead, it persuades, attracts and inspires our free will to consent to the grace that God wishes to give us. As Luc-Thomas Somme has remarked, this 'power to become children of God' is a gift ("He has 'given' them the power"), and in that sense passive in the one who receives it; on the other hand, it is active in the person who exercises it: by the infusion of grace a person receives from God the power to become and stay a son of God.[55] It is through Christ that this grace is produced, as we will later see.

Who receives from God this power to become a son of God? John has mentioned that this is given "to all who receive him", here he mentions "to all who believe in his name". Thomas mentions different interpretations here, but he prefers to read "all who believe in his name" as an explanation of what it is to receive him. Eph 3:17 ("That Christ may dwell in your hearts through faith") is the key to this explanation: we receive Christ in our hearts through faith, therefore to receive him is to believe in him.[57]

The final part of the sentence in John ("who were born, not of blood or of the will of the flesh or of the will of man, but of God" v. 13) is a reason for Thomas to speak about the way in which we become children of God. Our generation as children of God is not a carnal but a spiritual generation. Thomas mentions three differences between these forms of generation: carnal generation is called carnal because it is "from blood", whereas spiritual generation is not; carnal generation, because it is from the desires of the flesh, is bound up with original sin, which spiritual generation is not; and finally, carnal generation, because it is from man, produces children of men, whereas spiritual generation, because it is from God, produces children of God.[58] At a later point in the commentary, when commenting on "unless one is born again" (Jn 3:3), Thomas

---

[54] *In Io* 6:44 §935.

[55] L.-T. Somme, *Fils adoptifs de Dieu par Jésus Christ: La filiation divine par adoption dans la théologie de Saint Thomas d'Aquin,* Paris, Vrin, 1997, p. 147.

[57] *In Io* 1:12 §157.

[58] *In Io* 1:13 §163.

elaborates on this last difference. He notes that the Greek ἄνωθεν does not mean "again", but "from above". Christ is said to be born from above in two ways: both as to time ("if we may speak thus", Thomas tentatively adds) because he is begotten from eternity, and as to the principle of his generation, because he proceeds from the heavenly Father. Since our regeneration is in the likeness of the Son of God, and because that generation is from above, our generation also is from above: both as to the time, because of our eternal predestination, and as to its cause: it is a gift of God.[59]

We saw before that spiritual regeneration will become the central notion that Thomas will use in the *divisio textus* for Jn 3-11, and that will be presented in all its theological depth in the commentary on the beginning of Jn 3. It is here in the commentary on Jn 1 that Thomas introduces it, pointing forward to what is to come. As he will do later, he adds a remark here on baptism. It is in virtue of baptism that we are reborn as sons of God: in that sense, "he gave them the power to become children of God" can be read as referring to baptism. Read like this, Thomas writes, these verses show in a way the order of baptism: the first thing that is necessary is faith ("whoever received him", i.e. "to all who believe in his name"), which is why catechumens are instructed about the faith so that they may believe in his name, the second is baptism ("he gave power to become children of God"), which is the actual spiritual regeneration.[61] We will see that Thomas has more to say about baptism later in the commentary on Jn 1 (at the verses that speak of the baptism of Christ), but the theme of spiritual regeneration and baptism, announced here, will be fully explored when Thomas comments on the conversation between Jesus and Nicodemus in Jn 3. That will be the foundation for the commentary on Jn 3-11, as the *divisio textus* shows.[62]

---

[59] *In Io* 3:3 §435.

[61] *In Io* 1:13 §164. Cf. *In Io* 9:6-7 §1311, where Thomas quotes a a mystical reading from Augustine of the man born blind having his eyes anointed with saliva and then being sent to wash in the pool of Siloam as referring to the way from being a catechumen to baptism.

[62] For baptism, see e.g. *In Io* 3:5-6 §439-448. Herwi Rikhof has shown that Thomas's use of regeneration is the key to understanding the development from more juridical language in Thomas's writing on divine adoption in the *Scriptum* to more biblical language in the *Summa Theologiae*: H. Rikhof, 'Thomas on Divine Adoption', in: H. Goris, H. Rikhof, H. Schoot (eds.), *Divine Transcendence and Immanence in the Work of Thomas Aquinas*, Leuven, Peeters, 2009, p. 163-93. The centrality of the concept of regeneration in the commentary on John seems to strengthen Rikhof's thesis.

4. The Way of the Incarnation (Jn 1:14a)

With v. 14a ("And the Word was made flesh, and made his dwelling among us") we come to Thomas's discussion of the incarnation itself. Thomas structures his exposition of the first *clausula*, "And the Word was made flesh", in three parts. First, he relates it to three different phrases that went before, then he briefly discusses three Christological heresies that are associated with the interpretation of this *clausula*, and finally he discusses three questions.

"And the Word was made flesh" can be read as the continuation of "He came unto his own" (v. 11), Thomas argues, in which case it is an explanation of how the Word came: not by changing location, but being made flesh. It can also be read in relation to "he gave them power to become the sons of God", in which case the incarnation is to be understood as the cause for this possibility: because the Word was made flesh, it is possible for people to become children of God. Finally, "The Word was made flesh" can be read in relation to the earlier clausula "who are born from God" (v. 13), in which case Thomas values it for its power to astonish. If people might find it difficult to believe that they might be born from God, the even less likely remark that the Word was made flesh is added to say: do not wonder if men are born from God because God became man.[63]

These three ways of relating the verse to what came before all have their origin in patristic commentaries.[64] For Thomas, they are a way of making three points about the verse he is commenting on, but it also shows something about the way Thomas reads the Fourth Gospel: the fact that he does not choose between the interpretations shows how for him, the verse can be related to several texts that went before; these explanations are acceptable side by side since they all help the understanding of what the evangelist is presenting.

When compared to the commentaries by Albert and Bonaventure on Jn 1:14a, Thomas's commentary is substantially longer. The main difference is that Thomas discusses a series of Christological heresies at this point in the commentary, something neither Albert nor Bonaventure does.[65] For

---

[63] *In Io* 1:14 §165.

[64] The first is a reference to Augustine, *De Trinitate* IV, 19; the second to Chrysostom, *Hom. In Io* 11:1; and the third to Augustine, *Tract. in Io* 2,15. The latter two can be found in the *Catena Aurea* as well.

[65] A similar list to that of Thomas can however be found in the Commentary on John by William of Alton. Cf. T. Bellamah, *The Biblical Interpretation of William of Alton*, Oxford, Oxford University Press, 2011, p. 143-145.

Thomas, Jn 1:14a seems to be one of the biblical texts par excellence that help to understand the incarnation, as can be seen as well from other places in his works where he discusses the incarnation: this verse usually features prominently in those discussions.[66]

Thomas starts by mentioning three misinterpretations fairly briefly. Eutyches defended the monophysite interpretation that the Word or something in the Word was turned into flesh, leading to a mixture of natures in Christ. Thomas here argues from the immutability of God that this is impossible: against Eutyches, it must be said that the Word assumed flesh, not that the Word itself is that flesh.

Arius said that in the incarnation, there was no soul in Christ but that the Word assumed only human flesh without a soul. Thomas argues against this position that Scripture often mentions the soul of Christ and mentions affections of the soul such as being sad and sorrowful (Mt 26:37-38) that cannot exist in the Word of God, nor in flesh alone. Furthermore, whereas a soul is united to a body as its form, God, being incorporeal, cannot be the form of a body. Finally, because a soul is united to a body as its form, a body without a soul is a body only in an equivocal sense: without a soul, a body is a corpse rather than a body. Therefore, if the Word did not assume flesh with a soul, it did not assume flesh at all.

For the same reason that the flesh assumed by the Word must be authentically human, the soul that gives it its form must be both a sensitive and intellectual soul. Thomas is arguing here against the reading of Apollinaris of Laodicea, who recognized a sensitive soul in Christ that could undergo emotions, but stated that this soul lacked reason and intellect and that in the man Christ, their place was taken by the Word of God. Thomas's arguments here parallel those against Arius. First, Scripture tells that Christ marvelled (Mt 8:10), which is a rational activity. Furthermore, without an intellectual soul, there is no human flesh, no authentic human person, and one could not say: "God became man". Finally, Thomas implicitly quotes the soteriological rule that Gregory of Nazianzus had formulated in his discussion with Apollinaris: "What has not been assumed, has not been healed".[67]

---

[66] The example of *ScG* bk IV, ch. 28-38 might suffice: In these eleven chapters in which Thomas discusses the Christological heresies, Jn 1:14a is referred to no less than nine times.

[67] *In Io* 1:14 §166-168. The quotation is from Gregory of Nazianzus, Letter 101,7. The mentioning of wonder and Mt 8:10 shows that Thomas in the commentary on John takes the same position as he does in the *Summa Theologiae* on Christ's acquired knowledge. Cf. *STh* III q. 9 a. 4 and the discussion of Christ's wonder in *STh* III q. 15 a. 8. Cf. the literature mentioned in P. Gondreau, 'Anti-Docetism in Aquinas's *Super Ioannem*, St. Thomas as Defender of the Full Humanity of Christ', in: M. Dauphinais,

Three questions

While the discussion of these three heresies is brief and standard, Thomas offers more depth with three questions he adds. The first question continues the discussion with Arius and Apollinaris and asks why John only mentions flesh if the Word did assume flesh with a rational soul. Thomas gives four very different reasons. The first is an anti-Manichaean point: according to the Manichaeans, it would not have been fitting for the Word of God to assume flesh. To exclude this dualist position, the Evangelist explicitly mentions 'flesh'. Thomas adds that both at the incarnation and at the resurrection, it is important to exclude dualist explanations. Therefore, at the resurrection, the flesh of Christ will again be explicitly mentioned (Lk 24:39). Secondly, flesh is mentioned to show the greatness of God's kindness to us. Being immaterial, the rational soul has greater conformity to God than does flesh. That the Word would assume a rational soul already would have been a sign of great compassion, but to assume flesh as well, is a sign of compassion that is much greater, that Thomas even calls "incomprehensible", referring to 1 Tim 3:16: "Obviously great is the mystery of godliness which appeared in the flesh".[68] Thirdly, there is a Christological reason: by mentioning flesh, the evangelist stresses the uniqueness of the union in Christ. Scripture teaches that Wisdom "passes into holy souls, making them friends of God and prophets" (Wis 7:27). The union of the Word of God with the flesh is unique to Christ, however. Finally, there is a soteriological reason. Scripture is leading again. Thomas refers to Rom 8:3: "The law was powerless because it was weakened by the flesh. God, sending his Son in the likeness of sinful flesh and in reparation for sin, condemned sin in his flesh". The restoration of man was needed especially because of the weakness of the flesh. By explicitly stating that the Word assumed flesh, the evangelist shows that the coming of the Word was directed towards our restoration.[69]

Based on four biblical texts, Thomas here gives a theology of the physicality of the incarnation. The reasons it gives are *convenientia*:

M. Levering (eds.), *Reading John with St. Thomas Aquinas*, p. 254-76, here p. 265 nt.29. For a nuanced account of Christ's human knowledge, cf. S.F. Gaine, *Did the Saviour See the Father? Christ, Salvation and the Vision of God*, London, T&T Clark, 2015, p. 129-158.

[68] "Inaestimabilis pietatis indicium" *In Io* 1:14 §169. Thomas gives this reason in the *Summa Theologiae* as well: *STh* III q. 5 a. 3 ad 1.

[69] *In Io* 1:14, §169.

reasons that show fittingness, that help our understanding.[70] Taken together, they show the depth of the use of the word 'flesh' at this point in the Gospel. It is a warning against dualist views on the human person: our physicality is part of the goodness of creation. It is a sign that God's compassion reaches right into our bodies. It speaks of the unique union of the Word in Christ, and it is fitting with regard to what was needed for our salvation.

After the first question investigated the word 'flesh', the second question looks into the verb 'was made' (*factum est*). Why is it said that the Word "was made" flesh, rather than "assumed" (*assumpsit*) flesh? Thomas states that "was made" is written to exclude the heresy of Nestorius, who sees two persons in Christ: the Son of God and the son of Mary. But that breaks the unity of Christ: If the person or *suppositum* of the Word is different from the person or *suppositum* of the man in Christ, then the Word has not become man. Thomas makes a comparison with the prophets: the prophets were "lifted up" in a prophetic act by which the Word becomes present in the prophet as the object of the prophet's knowledge and love. That lifting up is for the prophetic act, however; it is not a unity of *suppositum*, as it is in the Word incarnate.[71]

Thomas adds another interpretation, which acknowledges in Christ one person of God and man, but states that in him, there are two *hypostases* or *supposita*, one human and the other divine. In the literature, this position has become known as the *assumptus homo theory*. It is the first of three so-called Christological "opinions" that Peter Lombard had described in his *Sentences*.[72] It gives a certain individuality to the human nature over and against the divine nature of Christ: when "man" is said of Christ, it therefore does not supposit for the divine nature. That is the reason why Thomas mentions it here and dismisses it: even though it

---

[70] Thomas often uses these *convenientia* when speaking about God's work in the history of salvation. These arguments are sometimes underestimated, because they do not have an absolute character: to the answer "Could God have acted differently in situation x or y?" in an absolute sense the answer is almost always 'yes'. The strength of *convenientia*, however, is that within the contingency of creation, it can be shown to be reasonable why God did this rather than that. Cf. J.-P. Torrell, *Le Christ en ses mystères: La vie et l'oeuvre de Jésus selon saint Thomas d'Aquin*, Vol. 1, Paris, Desclée, 1999, p. 34-37.

[71] "non dixit assumpsit, ut ostendat quod unio verbi ad carnem non est talis qualis est assumptio prophetarum, qui non assumebantur in unionem suppositi, sed ad actum propheticum tantum". *In Io* 1:14 §170 (Text corrected by L. Reid). Cf. E.M. Sweeney, "Divine Revelation in the Commentary of St. Thomas Aquinas on St. John's Gospel", Unpublished doctoral dissertation, University of Navarra, 1981, typescript, p. 242.

[72] Peter Lombard, *Sentences*, Bk III, d. 6.

refuses to speak of two persons in Christ because it speaks of two supposits it leads to a kind of neo-Nestorianism since the union of a divine person and a human *suppositum* is an accidental union that cannot bear the expressions "God was made man" and "Man was made God".[73] While not the first to express doubts about the *assumptus homo theory*, Thomas was the first to dismiss it, already in his commentary on the *Sentences*. Both in the *Summa Theologiae* and in the commentary on John, he even calls the opinion heretical, based on his study of "the Fifth Council" (Constantinople II).[74]

On the third question, "How is the Word man?" Thomas gives a very brief reply: Christ is man in the way that anyone is, namely as having a human nature. He is a divine *suppositum* united to a human nature. One could recognize in this the core of the Subsistence Theory, the second *opinio* that Peter Lombard described in his *Sentences*, and that Thomas saw as the only correct, and later in his life even as the only orthodox of the three positions. He does add one other remark. The Word was made flesh through a union to flesh. A union, Aquinas explains, is a relation. "And relations newly said of God with respect to creatures do not imply a change on the side of God, but on the side of the creature relating in a new way to God".[75] Henk Schoot has shown that 'union' is used analogously when it is said of the incarnate Son. We cannot know exactly what it means to say that Christ is one because there exists no such union in the created world, even though this union has similarities with created kinds

---

[73] *In Io* 1:14 §171. For helpful discussions of Thomas's treatment of the three Christological opinions cf. H.J.M. Schoot, *Christ The 'Name' of God: Thomas Aquinas on Naming Christ*, Leuven, Peeters, 1993, p. 124-127; J. Wawrykow, 'Hypostatic Union', in: R. van Nieuwenhove, J. Wawrykow (eds.), *The Theology of Thomas Aquinas*, p. 222-251, here p. 235-237, and R. Williams, *Christ the Heart of Creation*, London, Bloomsbury, 2018, p. 12-35.

[74] "Et ideo haec opinio damnata est tamquam haeretica in quinto Concilio, ubi dicitur: si quis in domino Iesu Christo unam personam, et duas hypostases dixerit, anathema sit". *In Io* 1:14 §171. *STh* III q. 2 a. 3c. Cf. S. Coakley, 'Person of Christ', in: P. McCosker, D. Turner (eds.), *The Cambridge Companion to the Summa Theologiae*, p. 222-39, here p. 229; O.H. Pesch, *Katholische Dogmatik: Aus Ökumenischer Erfahrung*, Bd. 1/1 Die Geschichte der Menschen mit Gott, Ostfildern, Matthias-Grünewald-Verlag, 2008, p. 740-743. The development from *Scriptum* to *Summa contra Gentiles* to *Summa Theologiae* is the subject of J. Wawrykow, 'Hypostatic Union'.

[75] "Unio autem relatio quaedam est. Relationes autem de novo dictae de Deo in respectu ad creaturas, non important mutationem ex parte Dei, sed ex parte creaturae novo modo se habentis ad Deum". *In Io* 1:14 §172.

of union. What we can say is that it has a similarity with a mixed relation, which is what Aquinas points to when he speaks about change.[76]

Thomas gives two interpretations of the second clause of v. 14 ("and made his dwelling among us"). The first continues the discussion with the Christological heresies. Chrysostom and Hilary read it as a correction of a possible misunderstanding of "the Word was made flesh". That might be read as if the Word was converted into flesh, meaning that there would be no two distinct natures in Christ but some mixture between the divine and human nature. Chrysostom and Hilary stress "made his dwelling" as an expression of distinction: to dwell implies a distinction between the dweller and that in which it dwells. Thomas agrees with this reading but adds a warning: Chrysostom and Hilary stressed dwelling as a distinction in order to stay away from any mixture of the two natures. It should, however, not be taken in such a way that one falls into the opposite heresy of completely separating the human and the divine in Christ: that would be a return to Nestorius.[77] Thomas adds a remark that again belongs to the Subsistence theory: that in Christ, there is a distinction in nature, but not in person nor in hypostasis. The human nature of Christ was assumed into a oneness of person, Thomas explains. "He made his dwelling among us" must therefore be explained to mean that the nature of the divine Word inhabited our nature. Not according to hypostasis or person, which in Christ is one and the same for both the human and the divine nature.[78]

Next to the interpretation in which the two clauses that begin v. 14 balance each other out, Thomas gives a second interpretation: one might also say that in "The Word was made flesh", the evangelist deals with the incarnation of the Word and that with "he made his dwelling among us" speaks of the manner of life of the Word incarnate, that he lived on familiar terms with the apostles. Thomas gives two reasons for this interpretation. The first is that Christ not only wanted to be like humans in nature but also in his living with them on close terms (though without sin), in order to draw to himself people won over by the charm of his way of life.[79] We saw before that Thomas stresses that the Father draws us to himself, not by coercion but by attraction. The same is said here of the Son: it is not enough just to say that the Son became like us in being

[76] H. Schoot, *Christ The 'Name' of God,* p. 133-144.
[77] *In Io* 1:14, §173-174.
[78] *In Io* 1:14 §175.
[79] "Non solum enim in natura voluit assimilari hominibus, sed etiam in convictu et familiari conversatione absque peccato, cum eis voluit esse simul, ut sic homines suae conversationis dulcedine allectos traheret ad seipsum". *In Io* 1:14 §178.

human; Thomas sees reason to stress the attractiveness of Christ's way of life. This attraction extends to the whole of his life: He made his dwelling, he was at home among us.

Secondly, "he made his dwelling among us" can be read as a statement to make the testimony of the Evangelist more credible: John can witness to Christ because he lived on close terms with him. Thomas refers to 1 Jn 1:1: "We tell you ... what we have heard, what we have seen with our eyes".

5. Conclusion

In this chapter, we have closely followed Thomas in his commentary on Jn 1:6-14, the part of the Gospel that speaks of the incarnation, according to Thomas in his *divisio textus*.

The verses on John the Baptist help Thomas to elaborate on what he has already said about Christ as light. John the Baptist is a prime example of someone who participates in that light and so becomes a witness to it. Thus 'testimony' is introduced, a concept which will remain of crucial importance both in the rest of the Fourth Gospel and in Thomas's commentary on it.

The discussion of the reasons for the incarnation shows something of the uniqueness of the genre of the biblical commentary in Thomas's work. This is not an exhaustive theological treatment of why the divine Word became incarnate, nor does it want to be that. However, what it does do is to draw as much understanding as possible from the biblical text. From the Gospel of John, Thomas understands that a lack of knowledge was a fundamental reason for the incarnation; that this lack of knowledge is not a lack in God, because God is efficient in that He enlightens every man because God always was and is present in the world and can be recognized from creation. The lack of knowledge is on our human side: creatures cannot from themselves understand the Creator, the Old Testament and prophetic tradition which culminated in John the Baptist had given real, but not sufficient knowledge of God, and the sinfulness of human nature had not been able to receive the true light. Therefore, Thomas reads in the Fourth Gospel that the light became human to enlighten human nature darkened by sin, to give a full knowledge of the God that had been prefigured in the Old Testament, and to be known through himself by those who participate in Him.

The benefit of the incarnation is that we are made into children of God. The grace to become children of God is a gift that does not coerce but that draws us into communion with God. Thomas introduces this 'spiritual regeneration' here, in the context of his thinking about the incarnation, and so paves the way for the rest of the commentary, in which this spiritual regeneration will have a pivotal role to play.

The Word incarnate, who "made his dwelling among us", has shown through his living among us the attractiveness that is a life fully informed by God. In his treatment of how to understand the incarnation, Thomas does something we already saw him do in the very beginning of the commentary: to make ample use of heretical interpretations as a way of taking away misunderstandings of the incarnation to enlarge his student's understanding of the mystery.

Like the commentary on Jn 1:1-5, Thomas's commentary on Jn 1:6-14 touches on a broad array of theological topics: some it only introduces, to be developed later in the commentary, some it briefly mentions, others it treats more in-depth. Without the *divisio textus*, it is hard to understand why Thomas makes the choices he makes in the way he treats his topics. The *divisio textus* relates the different topics to the biblical text they originate from, relates the topics to each other and gives a framework for understanding the commentary. In the commentary on Jn 1:6-14, as well as elsewhere, the *divisio textus* is the key to understanding the commentary.

CHAPTER 4
SEEING AND HEARING

In our study of the *divisio textus* in chapter 1, we saw that in contrast to Bonaventure and Albert, Thomas reads the first chapter of John as a textual unity. For Bonaventure, from Jn 1:14b onwards, the manifestation of the incarnation becomes the central focus of the Gospel, all the way onto the end of Jn 11. For Albert, the category of testimony is paramount, starting already from Jn 1:6 onwards. The testimony of someone else, John the Baptist, is what gives Jn 1:6 to the end of chapter 1 its unity, according to Albert, whereas from Ch 2 onwards, the rest of the Gospel will focus on the testimony that Christ gives of himself in his life, passion and glorification.

For Thomas, the divinity of Christ is the central focus of the whole of chapter 1. From chapter 2 onwards, John will "relate the effects and actions by which the divinity of the incarnate Word was made known to the world".[1] For Thomas, Jn 1:14b-51 forms the bridge between Jn 1:1-14b, which spoke about the divinity of the Word and the incarnation, and the text from Jn 2 onwards, which speaks about the manifestation of the incarnate Word to the world. It forms this bridge by showing the ways in which the incarnate Word is made known.[2] The manifestation of the Word incarnate happens in two ways, Thomas states: by seeing and by hearing.

> These are the two ways in which the apostles got to know the incarnate Word: they obtained knowledge of him by what they saw and by what they heard of the testimony of John the Baptist.[3]

These two ways are first introduced: seeing in v. 14b ("and we have seen his glory, the glory as of a Father's only Son, full of grace and truth") and hearing in v. 15 ("John testified to him and cried out, 'This was he of

---

[1] "hic consequenter incipit determinare de effectibus et operibus quibus manifestata est mundo divinitas verbi incarnati". *In Io* 2:1 §335.

[2] "ostendit modum, quo Christi divinitas nobis innotuit". *In Io* 1:1 §23 (text corrected by L. Reid). Cf. *In Io* 1:14 §179.

[3] "Innotuit autem apostolis verbum incarnatum dupliciter. Primo quidem per visum acceperunt de eo notitiam; secundo per auditum ex testimonio Ioannis Baptistae". *In Io* 1:14 §179.

whom I said: he who comes after me ranks ahead of me because he was before me'"). After that, both these ways are clarified: seeing in v. 16-18 and hearing in v. 19-51.

This is an important structural remark: it lays bare a pattern that Thomas recognises in the Fourth Gospel. The incarnate Word is made known through seeing and hearing: it is seen in the signs and miracles that Jesus did and in the things Jesus underwent, his passion and death. It is heard in what others testify about Jesus and even more so in what Jesus says about himself in the discourses and dialogues in the Gospel.

It is an important structural remark in the more strict sense as well: it shows the unity and importance that Jn 1 has for Thomas in the whole of the fourth Gospel. Jn 1 shows the divinity of the Word, the incarnation, and the fundamental pattern in which the divinity of the Word incarnate is manifested. The rest of the Gospel shows this manifestation in the concrete "effects and actions" of Christ.[4] This contrast should not be made absolute: Jesus's coming to John the Baptist and the calling of the first disciples are as much things Christ did (and in the case of his baptism, underwent) as everything that will follow in the Gospel and in that sense they are "effects and actions" of Christ just as much as everything that follows from Jn 2 onwards. For Thomas, however, the verses 14b-51 in the first chapter of the Gospel show the *modus*, the way in which the divinity of Christ is made known and in that sense show in brief what will be seen throughout the rest of the Gospel.

Since Thomas reads v. 14b-51 as divided into these two modes, seeing in v. 14b and clarified in v. 16-18, and hearing in v. 15 and clarified in v. 19-51, I will first discuss the points that are relevant for my purposes in his commentary on v. 14b and v. 16-18, and then discuss those in the commentary on v. 15 and v. 19-51.

1. Seeing his Glory

The first way in which the divinity of the incarnate Word is made known, through seeing, is shown in v. 14b, and then clarified in v. 16-18, Thomas states. In these verses, he recognises a chiastic structure: the commentary on v. 14b, following the text, discusses "seeing Christ's glory" first, and then discusses "full of grace and truth". In what Thomas sees as the clarification of this in v. 16-18, the order is reversed: Thomas concentrates first on grace (v. 16-17) and then on seeing God (v. 18). I will follow Thomas's order of exposition.

[4] "effectibus et operibus" *In Io* 2:1 §335.

Thomas gives three interpretations for "We have seen his glory". First, It could be read as an argument for the authenticity of the evangelist. There are more such remarks in the Johannine *corpus*: Thomas mentions Jn 3:11 ("We know of what we speak, and we bear witness of what we see") and 1 Jn 1:1 ("We tell you ... what we have heard, what we have seen with our own eyes"). The role of testimony will be analysed more extensively when he discusses how the divinity of the incarnate Word is made known through hearing. For the part on 'seeing', the two other interpretations carry more weight: one draws on the commentary on John by Chrysostom, the other on that of Augustine.

Chrysostom interprets "And we have seen his glory" as showing another advantage of the incarnation, after the remark that we are given the power to become sons of God in v. 12. Thomas expresses it with an image borrowed from the book of Exodus. Just like our eyes cannot see the light of the sun, but can see it when it shines in a cloud or some opaque body, so our human mind cannot see the divine light in itself, but can see and contemplate it more easily when it is covered with 'the cloud of human flesh'. Thomas quotes Exodus 16:10, which also speaks of God's glory: "They looked towards the desert, and saw the glory of the Lord in a cloud".[5] The divine Word cannot be understood, just like the light of the sun is too bright to be seen directly. The humanity of Christ, however, makes the divine Word 'visible' to our human eyes. In this context, Henk Schoot writes: "Christ's humanity is a sacrament, a mystery of God because it reveals and hides the Word. This we may call Christ's unique mode of signification".[6] Later, when commenting on Jn 8:25 ("The source who is also speaking to you"), Thomas will make the same point in terms of hearing: "Man cannot hear the voice of God directly [...]. So, in order

[5] *In Io* 1:14 §181. The comparison with the appearance of the glory of the Lord in a cloud in Ex 16:10 actually stems from Augustine instead of Chrysostome, as Aquinas recognizes when he refers to it again in *In Io* 8:12 §1142. Chrysostom makes a different comparison, also with a scene taken from Exodus, to make the same point: "For if the men of old time could not even bear to look upon the glorified countenance of Moses, who partook of the same nature with us, if that just man needed a veil which might shade over the purity of his glory, and show to them the face of their prophet mild and gentle; how could we creatures of clay and earth have endured the unveiled Godhead, which is unapproachable even by the powers above?" Chrysostome, *Hom. In Io* 12,1. The reference is to Ex 34:29-35.

[6] H.J.M. Schoot, *Christ the 'Name' of God: Thomas Aquinas on Naming Christ*, Leuven, Peeters, 1993, p. 39.

for us to hear the divine Word directly, the Word assumed flesh and spoke to us with a mouth of flesh".[7]

References to the book of Exodus and the person of Moses are ubiquitous in this part of Thomas's commentary. Moses asked to see God's glory but received the answer that he would only get to see God's back (Ex 33:18-23), which Thomas paraphrases as "shadows and figures".[8] This is true not just for Moses, but for the prophets as well: "For the prophets saw a certain brightness, not through a revealed appearance, but in figures and obscure manners, as is said in Jn 12:41: Isaiah said this when he saw his glory".[9] The apostles, on the other hand, did see the brightness of the Word through his bodily presence, not in figures. Thomas will have more to say about seeing God's glory when he gets to v. 18 ("No one has ever seen God"), but for this moment, in connection with the commentary by Chrysostom, this is the main point: that there is development in salvation history, that while Moses's shining face and the cloud in Exodus prefigured a way in which God was to be seen, the apostles saw the glory of the Word in a new way, no longer in shadows and figures, but in the bodily presence of Christ.

Augustine interprets "We have seen his glory" differently. He reads it in terms of the gift of grace. Continuing the image of seeing, he states that the reason we could not see God's glory is that "there had dashed into man's eye, as it were, dust, earth; it had wounded the eye, and it could not see the light".[10] It is sin that prevents us from seeing. Christ healed our eyes, writes Thomas, "making an eye-salve of his flesh, so that with his flesh the Word might heal our eyes, weakened by the concupiscence of the flesh".[11] Thomas makes explicit what in Augustine remains implicit:

---

[7] "nam vocem Dei immediate homo ferre non potest, quia, secundum Augustinum, infirma corda intelligibile verbum sine voce sensibili audire non possunt. Unde dicitur Ex. c. XX: 'quis est homo, ut audiat vocem domini Dei sui?' Etc. Ad hoc ergo quod immediate ipsum divinum verbum audiremus, carnem assumpsit, cuius organo locutus est nobis". *In Io* 8:25 §1183 (text corrected by L. Reid).

[8] "Umbras et figuras" *In Io* 1:14 §183.

[9] "Prophete vero hanc quidem claritatem viderunt non tamen revelata facie sed in figuris et enigmatibus, infra xii: haec dixit Isaias, quando vidit gloriam eius". *In Io* 1:14 §183. (text corrected by L. Reid. The reference to 1 Cor 12 in the Marietti clearly is a mistake).

[10] "Irruerat homini quasi pulvis in oculum, irruerat terra, sauciaverat oculum, videre non poterat lucem". Augustine, *Tract. In Io* 2,16.

[11] "sanavit oculos hominum, faciens de carne sua salutare collirium, ut sic oculos ex concupiscentia carnis corruptos verbum sua carne curaret". *In Io* 1:14 §182 (text corrected by L. Reid).

that this image is based on the mystical sense of Jn 9, the healing of the man born blind. In the commentary on Jn 9:6, Thomas refers again to this passage in Augustine. There he calls it a *sensus mystice*.[12] The Word incarnate here stands for the 'saliva' from the Father, Thomas explains: "For clay is from the earth, but saliva comes from the head. Similarly, in the person of Christ, his human nature was assumed from the earth; but the incarnate Word is from the head, i.e., from God the Father".[13] Martin Sabathé has pointed out how in this image the intratrinitarian procession is integrated with the mission of the Word: the saliva that is the Word comes forth from the head, the Father. Joined to the earth, the saliva becomes clay, just as in the incarnation, the divine Word is joined to a human nature. This clay, the incarnate Word, then heals the blindness, the consequence of sin that made it impossible to see God's glory.[14] For Thomas, this is the reason why in the Gospel "the Word was made flesh" is immediately followed by "and we have seen his glory:" "As if to say: as soon as the salve was made, our eyes have been healed".[15] The mystical sense thus functions as a reminder that the Word became incarnate as a remedy to our sins, which is the point of Augustine's interpretation: he reads the text in terms of sanctifying grace.

With the metaphor of the light becoming visible to human eyes because it shines into a cloud, Chrysostom gives Thomas a way to show that the incarnation makes the divine Word 'visible' to our human eyes. Augustine, with the *sensus mystice* of the saliva that heals our eyes, gives Thomas a way to show that the Word incarnate will take away the obstacles of sin and give us the grace that makes it possible to see God's glory. Thomas will develop this double take on the incarnation in the commentary on the verses that follow: the Son appears in the world, both as manifestor and as saviour.[16]

---

[12] *In Io* 9:6 §1311. Augustine himself calls it 'magnum mysterium'. *Tract. in Io* 44,2.

[13] "Lutum quidem de terra est, sputum autem a capite derivatur. Ita in persona Christi, natura quidem humana assumpta de terra est; verbum vero incarnatum a capite est, scilicet a Deo patre". *In Io* 1:14 §182.

[14] M. Sabathé, *La Trinité rédemptrice dans le commentaire de l'évangile de saint Jean par Thomas d'Aquin*, Paris, Vrin, 2011, p. 491-492.

[15] "Quasi dicat: statim facto collirio curati sunt oculi nostri" *In Io* 1:14 §182 (text corrected by L. Reid). Thomas uses the word *statim* again a few lines further on: "Hoc ergo lutum statim cum appositum fuit oculis hominum, vidimus gloriam eius". Cf. M. Sabathé, *La Trinité rédemptrice*, p. 387.

[16] "filius apparuit non solum ut manifestator, sed ut salvator". *In Io* 1:32 §270. In the English translation by Larcher and Weisheipl, the word *solum* has been left untranslated, which leads to an unfortunate change of meaning.

Returning to "we have seen his glory", the glory of the Word incarnate is unique, Thomas states, because it is "the glory as of the only-begotten". Thomas returns to Moses as an example of a person who was in glory because, in Exodus, it is said of him that "his face shone" (Ex 34:29). The glory of the Word is unique, however, in four ways. Thomas here first thinks of the transfiguration on the mount, where, according to 2 Peter, Christ "received honour and glory from God the Father" (2 Petr 1:17). This testimony which the Father gave to the Son is unique. Secondly, the uniqueness is shown in the service the angels pay to him (Mt 4:11). Thirdly, it is brought out by the submission of nature. Because "all things were made through him" the winds and the sea obey him (Mt 8:27), which is unique to the Word incarnate. And finally, it is seen in the way Christ taught and acted. Moses and other prophets did not teach from their own authority but on the authority of God. Christ teaches on his own authority; he "speaks as the Lord and as one having power, i.e. by reason of his own power".[17] The same is true for the miracles Christ worked: he worked them by his own power.

The four ways Thomas mentions as showing the uniqueness of the Word are ways in which the divinity of Christ becomes visible. At his baptism and again at the transformation on the mount, the Father testifies to it, and it becomes visible because the angels serve him and nature submits to him. It becomes recognisable in Christ's teaching and miracles, in what we can hear and see. That Thomas has the divinity of Christ in mind here becomes clear with a distinction he introduces at this point in the commentary. Scripture does not only speak of Christ as "only-begotten" but also as "the first-born of many brothers" (Rom 8:29). Thomas makes the distinction by stating that when we speak about Christ as "only-begotten", we speak about him as God: "Just as it belongs to the whole Blessed Trinity to be God, so it belongs to the Word of God to be God begotten".[18] Sonship here is attributed to the Word according to nature, and in that sense, he is the only Son of God: "because, since he alone is naturally begotten by the Father, the begotten of the Father is one only".[19] Speaking about the Word as only-begotten therefore is Trinitarian speech. Speaking of him as "the first-born of many brothers", however, is speaking in terms of participation: others are called sons of God by a

---

[17] "Christus vero loquitur tamquam dominus et potestatem habens, idest propria virtute". *In Io* 1:14 §186.

[18] "sicut totius sanctae Trinitatis proprium est esse Deum, ita verbo Dei proprium est quod sit Deus genitus". *In Io* 1:14 §187.

[19] "quia cum ipse solus sit naturaliter genitus a Patre, unus tantum est genitus Dei". *In Io* 1:14 §187.

likeness to him, by participation, and in that sense, he is "the first-born of all". Thomas summarises: "So, Christ is called the only-begotten of God by nature; but he is called the first-born insofar as from his natural sonship, by means of a certain likeness and participation, sonship is granted to many".[20]

Full of Grace

The incarnation makes it possible for us to see the glory of the only-begotten Son. What is this glory? For Thomas, the continuation of verse 14 is a clarification of what went before: saying that the Word incarnate is "full of grace and truth" is what it means to say that it is full of glory.[21] According to Thomas, grace and truth can be explained with regard to Christ in three ways. Thomas explains both but focusses most of his attention on grace in the commentary. Therefore, I will restrict myself to what he says about grace.

Thomas starts this second discussion of grace in the commentary with the fundamental remark that "grace is given to someone so that he might be joined to God through it".[22] We are joined to God in different ways: we are joined to God as creatures because we participate in a natural likeness. We can be joined to God through the gift of faith, through which God dwells in our hearts, or through the gift of charity. These ways of being joined to God are imperfect: participating in natural likeness is not a perfect union, faith does not allow us to see God as He is, and our charity is always finite, and therefore not capable of infinitely loving the infinitely lovable God. The perfect way of being joined to God is Christ, in whom God assumed human nature in order for man to be God in the unity of a person. This is the first way in which Christ is full of grace. The perfect union with God is the hypostatic union of Christ, which is why he

---

[20] "Sic ergo Christus dicitur unigenitus Dei per naturam, primogenitus vero inquantum ab eius naturali filiatione per quamdam similitudinem et participationem filiatio ad multos derivatur". *In Io* 1:14 §187. Thomas does not mention Col 1:15 here, in which Christ is called 'the firstborn of all creation'. In his commentary on that verse, Thomas relates Christ not only to human beings, but to all creatures: Christ is called firstborn of all creation because he is the Word representing God, and thus every creature known by God, and the principle of every creature. Cf. *In Col* 1:15 §35.

[21] "Consequenter cum dicit 'plenum gratiae et veritatis', ipsam gloriam verbi determinat, quasi dicat: talis est eius gloria quod plenus est gratia et veritate". *In Io* 1:14 §188 (text corrected by L. Reid).

[22] "Ad hoc datur gratia alicui ut per eam Deo coniungatur". *In Io* 1:14 §188 (text corrected by L. Reid). The first discussion of grace was in the commentary on "He gave them power to become sons of God:" *In Io* 1:12 §150-156. See above, p. 122.

is “full of grace”, in need of no special grace, because He is God in person.[23]

The second way in which Christ can be explained to be full of grace is in relation to his soul. Thomas here refers to Jn 3:34 (“for he gives the Spirit without measure”), interpreting the ‘without measure’ as specifically referring to Christ: it is because Christ received the gifts of the Holy Spirit without measure, that his soul can be said to be full of grace.[24] Thomas uses an analogy from Augustine to make his point: just as all the senses are found in the head, whereas there is only one sense present in the rest of the body (the sense of touch), so all graces can be found in Christ, the head of the Church, whereas there is only one gift of grace common to all the saints, which is the gift of charity.[25]

The third way in which Christ can be explained to be full of grace is in relation to his dignity as head of the Church. It is as head of the Church that it belongs to Christ to pour grace into others. Christ is “full of grace” in this sense in so far as he gave justifying grace, which the old law could not give. Thomas here already points forward to v. 17 (“The law indeed was given through Moses; grace and truth came through Jesus Christ”) and refers to Rom 8:3 for the inability of the law to justify: “For God has done what the law, weakened by the flesh, could not do: by sending his own Son in the likeness of sinful flesh, and to deal with sin, he condemned sin in the flesh”.[26]

---

[23] “Sed in Christo est plena coniunctio, secundum quod humana natura assumitur a Deo ut homo sit ipse Deus per unitatem persone. Fuit ergo plenus gratiae, inquantum non accepit a Deo aliquod donum gratuitum speciale, sed quod esset ipse Deus”. *In Io* 1:14 §188 (text corrected by L. Reid).

[24] “Anima Christi fuit plena gratia quia omnia dona Spiritus sancti absque mensura recepit, infra III ‘Non enim ad mensuram’ etc”. *In Io* 1:14 §189 (text corrected by L. Reid).

[25] “Et secundum quod dicit Augustinus, in singulis membris corporis est unus sensus communis, scilicet sensus tactus, in capite vero sunt omnes sensus, ita omnes gratie superabundantur sunt in capite Christo; in aliis vero sanctis est unum gratuitum donum commune omnibus, scilicet caritas, alia vero aliis specialia quia divisiones gratiarum sunt, I Cor xii, sed Christus habuit omnem gratiam Spiritus sancti, Is xi ‘Egredietur virga de radice Iesse et flos, scilicet Christus, de radice eius’ etc., ‘spiritus timoris Domini’ etc”. *In Io* 1:14 §189 (text corrected by L. Reid). In the *Scriptum* Thomas contrasts this view with the view of Origen that in the saints all five spiritual senses are present: *I Sent*, d. XIII, *expositio textus*, but neither here nor in the *Summa Theologiae* does he return to it when he refers to Augustine’s metaphor. Cf. *STh* III q. 8 a. 1c.

[26] “Dicitur ergo plenus gratia inquantum fecit gratiam iustificando, nam lex vetus infirmabatur nec iustificare poterat. Sed Christus iustificavit, infra eodem ‘gratia et

The three ways in which Thomas explains Christ to be full of grace are interrelated and show one way in which for Thomas Christology in the strict sense, the theological thinking about the person of Jesus Christ, is related to soteriology. It is because Christ's union with God is perfect that his human soul can receive the fullness of divine grace. For a human soul to receive fullness of grace means to be perfectly joined to God: that is, after all, the reason why grace is given in the first place, as Thomas started out by saying. This perfect way of being joined to God is the mystery of the hypostatic union, and the fullness of habitual grace in Christ's soul is an effect of this, as Thomas states in the *Summa Theologiae*.[27] It is this fullness of grace in the human soul of Christ that makes it possible for his human nature to be instrumental in causing grace in others by being head of the Church.[28]

The three ways in which, according to Thomas's account, Christ was full of grace, find a close parallel in three ways in which Christ is full of truth. The human nature in Christ attained to the divine truth so that while in other human beings we find participated truths, Christ is truth himself. As to Christ's soul, Thomas states that Christ knew every truth both human and divine from the instance of his conception. And as head of the Church, Christ can be said to be full of truth because he fulfilled the figures of the old law, and his teaching was not in figures but openly. I will not go deeper into these ways in which Christ can be said to be full of truth because while Thomas does mention them, his focus in this part of the commentary is on grace.[29]

Grace in the commentary on Jn 3:34

At this point, it is helpful to briefly study a fragment from another part of the commentary because it is insightful in the way the commentary works. As always, the *divisio textus* is the point of departure. In my discussion of the *divisiones textus* that Albert, Bonaventure and Thomas give of the fourth Gospel, I noticed that contrary to the other two theologians, Thomas reads John 1 as a unified whole that as a whole states the divinity of Christ, which is what this Gospel wants to make known principally in the first place. Contrary to Albert and Bonaventure, for Thomas John 1 is

veritas' etc., Rom xiii: 'Quod impossible erat legi, in quo infirmabatur per carnem, Deus filium suum mittens in similitudinem carnis peccati, de peccato damnavit peccatum in carne' etc". *In Io* 1:14 §190 (text corrected by L. Reid).

27 *STh* III q. 6 a. 6c.

28 Cf. *STh* III q. 8 a. 1 ad 1.

29 *In Io* 1:14 §188-190.

as it were a summary of the whole of the Gospel. That this is so can be seen from the *divisio textus*, where Thomas states that the Gospel should be divided into two parts: Jn 1, in which the evangelist states the divinity of Christ, and Jn 2-21 in which he shows the divinity of Christ by the things Christ did in the flesh.[31]

John 1 for Thomas introduces all the essential themes of Trinitarian theology, Christology and theology of grace that are subsequently developed further in the chapters that follow. That this is Thomas's view on the Gospel can be seen from the fact that Thomas's commentary works in the same way: the core theological topics that are introduced in chapter one are subsequently developed in further chapters. We will see examples of this in the next chapter, but we can see one here already, for Thomas returns to the threefold ways in which he says Christ is full of grace when he comments on the verse "for God does not bestow the Holy Spirit in fractions" (Jn 3:34). The context is the controversy after Jesus starts to baptise people as John does (Jn 3:31-32). Thomas reads the remarks the disciples of John the Baptist make to John as a double question: they complain about what Christ is doing ("He is here baptising") and about his increasing fame and reputation among the people ("and all the people are flocking to him" Jn 3:26). The answer the baptist gives to his disciples addresses both these points, Thomas explains in the *divisio textus*: first John answers the question about Christ baptising (Jn 3:27-29) and then about the question of Christ's growing fame (Jn 3:30-36).[32] In answer to this second question, John provides his students with the reasons for Christ's growing fame: his origin ("The one who came from above", v. 31), and his teaching ("He testifies to what he sees and to what he hears", v. 32), that is, his ability to proclaim divine truth. It is in this context, Christ's ability to proclaim divine truth, that Thomas places Jn 3:34b ("God does not bestow the Spirit in fractions"): "The ability to proclaim divine truth is present in Christ in the highest degree because he does not receive the Spirit in a partial way; and so he says: 'For God does not bestow the Spirit in fractions'".[33]

As we saw, Thomas already referred to this verse when he mentioned how the soul of Christ is full of grace because it has received the gifts of the Holy Spirit without measure. Jn 3:34 allows Thomas to say a bit more about the relation of Christ to the Holy Spirit. Speaking about Christ as God, one would have to say that God the Father gives the Holy Spirit to

[31] *In Io* 1:1 §23.
[32] *In Io* 3:27 §513.
[33] *In Io* 3:34 §541.

God the Son without measure in the sense that the Father gives to the Son the power to bring forth (*spirandi*) the Holy Spirit from eternity so that the Holy Spirit comes forth from the Son as much as from the Father. To this eternal forthcoming from the Father and the Son corresponds a mission in time, which for the Holy Spirit means the mission to manifest Christ in as much as the Spirit proceeds from him. The relation between eternal procession and mission in time is what Thomas recognises in Jn 16:14, which he quotes here: "He will give glory to me, because he will have received from me".[34] Speaking about Christ as man, Thomas states that Christ has the Holy Spirit as sanctifier. Here Jn 1:14 and Jn 3:34 strengthen each other: saying that Christ did not receive grace in a certain degree, as other humans do, is saying that God has not bestowed the Spirit in fractions on Christ.[35]

Having put these remarks about Christ and the Holy Spirit in place, Thomas expands on the three kinds of grace in Christ that he mentions in the commentary on Jn 1:14. The grace of union is not habitual grace; it is not a quality of the soul, but it is "a certain gratuitous gift" that causes Christ in his human nature to be the Son of God, "not by participation but by nature, insofar as the human nature of Christ is united to the Son of God in person". To be united to the divine nature is an infinite gift because the divine nature is infinite.[36] Thomas is careful in his wording here: he does not try to define this grace of union but only gives a negative reason why the union is called a grace: Christ had it without any preceding merits. It is gratuitous, freely given, and as gratuitous, this grace and gift of union is attributed to the Holy Spirit.

[34] In the commentary on John, Thomas does not use the distinction between 'missio visibilis' and 'missio invisibilis', that he makes in the *Summa Theologiae*. From the context here of the Spirit who makes Christ known (for example at his baptism) it is clear that he has the visible mission of the Holy Spirit in mind. Cf. *STh* I, q. 43. On this *quaestio*, cf. H. Rikhof, 'Trinity', in: R. van Nieuwenhove, J. Wawrykow (eds.), *The Theology of Thomas Aquinas*, Notre Dame, University of Notre Dame Press, 2005, p. 36-57, here p. 40-49.

[35] *In Io* 3:34 §543.

[36] "Nam gratia unionis, quae non est habitualis, sed quoddam gratuitum donum, datur Christo, ut scilicet in humana natura sit Deus filius Dei non per participationem, sed per naturam, inquantum ipsa humana natura Christi unita est filio Dei in persona: quae quidem unio gratia dicitur, quia nullis praecedentibus meritis hoc habuit". *In Io* 3:34 §544 (text corrected by L. Reid). §544 is very similar to *Comp. Theol.* Ch 215, which has the same expression "non per participationem, sed per naturam". The wording is clearer in *STh* III q. 7 a. 11 ad 1.

With regard to Christ's soul, grace is habitual, and because this grace is a created gift, it is finite. How can we then understand that Christ did receive the Holy Spirit, that is to say, grace, "without measure?" In his reply to this question, Thomas looks at it from three perspectives.

The first perspective is that of Christ, who receives this grace. As to his human soul, the capacity to receive grace is finite. Thomas argues, however, that this human capacity is completely filled because there is no measure on the part of the one who gives the grace. Thomas compares it to someone who takes a bucket to a river: while the bucket can contain only a limited amount of water, the river provides an unlimited amount. When the bucket is overflowing, one might say that it has received water "without measure:" while there is a limit to the amount of water the bucket can hold, that capacity is filled completely, there is no limit to the giver: it has received as much as it can hold. So with grace in the human soul of Christ: while it is finite as to the capacity of the receiver, it is given in an infinite way, without measure.

The second perspective is that of the gift that is given. Here Thomas interprets "without measure" in the sense of "complete", of having the entire fullness of the gift, even though the gift itself might be finite. Thomas mentions a colour as an example. Being white is not something infinite, but when something is entirely white, it can be said to have "whiteness" without measure: it could not be more white than it is. Contrary to human persons who receive grace in different measures (Thomas refers to 1 Cor 12: we all receive different gifts), Christ received everything that pertains to the nature of grace. In that sense, the created grace he received, even though finite in nature, was "without measure".

From the perspective of its cause, the habitual grace in the soul of Christ is infinite because its cause is: for his soul is united to the divine Word, the infinite source of all creation. The image Thomas uses here is of a fountain that could produce an infinite source of water. If someone has such a fountain, he can be said to have water "without measure" because its source is infinite.

Finally, capital grace, the grace Christ has as head of the Church, is infinite "as to its influence" (*quantum ad influentiam*). Because Christ has the Spirit without measure, he can pour out the gifts of the Spirit without measure. Or, as Thomas writes, referring to 1 Jn 2:2 ("He is the offering for our sins; and not for ours only, but also for those of the entire world"): "the grace of Christ is sufficient not merely for the salvation of some men, but for all the people of the entire world, and even for many worlds, if they existed".[37]

The exposition of Jn 3:34 adds two things to the commentary on Jn 1:14. While the commentary on Jn 1:14 mentions the Holy Spirit, it is in the commentary on Jn 3:34 that Thomas goes into the working of the Holy Spirit and in that way deepens the Trinitarian character of his students's theology: it is the Spirit that manifests Christ and sanctifies him as to his human nature, and it is to the Holy Spirit that the gift or grace of the union between the Divine Word and the human nature of Christ is attributed. Furthermore, Jn 3:34 helps Thomas to keep in view that when we speak of grace in Christ, in whatever form, we are speaking of the grace that is the Holy Spirit, that is infinite in character, given "without measure".

Secondly, the "without measure" of Jn 3:34 challenges Thomas to give a more detailed account of what is finite and infinite in the grace of Christ. From eternity, the Father gives to the Son the power to bring forth the Spirit. The union of the divine Word with a human nature in the incarnation is a gift that cannot be measured. As to his human soul, Christ was completely filled with the Holy Spirit, in every aspect, receiving all gifts, filled in such a way that it could overflow to others, which was necessary for his mission to be the Saviour of the world, of all people, as head of the Church. All this has to be said in order to do justice to the person of Christ, and at the same time, it has to be taken into account that when speaking about the human nature of Christ, about his soul, and about Christ as the head of the Church, we are speaking of a created, finite reality, that receives the infinite gift of the grace of the Holy Spirit in a finite human way: *quidquid recipitur, ad modum recipientis recipitur*.

Grace upon Grace

Let us return to the commentary on Jn 1. Thomas reads Jn 1:16-18 as an explanation of Jn 1:14b: the divinity of Christ made known to the apostles through sight. "Seeing his glory" is seeing Him "full of grace and truth". In the exposition of v. 14b, the main focus was on grace, and in the exposition of v. 16-18 that is again the case. John does two things here, Thomas writes: he shows Christ to be the fountain, the origin of all grace, and he shows the distribution of grace in us through Christ.

---

[37] "ut scilicet gratia Christi non solum sufficiat ad salutem hominum aliquorum, sed hominum totius mundi, secundum illud I Io. II, 2: 'ipse est propitiatio pro peccatis nostris, et non pro nostris tantum, sed etiam totius mundi', ac etiam plurium mundorum, si essent". *In Io* 3:34 §544.

That Christ is the origin of grace is the conclusion Thomas draws from "of his fullness we have all received, grace upon grace". A comparison with two other people who are called "full of grace" in Scripture, St. Stephen (Acts 6:8) and the virgin Mary (Lk 1:28), is helpful here. According to Thomas, the same expression "full of grace" has to be interpreted in different ways when it is used for Stephen, Mary and Christ: in St. Stephen it says something about his holiness, which makes it possible for him to act meritoriously. In Mary it flows over and becomes bodily in her womb. Thomas carefully notes, however, that she is never the origin of grace in others. That only can be said about Christ: only from him does grace overflow to others in such a way that he can be called the author and maker of grace (*gratie actor et factor*) in others.[38]

In previous chapters, we have seen how prepositions in the Gospel text often are taken up by Thomas to make theological distinctions in his exposition. Thomas's commentary on Jn 1:16 ("Of his fullness we have all received, grace upon grace") is another telling example. Thomas notices that the word "of" (*de*) can have a triple meaning and uses this as an explanation of how Christ is the origin of grace. First, "*de*" can signify efficiency in the sense of an origin: a ray proceeds from the sun. Read this way it shows how the man Christ is the author of grace, the cause of grace in all creatures.[39]

'From' can also refer to a portion, as when we say "from this bread or wine". In this sense, it refers to participation: we have received from the fullness of grace which is in Christ in the sense that we participate in what is fully present in Christ.

The final way (the second in Thomas's enumeration) is the most interesting one. It is not present either in the *Glossa* or in the *Catena Aurea* or in the commentary by Albert or that by Bonaventure. Thomas writes:

> In a second way, [this preposition *de*] refers to consubstantiality, because although habitual gifts are different in us than in Christ, yet it is one and the same Holy Spirit who is in Christ and who fills all the saints: 'One and the same Spirit produces all these' (1 Cor 12:11); 'I will pour out my Spirit upon all flesh' (Jl 2:28); 'If anyone does not have the Spirit of Christ, he does not

[38] *In Io* 1:16 §201.
[39] *In Io* 1:16 §202.

> belong to him' (Rom 8:9). For the unity of the Holy Spirit produces unity in the Church.[40]

Thomas uses the word 'consubstantiality' here to refer to Christ and the Holy Spirit having the same divine nature: the fullness of Christ is the Holy Spirit. Habitual gifts might be different in Christ and in us (if only because even the saints only receive some of the gifts, while Christ received "the fullness of grace", as we saw before), but there is a principle of unity: that principle is the Holy Spirit.

The argument in a very concise way does seem to consist of two steps. The *de* in "of his fullness" refers to the consubstantiality between Son and Holy Spirit. It is because the Son and the Holy Spirit are consubstantial, that "of his fullness" (which in the context naturally is read as "of the fullness of the Son") can also be read as referring to the Holy Spirit: of the fullness that is the Holy Spirit we have all received grace upon grace. The second step is the remark that it is the same Holy Spirit that is in Christ and in the saints ("we have all received"), therefore bringing unity between the head and the members of the Church.

The quotations from Scripture are especially significant, here: not only are all three of these references taken from key texts in Scripture about the Holy Spirit, but they all also speak about the Holy Spirit as bringing about unity, either by inclusion (as in the case of the quotations from 1 Cor 12 and Jl 2) or exclusion (in the case of the quotation from Rom 8). Jean-Pierre Torrell has shown how in the context of the image of the Church as the body of Christ, "the role of the Holy Spirit is to establish the "continuity" between Christ the Head and the faithful members, for he has the property of remaining numerically *one and the same* in the Head and in the members".[41]

At this point in the commentary, Thomas makes one final subdivision that is worth mentioning. The *divisio textus* becomes fairly intricate here, but

---

[40] "Secundo vero consubstantialitatem, quia licet dona habitualia alia sint in nobis quam in Christo, tamen Spiritus Sanctus, qui est in Christo unus et idem replet omnes sanctos. I Cor. XII, 11: 'haec omnia operatur unus atque idem Spiritus'; Ioel. II, 28: 'effundam de Spiritu meo super omnem carnem' etc.; Rom. c. VIII, 9: 'si quis Spiritum Christi non habet, hic non est eius'. Nam unitas Spiritus Sancti facit in Ecclesia unitatem". *In Io* 1:16 §202 (text corrected by L. Reid).

[41] J.-P. Torrell, *Saint Thomas Aquinas, Spiritual Master*, Washington D.C., Catholic University of America Press, 2003, p. 189. For a study on the role of Biblical quotations in Thomas's Biblical commentaries, cf. P. Roszak, 'The Place and Function of Biblical Citations in Thomas Aquinas's Exegesis', in: P. Roszak, J. Vijgen (eds.), *Reading Sacred Scripture with Thomas Aquinas: Hermeneutical Tools, Theological Questions and New Perspectives*, Turnhout, Brepols, 2015, p. 115-139.

it is worth bearing with him because it is in the *divisio*, as Thomas's interpretative framework for the commentary, that many of his interpretative choices become visible. We saw that for Thomas Jn 1:14b-51 is about how the incarnate Word is made known: through seeing (v. 14b) and hearing (v. 15), both ways then being expanded upon by the evangelist in v. 16-18 and 19-51, respectively. "Seeing his glory" in v. 14 was interpreted as seeing him "full of grace and truth", and in his exposition of v. 16-18, Thomas focuses mainly on grace. Christ is the origin of grace in ways in which others like Stephen and the virgin Mary are not. The rest of these verses 16-18, from "grace upon grace" are read by Thomas as two ways in which Christ, the origin of grace, gives us grace. We receive it from him as its author (v. 16-17) and as its teacher (v. 18). It is to this first part that we now turn.

It is from the fullness of grace in Christ that we receive "grace upon grace". For his explanation, Thomas turns once more to two of his favourite commentators, Chrysostom and Augustine.

With Chrysostom, Thomas reads v. 17 ("because, while the law was given through Moses, grace and truth have come through Jesus Christ") as an explanation of "grace upon grace" in v. 16: the first grace is Torah, the law given by Moses; the second grace is given by Christ. Thomas explains that this means Christ ranks above Moses in two ways: according to what they gave and according to the way it was given. What Moses gave was a symbol of the reality that Christ is, the shadow of the truth. It is important to notice, as Klimczak has done, that this does not mean that the *figura* that the law was, is unimportant or untruthful. Thomas calls it "a great grace" because it gave a true knowledge of the one true God. It is precisely this knowledge that distinguishes the Jews from the heathen. It could not bring salvation, however, nor was it supposed to do that: it showed what was to be done and avoided, but gave no help to fulfil these commandments; it promised the help of grace, but could not give grace itself; its ceremonies and precepts pointed forward to the grace of the New Covenant but could not give grace themselves. According to the way it was given, Thomas distinguishes Moses from Christ by stating that while Moses proclaimed the law, he was not the origin of it; Christ is the author of grace.[42]

[42] *In Io* 1:16-17 §205-206. Cf. P. Klimczak, *Christus magister: Le Christ maître dans les commentaires évangéliques de saint Thomas d'Aquin*, Fribourg, Academic Press Fribourg, 2013, p. 238-239.

We can be brief about the interpretation according to Augustine, here. In his *Tractatus* on John, he interprets "grace upon grace" as referring to the grace of faith in this life and the grace of eternal life, and Thomas has included this commentary in his *Catena Aurea*.[43] In the commentary, Thomas broadens this interpretation to include the distinction between prevenient grace and subsequent grace. In the *Summa Theologiae*, Thomas distinguishes five stages of the working of grace: it heals us from the effects of sin, it moves us to want to do good, it helps us to actually do that good, it helps us to persevere in the good, and finally it helps us to reach heavenly glory. Every earlier step is prevenient to the next, every next step subsequent to the earlier.[44] In line with Augustine's interpretation, Thomas recognises this distinction in the words "grace upon grace" in Jn 1:16.

No one has ever seen God

After the commentary on v. 16-17 showed Christ as author of grace, according to Thomas v. 18 ("No one has ever seen God; it is the only-begotten Son, who is in the bosom of the Father, who has made him known") shows him as teacher of grace. The first part of the verse challenges Thomas to think about what it means to 'see God'. For it seems that Scripture mentions several ways in which people see God. Thomas mentions four of those ways. One can see God in a created substance, as Abraham recognised God in the three men visiting him by the oaks of Mamre (Gn 18:1-8). One might see God through a representation in the imagination, as is clear from the many visions Scripture speaks about. Thomas mentions Isaiah seeing God seated on a high and lofty throne (Is 6:1). This is by no means an innocuous example since it was precisely this vision that Thomas used in the prologue to this commentary to understand John the evangelist as a contemplative. What Isaiah did or did not see has direct repercussions for understanding the writer of the Fourth Gospel. Thirdly, there is Rom 1:20, a favourite verse of Thomas's, which suggests to him that by abstracting from material things, one can see God through an intelligible species. Finally, God might infuse a spiritual light during contemplation. Thomas refers to a remark by Gregory the Great saying that through his deep contemplation, this is how Jacob saw God face to face when he wrestled with a man near the Jabbok (Gn 32:22-32).

Thomas reacts to these four ways Scripture speaks about people seeing God with a lengthy exposition, in which several points can be

---

[43] Augustine, *Tract. in Io* 3.9; Cf. *Catena Aurea in Io* 1:16.

[44] *STh* I-II q. 111 a. 3.

distinguished. Thomas is adamant in his first point: by none of these visions has the divine essence been seen. All of these visions require a created species representing the divine essence. Be it through our senses, through our imagination or through our intellect, we always use some created image to know God, and no created species can represent the divine essence, both because nothing finite can represent the infinite as it is and because God is his own *esse*, in him his wisdom and goodness and other divine attributes are one. All those attributes, however, can never be represented through one created thing. Therefore Thomas concludes that "we do not know what God is by all these acts of knowing, but what he is not, or that he is".[45] An explicit reference to Dionysius the Areopagite's *Mystical Theology* concludes this point.[46]

Does this mean that the divine essence will never be seen, neither by people here on earth nor by the angels and blessed in heaven? This is not an innocent question in Thomas's time. In 1241, the thesis that the divine essence is seen neither by people nor by angels had been condemned at the university of Paris.[47] Thomas gives three reasons for declining this thesis, three reasons that he also mentions in the *Summa Theologiae*: it is contrary to Scripture (Thomas refers to 1 Jn 3:2 and Jn 17:3); furthermore, one should not separate God's substance from God's glory which the saints see in heaven, as if the saints in heaven see God's light, but not his

---

[45] "per omnes illas cognitiones non scitur de Deo quid est, sed quid non est, vel an est". *In Io* 1:18 §211. The words Thomas uses here are of course strongly reminiscent of the beginning of the *Summa* as well: "primo considerandum est an Deus sit; secundo, quomodo sit, vel potius quomodo non sit" (*STh* I, q. 2 Intr.) and "quia de Deo scire non possumus quid sit, sed quid non sit, non possumus considerare de Deo quomodo sit, sed potius quomodo non sit" (*STh* I, q. 3 Intr.).

[46] P.-Y. Maillard has shown that from the four ways Thomas mentions of seeing God, three (the first, the second and the fourth) seem to go back to a tripartite distinction Augustine makes in his *De Genesi ad litteram* between a physical vison, a spiritual vision and an intellectual vision, while the third Thomas mentions is based on an Aristotelian epistemology. Maillard rightly warns that the fact that Thomas here cites Dionysius should not be used to construe an opposition between an 'apophatic Dionysius' and a 'cataphatic Augustine' (or even worse, between a 'negative theology' in the East and a 'positive theology' in the West), if only because, as Maillard shows, the apophatic remarks Thomas makes here can be found in Augustine's works as well, not least in his *Tract. in Io*. P.-Y. Maillard, *La vision de Dieu chez Thomas d'Aquin*, Paris, Vrin, 2001, p. 131-137.

[47] For more on the 1241 Parisien condemnation, cf. P.-Y. Maillard, *La Vision de Dieu*, p. 205-221, who defends the thesis that while Thomas does not think any of the Greek fathers fall under this condemnation, he seems to think that a number of western scholars starting with John Scot Eriugena do, as well as defenders of the so-called Second Averroism.

essence; finally human beings have a natural desire to know, and from the causes we recognise in the world there is a natural desire to know the first cause, God. To take away the possibility of knowing this first cause is to take away the possibility of human happiness: "Therefore, for the created intellect to be happy, it is necessary that the divine essence be seen".[48]

Thomas completes his discussion about seeing God with three concluding remarks. God can never be seen by our senses or imagination because God is not corporeal. Furthermore, in this life, God's essence can never be seen by our intellect either, because as long as we are on earth, we receive knowledge by making use of our body and our senses, and in that way, God's incorporeal essence cannot be seen. Finally, while the blessed see God, they do not comprehend Him. For someone comprehends something, Thomas writes, "when he knows that thing to the extent that it is knowable in itself; otherwise, although he may know it, he does not comprehend it". But God, being infinite in power, can never be known by a created, finite intellect in God's infinity, and therefore cannot be comprehended.[49]

To readers of Thomas's work, none of this will be very surprising: the apophatic character of Thomas's theology is well-known. Here it functions as an introduction that leads Thomas to a few clarifications about Christ. In the discussion of the commentary on Jn 1:10, we saw that Thomas there gives our lack of knowledge of God as the main reason for the incarnation. Here that point is restated in other words: because no one has ever seen God, it is necessary for us to receive wisdom.[50]

That Christ is the competent teacher who makes God known to us,

---

[48] "Necesse est ergo ad beatitudinem intellectus creati, ut divina essentia videatur" *In Io* 1:18 §212. Cf. *STh* I q. 12 a. 1. Theology in the twentieth century saw an extended discussion about the natural desire to see God, a discussion that was centered for a long time on two books by Henri de Lubac: H. de Lubac, *Surnaturel: Études historiques*, Paris, Aubier, 1946; H. de Lubac, *Le mystère du surnaturel*, Paris, Aubier, 1965. I will not enter that discussion here, but refer to two works that briefly discuss the desire to see God in the theology of Thomas: J.-P. Torrell, *Saint Thomas Aquinas, Spiritual Master*, p. 342-348; P.-Y. Maillard, *La vision de Dieu*, p. 180-188. For a presentation of the debates in the twentieth century, cf. F. Kerr, *After Aquinas: Versions of Thomism*, Oxford, Blackwell Publishing, 2002, p. 134-148.

[49] *In Io* 1:18 §213. In these three points, Thomas briefly summarizes what he had discussed at more length in *STh* I q. 12. For these three remarks, cf. a. 3 a. 11 and a. 7 respectively.

[50] "Sic ergo necessarium erat quod reciperemus sapientiam, quia Deum nemo vidit unquam". *In Io* 1:18 §214.

Thomas understands from what follows in the Gospel: "It is the only-begotten Son who is in the bosom of the Father, who has made him known". Thomas recognises in these words three characteristics of this teacher that all boil down to the mystery of the Trinity: that Christ is 'Son' shows that he is of the same nature as the Father, and therefore has unique knowledge of Him; before, we already saw that "only-begotten" is for Thomas a Trinitarian term, and he repeats that here. And finally, Thomas introduces a reading of "in the bosom of the Father" which he takes from St. Augustine: according to this explanation, "bosom" refers to the secret things of the Father. That Christ is "in the bosom of the Father" in his secrets is a way to speak about his consubstantiality with the Father; in other words, about his divinity. The three words, only-begotten, Son, bosom, all referring to the divinity of Christ, show him to be a competent teacher of the otherwise unknown secrets of God because he shares in God's divinity.[51]

Thomas adds two remarks. The first is that what had been said of creatures never being able to comprehend God is true of the soul of Christ as well. Comprehension is attributed only to "the only-begotten Son who is in the bosom of the Father", Thomas writes, confirming that that expression refers to the divine Word only. Only Father, Son and Holy Spirit comprehend God, not the human soul of Christ.[52]

The second remark is a combination of two quotations that can be found in the *Catena Aurea*, one by Augustine and the other by Chrysostom. Augustine had criticised people who stated that while the Father is invisible, the Son is visible. Thomas takes over the critique by using the argument of Chrysostom that he who is "the image of the invisible God" (Col 1:15) must himself be invisible. Thomas agrees, referring back to what he said before about the Son being among the hidden things of the Father: the Son is "naturally invisible" (*naturaliter invisibilis*), and Thomas adds that this "incomprehensibility of the Son" (*incomprehensibilitas filii*) is stated at many places in Scripture, including Is 45:15 ("Truly, you are a hidden God", which Thomas reads

[51] *In Io* 1:18 §215-218. For the origin of the explanation of "bosom" as "secrets" in Augustine, cf. his *Tract. In Io* 3,17, referred to by Thomas as well in *Catena Aurea in Io* 1:18.

[52] 'Comprehension' here is to be understood in the way it was used before, as knowing everything there is to be known about something. The distinction between *viator* and *comprehensor* is not what Thomas is speaking about here: in that sense, Christ's soul was *comprehensor* while on earth.

Christologically) and Mt 11:27 ("No one knows the Son except the Father").[53]

It is hard to find what Henk Schoot has called "negative Christology" expressed in more emphatic terms anywhere in Thomas's writings. The Son, the second person of the divine Trinity, remains utterly incomprehensible to us, both before and after the incarnation. That, for Thomas, is how the logic of Jn 1:18 works: it is because the Son shares in the incomprehensibility of the Father that he is "the competent teacher" (*sufficiens doctor*, §215) who teaches us first-hand about the Triune God.[54]

Conclusion: What has been seen?

With the exposition of v. 18, Thomas concludes his discussion on how the Word incarnate was made known by seeing. It seems to end in an aporia. Is there actually something that has been seen at all, and if so, what is that?

The commentary on v. 18 has made it abundantly clear that what has not become visible in the incarnation is the divine essence. Thomas's Christology remains an apophatic theology, and Thomas has no hesitation to apply the most apophatic verses of Scripture (like Is 45:15 and 1 Tim 6:16) to the incarnate Son. The divinity of Christ remains invisible, not just to our bodily eyes, but to our imagination and our intellect as well: in the precise meaning that Thomas gives to it, the divinity of Christ can never be comprehended by any creature, not *in via*, not even *in patria*. The incomprehensibility of Christ is the flip side of his divinity: it is as divine that Christ is unknowable. His divinity, unknowable as it is in itself, is the necessary prerequisite for stating that it is the Word incarnate that makes God known. Only because he shares in the divine mystery, in the secret of God, can Christ make us see God.

As we saw, Thomas carefully and continuously juxtaposes the commentaries by Chrysostom and Augustine in this part of the commentary. With his constant references to Exodus, Chrysostom stresses how in the incarnation, the human body of Christ God becomes 'visible' in a new way, how salvation history has led to this point. Augustine stresses that it is this Word incarnate that heals our eyes from sin, that gives us the grace to recognise God in Christ. Thomas juxtaposes

[53] *In Io* 1:18 §220. For Augustine and Chrysostome, cf. *Catena Aurea in Io* 1:18.
[54] *In Io* 1:18 §221-222.

these two commentaries because they belong together because "the Son appears in the world both as manifestor and saviour".[55] What is manifested is God's glory. What saves us is God's glory. It is this unique glory that becomes visible in the life of Christ: in the testimony given to him by the Father, in the submission of the angels and nature to him, in the way Christ taught and acted.

What is this glory? It is grace, that which is given so that someone may be joined to God through it. That union exists in Christ in a perfect and unique way in the hypostatic union: he alone is "full of grace". It is because of this hypostatic union that the human soul in Christ is full of grace and that this human nature can be instrumental in causing grace in others, in giving the Holy Spirit. It is the Holy Spirit who brings unity, who establishes the continuity between Christ the head of the Church, and the members: the same Holy Spirit that is in Christ fully and that shares with Christ the one divine nature, gives graces to the saints and thereby brings unity to the Church.

At the end of the commentary of this part of the Gospel, Thomas asks what Christ has made known except the one God that Moses had already made known. What did Christ add to Moses? Thomas's answer almost seems a throwaway remark: "It added the mystery of the Trinity and many other things that neither Moses nor any of the prophets made known".[56] What has been seen because of the incarnation? If 'seen' is understood as 'fully grasped', 'comprehended', the answer is: nothing. If 'seen' is understood as 'made known in a human, limited and participated way', the answer is: 'everything': the triune God, grace, and our salvation.

2. Hearing

Next to 'seeing', 'hearing' is the other way in which, according to Thomas, the fourth Gospel presents how the divinity of Christ is made known. 'Hearing' here predominantly means testimony: through witnesses, the divinity of the Word is announced. In Jn 1, that witness first and foremost is John the Baptist, and the first disciples at the end of the chapter. There is another way in which Christ was made known as well: through his baptism. The baptism of Christ is not just a way by which John the Baptist makes known who Christ is; for Thomas, the baptism itself has the character of a manifestation, as we will see. In what

---

[55] *In Io* 1:32 §270.
[56] *In Io* 1:18 §222.

follows, I will discuss three topics that are important to Thomas in his reading of Jn 1:15.19-51 in terms of testimony: the role of the witness, the process of conversion, and the fruit of the testimony. In a separate section after that, I will look at Christ's baptism as testimony.

Being a witness

When we discussed Thomas's commentary on the first time the fourth Gospel mentions John the Baptist, we noticed that Thomas stresses John's office as witness and participation as the necessary condition for being a witness: one can only manifest the truth in so far as one has a share in divine truth.[58] In addition to this, in the commentary on v. 15.19-51, there is another point that Thomas stresses about being a witness, which is that it requires the witness to point away from himself to the person his testimony is about.

After having given negative answers to three questions (that he is not the Messiah, nor Elijah, nor the prophet), John answers the question of who he is by calling himself a voice that cries in the wilderness. Thomas reads that reply as a sign of John's devotion. He is so full of Christ that he does not speak about who he is (by replying: "I am the son of Zachary", for example) but about the way in which he followed Christ: he is the voice that makes known the divine Word.[59] When asked about his office, John again takes the opportunity to bear witness to Christ.[60]

This Christ-oriented character of the witness is not just relevant for those who have seen Jesus; it is a task for all witnesses, including those who are preachers. When Andrew immediately after having begun to follow Jesus brings his brother Simon to Jesus, Thomas comments: "consider the devotion of Andrew: for he brought him to Jesus and not to himself (for he knew that he himself was weak); and so he leads him to Christ to be instructed by him. This shows us that the efforts of preachers should not be to win for themselves the fruits of their preaching, i.e., to turn them to their own private benefit and honour, but to bring them to Jesus, i.e., to refer them to his glory and honour: "What we preach is not ourselves, but Jesus Christ", as is said in 2 Corinthians (4:5)".[61]

---

[58] *In Io* 1:7 §117. See above, p. 107.

[59] *In Io* 1:23 §235-236.

[60] *In Io* 1:27 §245.

[61] "Andreae devotionem considera: quia duxit eum ad Iesum, non ad se (sciebat enim se infirmum), et ideo eum ad Christum adducit, ut ipse eum instruat; instruens simul per hoc, quod hic debet esse praedicatorum conatus, ut fructus praedicationis et studium non sibi vindicent, seu ad utilitatem et honorem proprium convertant, sed ut adducant ad Iesum, idest ad eius gloriam et honorem referant. II Cor. IV, 5: 'non enim praedicamus nosmetipsos, sed Iesum Christum'". *In Io* 1:42 §302. (text corrected by

Thomas recognises three places where John the Baptist compares himself to Christ. The first is when he calls himself "a voice that cries in the wilderness" (v. 23). In his commentary on this verse, Thomas returns to his exposition on the distinction between the internal word and the external, voiced word that was foundational in the commentary on v. 1. John calls himself the voice because he comes after the internal word but is instrumental in causing knowledge: we get to know someone else's internal words when they are spoken to us. The voice that John is makes God's internal, eternal Word audible.[62]

The second comparison is in v. 27: "He who comes after me, who ranks ahead of me, the strap of whose sandal I am not worthy to unfasten",[63] Jesus will come after John when it comes to preaching, baptising and dying, as the perfect follows the imperfect, Thomas interprets. Indeed, "the entire life of John was a preparation for Christ".[64] The remark about being unworthy to unfasten the strap of the sandal is read by Thomas as a way to speak about the superiority of Christ that goes beyond mere comparisons between humans: "You must not suppose that he ranks ahead of me in dignity in the way that one man is placed ahead of another, rather he is ranked so far above me that I am nothing in comparison to him".[65] Just as Abraham, Job and Isaiah completely lowered themselves when considering the infinite greatness of God, so does John in speaking of the divinity of Christ.[66] In speaking of God, comparisons break down because the divine and the creature are not on the same scale which would make a comparison possible in the first place. That is Thomas' reading of the image of being unworthy to loosen the strap of the sandal. With a mystical explanation of this verse by Gregory the Great incorporated in the *Glossa* and therefore widely quoted in medieval commentaries (Albert and Bonaventure both quote it as well) Thomas goes one step further. Gregory explains that the sandal, made

L. Reid). Cf. *In Io 1*:51 §333, where Thomas follows Augustine in reading the Angels Jesus mentions as preachers, and saying: "qui quidem ascendunt per contemplationem [...] et descendunt per populorum eruditionem: 'super filium hominis', idest ad honorem Christi: quia, ut dicitur II Cor. IV, v. 5: 'non enim praedicamus nos ipsos, sed Iesum Christum dominum nostrum'".

[62] *In Io* 1:23 §236.

[63] In Thomas's text: "Ipse est qui post me venit, qui ante me factus est, cuius ego non sum dignus ut solvam eius corrigiam calceamenti". Modern editions of the Bible usually leave out 'who ranks ahead of me'.

[64] *In Io* 1:27 §248.

[65] "Quasi dicat: non intelligatis ipsum mihi in dignitate praepositum sicut unus homo praefertur alteri, sed tam excellenter, quod nihil sum in comparatione ad ipsum". *In Io* 1:27 §249.

[66] Thomas refers to Gn 18:27 (Abraham), Jb 42:5 (Job) and Is 40:17 (Isaiah).

from the hide of dead animals, indicates our mortal human nature. Christ assumes this nature, and the strap of the sandal is the union of his divine and human nature. No one can unfasten that strap, that is to say, fully understand and explain it. There is, therefore, in Christ a double mystery: the mystery of his divinity and the mystery of the union of the two natures, neither of which can be fully understood.[67]

The third comparison, at the verse "After me is to come a man who ranks ahead of me because he existed before me" (v. 30), shows the same pattern: Christ is like John in his humanity, even though Christ's humanity is perfect in many ways, he ranks ahead of John in dignity, and is before John in eternity, existing before him.[68] The last part of the comparison is the important part for Thomas because he uses it as an argument against two errors that both deny the divinity of Christ: that of Arius and that of Paul of Samosata, who without qualification, absolutely said that Christ did take his beginning from Mary.

In the commentary on these verses, Thomas portrays John the Baptist as the perfect example of a witness, someone who points away from himself to Christ and his divinity. It is through hearing the testimony of people like John the Baptist that we come to know the divinity of Christ.

The process of conversion

The second point that Thomas pays close attention to when speaking about testimony as a way into getting to know the divinity of Christ is the process of conversion. He explicitly mentions the importance of the process in his commentary on v. 15, the first time John the Baptist's words "He who comes after me, ranks ahead of me" appear in the Gospel. Thomas writes:

> Here we should note that John follows the custom of the good teacher who does not immediately give to his students the most profound and hidden knowledge but gradually proceeds from the things that are manifest to them to more profound teachings; thus, John does not immediately say that Christ is the Son of God, but first ranks Him higher than himself, in order to lead them, hearing this, to higher things.[69]

---

[67] *In Io* 1:27 §250. Albert, *In Io* 1:27 p. 64. Bonaventure, *In Io* 1:27 n. 56. Cf. H. Schoot, *Christ the 'Name' of God*, p. 9-11.

[68] *In Io* 1:30 §260-262.

[69] "Ubi notandum est quod Ioannes servat morem boni magistri qui non statim profundissima et occulta scientie tradit discipulis sed paulatim ex manifestis eis procedit ad profundiora doctrine, sic et Ioannes non statim dicit Christum esse Filium Dei, sed primo pretulit eum sibi ut ex hoc ad altiora duceret audientes". *In Io* 1:15 §196 (text corrected by L. Reid).

The education that John the Baptist has given and continues to give to his disciples is itself somehow midway between the teaching of the law and the prophets (who announced the coming of Christ from afar), and the teaching of Christ himself, which was clear and openly made Himself known.[70]

It belongs to the good teacher that John the Baptist is, that he keeps brief when that is sufficient, and does not order his disciples what to do, but shows them the attraction and lets them draw their own conclusions. Thus John says: “Look! There is the lamb of God”. He does not need to say more because his disciples have been sufficiently instructed to understand his remark, and he does not order them to follow Christ but allows them to understand for themselves that it will be for their benefit if they follow Christ.[71]

Finally, Thomas pays attention to the effect words have on their hearers in the process. Twice John the Baptist describes to his disciples the dignity of Christ, which infinitely surpasses his own. But it is only when John calls Christ “the lamb of God” that his disciples convert and begin to follow Christ. “And this is because we are more moved by Christ’s humility and the sufferings he endured for us”.[72] When John mentions Christ’s divine dignity, his disciples receive important teachings that prepare them for meeting the Lord. But only when John the Baptist mentions Christ’s humility and the mystery of the incarnation, that is when his disciples begin to follow Christ.

The fruit of testimony

Testimony is not an end in itself: it needs to bear fruit. In the *divisio textus* of the stories of the calling of the first disciples in Jn 1:35-51, a pattern can be seen in how Thomas understands the process of testimony to bear fruit. When John the Baptist points his disciples towards Christ, in his *divisio textus* Thomas describes the fruit or result of this testimony in two steps: first, there is the beginning of it coming from John’s testimony at the moment when the disciples start to follow Christ (v. 37); secondly, it is consummated, completed by Christ in the conversation he has with them (v. 38-39).[73] When Andrew preaches the Messiah to his brother Simon Peter, Thomas structures the text according to the same pattern: the result begins with the preaching of Andrew (v. 40-41) and is

---

[70] *In Io* 1:15 §197.

[71] *In Io* 1:36 §283.

[72] “quia humilia, et quae pro nobis passus est Christus, magis movent nos;” *In Io* 1:37 §285.

[73] *In Io* 1:37 §284.

completed when Christ meets Simon (v. 42).[74] Finally, when Philip starts to speak to Nathanael about Christ, the pattern returns for a third time: the testimony begins to bear fruit in the conversation between Nathanael and Philip (v. 45-46) and is consummated by Christ (v. 47-51).[75]

The pattern here is too strong to be coincidental. Apparently, this is what testimony does, according to Thomas: it bears fruit when it brings someone to Christ and finds its fulfilment in Christ acting himself. But the reason Thomas gives for this pattern in the case of John the Baptist and his disciples differs from the latter two cases. In what follows, I will discuss these three examples of testimony bearing fruit.

The reason Thomas gives for Christ to bring the testimony of John the Baptist to completion lies in the relation of the Old Testament to the New. Thomas quotes Heb 7:19: "The law brought nothing to perfection". Thomas reads the question Jesus asks John's disciples as an examination of their intention: "What are you looking for?" When they show their intention, he makes them into more intimate friends and shows that they are worthy to hear him.[76] Thomas sees the two disciples giving a double answer: they call him "Rabbi", teacher, indicating that they want to learn something. In the question they then ask Jesus, they show the second thing they look for in following him: "Where do you live?" They want to come back to him more often.

This is the literal exposition Thomas gives. He adds a double spiritual sense. Read allegorically, God's home is in heaven. When they ask where Christ lives, the disciples want to follow him on his way to his heavenly home. In the tropological sense, the question is put upside down, as if they ask: "What should we do, what qualities should we have, so that you may live in us?" The answer of Christ "Come and see" invites them to experience: in the literal sense, they are invited to join him. In the mystical sense, whether it be the allegorical sense that asked where God lives or the tropological sense that asked how God can come to live in us, it is an invitation to experience as well, because, as Thomas explains, the dwelling of God, whether by grace in this life or in glory, cannot be explained in words, but only be known from experience. Christ, therefore, answers: "Come", by believing and working, "and see", by experiencing and understanding.[77] Both the reference to experience and the paraphrase

---

[74] *In Io* 1:40 §298

[75] *In Io* 1:45 §315.

[76] *In Io* 1:38 §288. In a beautiful article, Ferdinand de Grijs started with Thomas's commentary on Jn 1:35-39 to make some remarks about 'a hermeneutics of Christ:' F. de Grijs, 'Kom en zie waar ik woon!: Aantekeningen bij een hermeneutiek van Christus', in: *Jaarboek Thomas Instituut Utrecht* 17 (1997), p. 49-61.

[77] *In Io* 1:39 §292.

of 'come and see' are implicit quotations from the *Glossa*, but Thomas adds his own interpretation by noting that we can attain this knowledge by experience in four ways, all of them referring to a verse from Scripture that has either the word "come" or the word "see" in it: by doing good works ("When shall I come and appear before the face of God" Ps 42:3), by stillness of our mind ("Be still and see" Ps 46:11), by tasting the divine sweetness, which Thomas understands to be a reference to the sacraments ("Taste and see that the Lord is sweet" Ps 33:9) and by acts of devotion ("Let us lift up our hearts in prayer" Lam 3:41, which Thomas relates to "Feel and see" in Lk 24:39).

The testimony that John the Baptist has given of Jesus has thus come to completion in two parts: his testimony has brought the disciples to Jesus, and the conversation with Jesus has opened the way for the disciples to know him, to begin the learning process that they asked for: they start to learn where Christ lives.

In the case of Andrew, we saw that the coming to fruition of his testimony begins with him bringing his brother Simon to Jesus (v. 41): he does not keep the treasure to himself, nor does he in his preaching to his brother want to bring him closer to himself. Being the good witness that he is, he intends to bring Simon to Jesus. The second step of the coming to fruition of the testimony happens in Jesus's remark: "You are Simon, son of John; you are to be called Kephas (which is translated: Peter)" (v. 42). What happens here, according to Thomas, is that "Christ, wishing to raise him up to faith in his divinity, begins to perform works of divinity, making known things that are hidden".[78] Thomas recognises three secrets here: a secret in the present, that Christ knows his name, his identity; a secret in the past, that Christ knows his history, his ancestry ("son of John"), and a secret in the future: that Christ knows what he will be called in the future, his future destiny. In this part of the commentary, which, as Thomas has indicated in the *divisio textus*, is about how the divinity of Christ is made known through hearing, through testimony, Christ makes his divinity known by making known things that are hidden.

The three-part revelation of hidden things returns in Thomas's commentary on the conversation between Christ and Nathanael in v. 47-51. To Nathanael, Christ makes known hidden matters in the present ("Here is a true Israelite, in whom there is no guile"), hidden matters in the past ("Before Philip called you, I saw you when you were sitting under

[78] "Christus, ad fidem divinitatis eum elevare volens, incipit quae divinitatis sunt opera facere, occulta praedicans". *In Io* 1:42 §303.

the fig tree"), and hidden matters in the future ("You will see greater things than this").[79] The literal sense here, according to Thomas, is that Christ reveals his knowledge of secrets that related only to Nathanael. That Christ knows these shows his divine power, states Thomas, for "The eyes of the Lord are far brighter than the sun" (Sir 23:28).

In a mystical sense which Thomas borrows from Augustine, the fig tree signifies sin. 'Sitting under the fig tree' means under the shadow of sin. The meaning of the verse then becomes: "Before you were called to grace, I saw you, with the eye of mercy; for God's predestination is on people even when they are living in sin".[80] Nathanael is being brought to faith in Christ's divinity by Christ, who reveals hidden things to him: secrets about his person, past, present and future, and secrets about his eternal predestination.

Why this stress on revealing secrets? I think there are two reasons for this. Thomas gives the first in the commentary on v. 47. He states that there are two ways by which people are converted to Christ: some are converted by miracles they have seen and things they have experienced. Others are converted through internal insights, through prophecy and foreknowledge of things that lie hidden in the future. Thomas calls this second way "more efficient" (*efficacior*) than the first because the first might be deceptive. Demons or people under their influence can pretend to do astonishing things, marvels, but predicting the future can only be done by divine power, says Thomas, referring to Is 41:23 ("Tell us what is to come, and we will say that you are gods") and 1 Cor 14:22 ("Prophecies are for those who believe").[81]

The second reason can be found in the commentary on Jn 15:15 ("I have called you friends, for all that I have heard from my Father I have made known to you"). For Thomas, it is a true sign of friendship that friends reveal their secrets to each other. The knowledge Christ receives from the Father is his own being, his divinity. Sharing his knowledge, therefore, means making the disciples *capax Dei*, giving them a share in his divinity.[82]

---

[79] *In Io* 1:47 §321. Cf. §325, §329.

[80] "antequam ad gratiam vocatus esses, ego vidi te, scilicet oculo misericordiae: nam ipsa Dei praedestinatio in hominibus est etiam quando sunt in peccato". *In Io* 1:48 §326 (text corrected by L. Reid).

[81] *In Io* 1:47 §320.

[82] *In Io* 15:15 §2016-2017.

Christ's baptism as testimony
In the testimony of John the Baptist, what he has to say about the baptism of Jesus deserves special attention. First of all, just like in other parts of his testimony, John the Baptist manifests something about Christ. John calls Christ 'The lamb of God' twice in Jn 1. We saw that Thomas in his commentary on the first time this expression is used, focused on the effect it had on the listeners, John's disciples: they had already heard of his dignity, but when they hear of his humility and his future sufferings (and according to Thomas, they understood all this from hearing him called 'lamb of God'), they are moved to follow him.[83]

In his commentary on the second time the expression 'lamb of God' is used, Thomas has a little more to say on what it refers to. According to Thomas, the lamb was the principal sacrifice among the sacrifices offered daily in the temple, whereas the other offers are additions to it. Thomas sees in this a signification of Christ's sacrifice as the principal sacrifice, whereas the martyrs who suffered for their faith have contributed something to the salvation of the faithful in so far as their sacrifice was a participation in that of Christ. The addition "of God" to "lamb" is crucial here, Thomas explains, because it is the divine nature of Christ that gives this sacrifice the power to clean us from our sins and sanctify us.[84] John's witness manifests the divinity of Christ as saving and sanctifying.

John's baptism as testimony
It is not just John testifying what he saw that is relevant to Thomas, however. The event of Jesus's baptism that John evokes is itself a witness. It is during this baptism that the power of the Father was present in the voice, and the Holy Spirit was present in the dove, showing the power and the dignity of Christ all the more. Earlier, Thomas had stated that what Christ added to Moses was that He made known the Trinity: it is at the event of his baptism that this manifestation begins.[85]

The logic with which this happens is the logic of the relations of origin in God, Thomas explains: just as the Son who exists by the Father manifests the Father (Thomas refers to Jn 17:6 "Father, I have manifested your name"), so the Holy Spirit who exists by the Son, manifests the Son.

---

[83] *In Io* 1:37 §285.
[84] *In Io* 1:29 §257. Thomas adds that 'God' can signify both the Son, because it is offered by Christ who is God, or the Father because it is the Father who provided with an oblation that satisfied for sins, but the first interpretation that it is the divinity of Christ that gives this sacrifice the power to cleanse and sanctify is the principal one.
[85] *In Io* 1:31 §266. Cf. *In Io* 1:18 §222.

The baptism of Christ, therefore, manifests the divinity of Christ, the Trinity and the relations of origin in the Triune God.[86]

The role of the Holy Spirit in this is that of making Christ known, Thomas stresses. Against adoptionism, he states that the Holy Spirit descended on Christ not for the benefit of Christ, but for ours, so that the grace of Christ may be known to us.[87] Christ always was full of the Holy Spirit, and therefore the descent of the Spirit on Christ at his baptism cannot be understood in terms of a 'more', of something being added to Christ. That does not mean that the Holy Spirit has nothing to do with the human nature of Christ. Quite the opposite: Christ in his human nature never was not full of the Holy Spirit, so that his baptism should not be read in terms of an addition or change in this respect.

Manifestation is the reason why the appearing Holy Spirit had to be visible and appeared in the form of a dove. Thomas cites several reasons why the Holy Spirit appeared as a dove rather than in some other form and, more importantly, contrasts this appearance with the incarnation of the Word. The Holy Spirit here only becomes visible to manifest, to make known, and for that, the assumption of any suitable visible form suffices: there is not a unity of person of the Holy Spirit and the dove like there is in the incarnation. In the incarnation, there is a unity of person, however, because "the Son did not just appear as a manifestor, but as a Saviour".[88] I have referred to this remark before, but it is in this context of Thomas mentioning the incarnation that it appears, and it is fundamental for his Christology. As Klimczak remarks: "The realism of the incarnation is the foundation and the guarantee for the realism of salvation".[89] Thomas's continuous attentiveness for the human and divine natures of Christ are not the sign of an odd curiosity into the person of Christ but are the foundation to understand that and how we are saved. A quotation from a Christmas sermon of Leo the Great supports this: "It was appropriate that he be God and man: God, in order to provide a remedy; and man, in order to offer an example".[90]

Regarding the divinity of Christ, there is one more remark Thomas makes about the baptism of Christ: that it is his divinity that gives our baptism its power. Christ in his divinity cleanses the soul interiorly from sin, which is signified by the water with which we are baptised. According to

---

[86] *In Io* 1:32 §268.
[87] *In Io* 1:33 §274.
[88] *In Io* 1:32 §270.
[89] P. Klimczak, *Christus Magister*, p. 167.
[90] *In Io* 1:32 §270. The quotation is from Leo the Great, sermon 21.

the same logic, it is only Christ who can institute sacraments: sacraments give invisible grace, which only God can give. Therefore, the baptism of Christ is directly linked to ours: it made known how Christ works in us. "And so John, in stating that the Holy Spirit came down upon Christ, teaches that it is Christ alone who baptises interiorly by his own power".[91]

3. Conclusion

In his *divisio textus* of the Fourth Gospel, Thomas states that Jn 1:14b-51 show the modus by which the divinity of Christ is made known: it is made known by seeing and by hearing. Commenting on Jn 3:11 ("Amen, amen I say to you: we know of what we speak and we bear witness of what we see"), Thomas returns to these two senses: they are essential because a qualified witness bases his testimony on them.[92]

In his discussion of this double way by which the divinity of Christ is made known, three points appeared again and again in Thomas's commentary. The first is the tension between manifestation and the hiddenness of God. Thomas does not solve the tension but keeps it: in Christ, we do get to know God in a new and definitive way. We get to know God as Father, Son and Holy Spirit. However, that knowledge is knowledge of a mystery, just as both the divinity of Christ and the unity of the divine and human nature in Christ remain incomprehensible to us.

The second point is Thomas's attentiveness to process. Both when he speaks about salvation history, about what was revealed to Moses and what has been revealed in the Word incarnate, and when he speaks about the calling of the first disciples, Thomas, like a good teacher, has a sensitivity for the process that education is, and recognises it in Scripture.

Finally, what Thomas underscores again and again in this part of the commentary is the relation between Christology and soteriology, between manifestation and salvation. Behind the stress on the divinity of Christ is not a matter of curiosity in the person of Christ but a longing to understand the salvific history of Christ.

Pim Valkenberg wrote about the section about the mysteries of the life of Christ in the third part of *Summa Theologiae*: "The reason why Aquinas inserted such a section in his *Summa*, absent in his earlier systematic works, is that his ongoing reading and explaining of Scripture

---

[91] "Et ideo didicit Ioannes per hoc quod Spiritus Sanctus descendit super eum, quod Christus solus interius est qui sua virtute baptizat". *In Io* 1:33 §276 (text corrected by L. Reid).

[92] *In Io* 3:11 §462.

as *Magister in sacra pagina* taught him to concentrate more on the soteriological meaning of the life of Christ".[93] That development can be seen in Thomas's commentary on Jn 1, which gives in a nutshell what will be developed in the subsequent chapters of the commentary. To these chapters we now turn.

93 P. Valkenberg, 'Scripture', in: P. McCosker, D. Turner (eds.), *The Cambridge Companion to the Summa Theologiae*, Cambridge, Cambridge University Press, 2016, p. 48-61, here p. 58.

CHAPTER 5
THE DIVINITY OF CHRIST

In previous chapters, we have analysed Thomas's commentary on Jn 1 and presented it as the commentary on the whole of the Gospel in a nutshell. That hypothesis needs to be tested in this last chapter.

At the beginning of the commentary on Jn 2, Thomas gives his *divisio textus* for the rest of the Gospel:

> Above, the Evangelist showed the dignity of the incarnate Word and gave various evidence for it. Now he begins to relate the effects and actions by which the divinity of the incarnate Word was made known to the world. First, he tells the things Christ did, while living in the world, that show his divinity. Secondly, he tells how Christ showed his divinity while dying; and this from chapter twelve on.[1]

In this chapter, we will take this *divisio textus* as our main guide by looking at the *divisio textus* of Jn 3-11 and how it directs Thomas's focus on the divinity of Christ in these chapters. We will look at the commentary on Jn 12-21 by studying the interpretation Thomas gives in these chapters of the Johannine concept of glorification.[2]

The *divisio textus* of Jn 3-11 and Thomas's treatment of glorification in the commentary on Jn 12-21 will provide us with good opportunities to test and deepen the hypotheses about the importance of

---

[1] "Supra Evangelista ostendit dignitatem verbi incarnati, et evidentiam eius multipliciter; hic consequenter incipit determinare de effectibus et operibus quibus manifestata est mundo divinitas verbi incarnati, et primo narrat ea quae Christus fecit in mundo vivendo, ad manifestationem suae divinitatis; secundo quomodo Christus suam divinitatem demonstravit moriendo; et hoc a XII cap. et ultra". *In Io* 2:1 §335.

[2] I will not go into the commentary on Jn 2, here. In his *divisio textus*, Thomas makes clear that he reads Jn 2 as showing the divinity of Christ in relation to the power He had over nature. From Jn 3 onwards, the Gospel shows the divinity of Christ in relation to the effects of grace: *In Io* 2:1 §335. This *divisio textus* makes clear that Thomas gives an interpretation of Jn 2 in which two instances of Christ's dominion over nature are central: the changing of water into wine and Christ's future resurrection, signified in the cleansing of the temple. Cf. S. Mangnus, 'On Heresies and Hermeneutics: Thomas Aquinas on John 2', in: A. Ghisalberti, A. Petagine, R. Rizzello (eds.), *Letture e interpretazioni di Tommaso d'Aquino oggi: Cantieri aperti*, Torino, Annali Chieresi, 2005, p. 59-68.

the *divisio textus* and the idea that the commentary on Jn 1 is the commentary in a nutshell, while following the general division Thomas gives of the commentary on Jn 2-21. There is another topic pertinent to our study, however, that Thomas emphasizes throughout the whole of the commentary: the relation of the Son to the Father. That Thomas returns to it throughout the commentary is unsurprising, because it is a theme that John the evangelist returns to throughout his Gospel. For our study, this topic is pertinent since for Thomas the divinity of Christ is based on the equality of the Father and the Son. However, in the Fourth Gospel, there are texts that suggest a subordination of the Son to the Father. In commenting on these texts, Thomas suggests two strategies for dealing with this suggestion of inferiority in the Son *vis à vis* the Father. We will look into Thomas's remarks on the relation of the Son to the Father in between the two sections that deal with the commentary on Jn 3-11 and Jn 12-21 respectively.

1. Spiritual Regeneration and Gifts

In Thomas's interpretation of the fourth Gospel, Jn 3-11 forms a textual unity. We have seen before how he structures this part of the Gospel in his *divisio textus*: following Jn 2, which according to Thomas treats of the power of Christ's divinity over nature, these chapters show Christ's divine power in relation to our reformation by grace, which Thomas calls the evangelist's 'principal subject'.[3] This reformation by grace, Thomas writes, happens through spiritual regeneration and through the conferring of gifts to those who are regenerated. This then gives the subdivision of Jn 3-11: Jn 3-4 speak of spiritual regeneration, whereas in Jn 5-11 the gifts are discussed. Thomas then further subdivides these two parts by saying that Jn 3 treats spiritual regeneration in relation to the Jews and Jn 4 in relation to the gentiles.[4] Thomas takes the notion that parents give three things to their children, life, food and education, to subdivide Jn 5-11: Christ gives to those who are spiritually reborn spiritual life, spiritual food and spiritual education. This leads Thomas to the *divisio textus* that Jn 5 considers spiritual life, Jn 6 spiritual food, and Jn 7-11 spiritual teaching.[5]

[3] "De qua principaliter intendit". *In Io* 3:1 §423 (text corrected by L. Reid).
[4] *In Io* 3:1 §423.
[5] *In Io* 5:1 §699.

As is usual with *divisones textus*, this structure is original: Albert and Bonaventure give a different structure for this part of the Gospel.[6] As such, it gives an important insight in Thomas's interpretation of this part of the Gospel. Thomas interprets these chapters on what could be called the public life of Christ as a theological model for how the divine Word works in the faithful. 'Theological model' should not be interpreted here as a contrast to a historical interpretation of the Gospel. Thomas's interpretation is focused neither on arguing for nor against the historical accuracy of the Gospel account: he seems to take that for granted, sometimes reproduces patristic harmonizations of the Gospels to account for differences between them, predominantly from Augustine's *De consensu Evangelistarum*. Apart from that, however, the historical accuracy is not a theme with which Thomas is very much occupied in the commentary on John.

The public life of Jesus is a theological model in the sense that what John describes as the events of the public life of Jesus Christ, shows us how the divine Word works in the life of every believer. This is Thomas's main interest in these chapters from the fourth Gospel: they show us, not just how Jesus Christ worked in the years that, according to John's chronology, passed by between Jesus meeting Nicodemus by night (Jn 3:2) and the day on which the Pharisees and chief priests started to plan to put him to death (Jn 11:53), but how the Word incarnate, the second person of the Trinity, works in the life of every believer in every time.

It is the *divisio textus* of the commentary that guides the reader towards this systematic interpretation of the Fourth Gospel. The theological question behind these chapters for Thomas seems to be: how does the grace of the divine Word reform us? The answer the fourth Gospel gives, according to Thomas, is: it reforms us through spiritual regeneration, first, and, second, through the giving of gifts to those thus reformed afterwards. The conversations Jesus has with Nicodemus and the Samaritan woman at the well on water and the Spirit show the first;

---

[6] Bonaventure treats Jn 1:43-11:46 under the heading of the witness that Christ gives of himself, and then subdivides Jn 1:43-4:54 according to the different people addressed by Christ (1:43 - 4) and according to the manifestation of the Word: as healer (Jn 5), conserver (Jn 6), director (Jn 7-10) and vivifier (Jn 11). Cf. Bonaventure, *In Io* 11:43, n. 89 and *In Io* 5:1 n. 1.
The structure Albert gives of Jn 2-11 is closer to that of Thomas. He reads Jn 2-11 as showing the different aspects of the manifestation of the Word: his power in Jn 2-6, his enlightenment as wisdom in Jn 7-10. According to Albert these two then lead to a conclusion of the Word being life-giving in Jn 11. Cf. Albert, *In Io* 2:1, p. 87.

the spiritual life, spiritual food and spiritual teaching Jesus is shown to give in Jn 5-11, show the second.

Jn 3-4: spiritual regeneration

Thomas reads Jn 3 as an explanation of what spiritual regeneration is. He mentions a threefold spiritual regeneration. There was a spiritual regeneration in the Old Law, but it was symbolic and imperfect. In the new Law, there is an evident spiritual regeneration, although imperfect as well: through baptism we are renewed inwardly, through grace, but not outwardly. Therefore we can and do see the kingdom of God and the mysteries of eternal salvation, but imperfectly. Perfect regeneration happens *in patria*, in heaven, when we will be renewed both inwardly and outwardly.[7]

It is clear that under the New Law, spiritual regeneration is closely related to the sacrament of baptism, so much so that Thomas sometimes seems to use the terms as synonyms.[8] More often, it seems that Thomas uses the term 'spiritual regeneration' to describe the effect the sacrament of baptism has on those who receive it, what it does to someone.[9] In that sense, spiritual regeneration is to be understood as the *res tantum* of the sacrament of baptism.[10]

In the commentary on John 3, Thomas gives an explanation of spiritual regeneration which boils down to three questions: what the need for it is, what its quality is, and what its cause.[11] These three questions focus on us, the receivers of grace, on the Holy Spirit, and on Christ, respectively.

Thomas describes our need for spiritual regeneration by stating that without it, one cannot know the secrets of divinity, or in the words of John, 'Unless one is born again, he cannot see the kingdom of God' (Jn 3:3). In this verse, Thomas explains, Christ is gently leading Nicodemus to a deeper comprehension of himself with the analogy of seeing: just as physically we can see bodily things, so in our spiritual life there is a form of spiritual vision. This vision, Thomas states, comes through the Holy

---

[7] *In Io* 3:3 §433.

[8] See e.g. *STh* III q. 66 a. 2c: "Baptismus, qui est spiritualis regeneratio…"

[9] See e.g. *STh* III q. 68 a. 9 ad 1: "regeneratio spiritualis, quae fit per baptismum, quodammodo similis est nativitati carnali…"

[10] Cf. *STh* III q. 66 a. 1c. There Thomas states that inward justification (*iustificatio interior*) is the *res tantum* of the sacrament of baptism. I take it that *iustificatio interior* and *spiritualis regeneratio* are different descriptions of the same reality.

[11] This is the *divisio textus* of the commentary on Jn 3:1-21, as Thomas gives it in *In Io* 3:1 §423. Thomas calls the rest of the chapter (Jn 3:22-36) "Christ completes what he taught by deeds", putting the stress on Christ as one who baptizes.

Spirit; and since the Holy Spirit is given through spiritual regeneration, that regeneration is necessary to see God.[12]

Why does spiritual regeneration come through the Spirit? This is the second question Thomas mentions, and it focusses on the Spirit. The answer to this question is what Thomas calls the 'quality' (*qualitas*) of spiritual regeneration. Regeneration means being generated in the likeness of the one generating, that is to say: regeneration is generation as children of God, in the likeness of the Son of God. Spiritual regeneration means receiving the likeness of Christ by sharing in his Spirit. How does this happen? Being made like the true Son comes about by us having his Spirit. Someone who receives the Holy Spirit, is regenerated in the likeness of the Son of God by receiving His Spirit. We become Christlike, and therefore children of God whose Son He is, by receiving His Spirit. Therefore, Thomas concludes, spiritual regeneration comes from the Spirit.[13]

Finally Thomas mentions a twofold cause for spiritual regeneration: the incarnation and the passion of Christ. Thomas states that spiritual regeneration has a hidden source and a hidden end: it has his origin in God and leads us to God. By descending from heaven, Christ opened the way for us to participate in the movement back to heaven through the Holy Spirit.[14] Spiritual regeneration is the fruit of the passion in the sense that believing in the crucified Christ frees from sin, and preserves for eternal life.[15]

In the commentary on Jn 4 Thomas begins with stating that the grace of spiritual regeneration is given to the gentiles through teaching and through miracles.[16] The teaching shows the different elements at play when spiritual regeneration is received: the gift, the way it is given, and the giver. Thomas's exposition on these three elements shows that it is another way of concentrating on the three who are involved in the process of spiritual regeneration: the Holy Spirit, us and Christ. In other words, what Thomas does here is parallel to what he did in the commentary on Jn 3: what spiritual regeneration is, is clarified by relating it to the Holy Spirit, to Christ, and to us.

[12] *In Io* 3:3 §431-432.
[13] *In Io* 3:5 §442.
[14] *In Io* 3:13 §468.
[15] *In Io* 3:15 §475.
[16] *In Io* 4:1 §549.

The gift, living water signifies the grace of the Holy Spirit.[17] Comparing spiritual water as the grace of the Holy Spirit with natural water, Thomas notes the different effects natural and spiritual water have on our natural and spiritual thirsts, respectively. When we drink natural water, we will thirst again after a while: the natural effect of quenching thirst does not last. The effect of spiritual water does not end, because it has an eternal cause, which is the Holy Spirit. In another way, living water does produce thirst, however: when we receive the grace that is spiritual water in this life, we receive it imperfectly, and we thirst for more, a thirst that will be quenched in glory. In that sense, while the direction of natural water is to fall downwards, the direction of spiritual water is upwards: it leaps up inside us like a fountain and leads us to God.[18]

In the commentary on Jn 3, the question Thomas discussed regarding us was why we need spiritual regeneration. In the commentary on Jn 4, Thomas discusses the question how we obtain it. Thomas replies: "In the case of adults, living water, i.e. grace, is obtained by desiring it, i.e., by asking".[19] This asking, Thomas interprets, is what prayer is.[20] The desire, and the prayer that flows from it, is caused by two things, Thomas says: a knowledge of the good to be desired and a knowledge of the giver. In the conversation with the Samaritan woman, Jesus gives both the knowledge of the good to be desired, and the knowledge of the giver to her, when he says: "If you knew the gift of God, and realized who it is who says to you, 'Give me a drink', you perhaps would have asked him,

---

[17] *In Io* 4:10 §577. In the commentary on Jn 3, Thomas had already given three reasons why water is necessary for our spiritual regeneration. In order that our bodies may be regenerated and not just our souls, water is involved to regenerate our bodies. Secondly, there is an epistemological reason: we know spiritual things through sensible things: the washing and cleansing of the water shows us that through baptism we are washed and cleansed in a spiritual way. And finally, Thomas gives a sacramental reason: since the sacraments have their efficacy from the power of the incarnate Word, it is fitting that at baptism, we are submerged in water just as Christ was buried in the earth for three days: *In Io* 3:5 §433.

[18] *In Io* 4:13-14 §586-587. The comparisons Thomas makes between natural and spiritual water are all traditional; the question on whether this water does or does not stop us from becoming thirsty again, for example, a question caused by the contrast between Jn 4:14 (which suggests that we will no longer thirst) and Sir 24:29 (which suggests that we will), can be found both in the commentaries of Albert and Bonaventure.

[19] "ad habendum aquam vivam, idest gratiam, in adultis per desiderium pervenitur, idest per petitionem". *In Io* 4:10 §578.

[20] *In Io* 4:19 §595.

that he give you living water" (Jn 4:10).[21] The desire, and the prayer that flows from it, is itself already a gift of God. This prayer, in order for it to be true worship, should be 'in spirit and truth': it needs to be spiritual, and it needs to be truthful in two senses: united to the truth of faith, and without pretense or hypocrisy. It is this prayer, which unites the fervor of love, the truth of faith and a correct intention, that fits God, who is spirit and truth.[22]

Finally, after the gift of water (the grace of the Holy Spirit) and the way we achieve it (through prayer), there is the giver of the gift, Christ. Thomas is brief here. When the Samaritan woman confesses her belief in the coming Messiah, Jesus replies 'I who speak to you am he' (Jn 4:26). Thomas's exposition here is not so much about the person of Christ, but about the way he makes himself known. To the Samaritan woman he did this gradually. If he had done so all at once, the woman might have thought he spoke out of vainglory, Thomas remarks. Instead what He did was take time, go step by step in a process of leading her to knowledge of himself. Thomas contrasts this to the Pharisees who asked Jesus whether he was the Christ (Jn 10:24). To them, Jesus does not reveal himself, because their intention is not to learn, but to test him.[23]

In my presentation of the commentary on Jn 3 and 4 so far, I have focused on what Thomas in his *divisio textus* points towards as the main topics under discussion in the conversations Jesus has with Nicodemus and the Samaritan woman at the well, respectively. Thomas interprets Jn 3:22-36 ('Jesus baptises') and Jn 4:43-54 ('the future conversion of the gentiles through miracles') as actions that correlate with the teaching Jesus has given in these respective chapters. [24] That does not make them unimportant, as if they were 'mere' external confirmations: Thomas often finds theologically interesting aspects in John's depiction of these actions of Christ, or in the conversations and speeches that follow them.[25] More

[21] *In Io* 4:10 §579.

[22] *In Io* 4:23 §611 and *In Io* 4:24 §615.

[23] *In Io* 4:26 §619.

[24] I have argued elsewhere that for Thomas, just as with the Samaritan woman at the well in Jn 4:1-42, Jesus gives his teaching to the royal official in Jn 4:43-54 gradually: both stories are (among other things) stories of how faith does grow with the gradual teaching Christ gives. Cf. S. Mangnus, 'When Thomas reads a Story…: Aquinas on Jn 4,43-54 and its Implications for reading his Biblical Commentaries', in: *Jaarboek Thomas Instituut Utrecht 2003* (2004), p. 9-29.

[25] An example of this from the commentary on Jn 3 is Thomas's interpretation of 'God does not bestow the Spirit in fractions' (Jn 3:34) which we have discussed before.

importantly, at several points in the commentary Thomas remarks how in John words and signs always go together, and together form the teaching that Christ gives.[26] There are two reasons for this. The first is epistemological: we learn about invisible things through visible ones. And so what is invisible is made known through the visible.[27] Secondly, Thomas states that salutary grace is given to the gentiles in two ways: through teaching and through miracles. John confirms that by showing these two together.[28] In order for the knowledge of God's salvation in Christ to reach all people, Christ does all these things.

In the previous chapters, I have showed the Trinitarian character of Thomas's interpretation of John 1. This Trinitarian starting point forms the basis for Thomas's reading of Jn 3-4, which speak of what Thomas calls the divine power of Christ in relation to our reformation by grace,[29] how Christ in his divinity brings us to new life through the grace of baptism. The structure that the *divisio textus* offers shows that Thomas reads Jn 3-4 in a Trinitarian way, concentrating in both chapters on us, receivers of grace, on the Holy Spirit, and on Christ.

Regarding us, we need to be reborn spiritually, because without it, human beings cannot see God. The way we receive it is through prayer, which for Thomas in this context is petitionary prayer.

Regarding the Holy Spirit, spiritual regeneration means we receive the Holy Spirit, and become children of God, in the likeness of the Son, because we share in His Spirit. Receiving the Spirit is sufficient, because its effects remain; it deepens our thirst for God, and leads us upwards toward Him.

Regarding Christ, the origin and goal of our spiritual regeneration is hidden in God: the incarnation of the Son of God has opened the way for us to God, while our faith in the passion of Christ frees us from sin and preserves us on the way back to God. In order for us to be able to receive this faith, Christ gently makes himself known to us, sometimes,

---

[26] Thomas makes the remark about how in John teaching and some visible action often go together in *In Io* 5:1 §699, and subsequently uses this as recurring principle for his *divisio textus* of Jn 5-11: Jn 5, on spiritual life, is divided that way (*In Io* 5:1 §699), Jn 6 on spiritual food is (*In Io* 6:1 §838), and in the chapters on spiritual teaching (Jn 7-11) it occurs twice: In the division of the chapters on the enlightening character of that teaching in Jn 8-9 (*In Io* 8:1 §1118) and in those on the lifegiving character of teaching in Jn 10-11 (*In Io* 10:1 §1364).

[27] *In Io* 5:1 §699.

[28] *In Io* 4:1 §549.

[29] *In Io* 3:1 §423.

as with the Samaritan woman, gradually. This is the structure of Thomas's commentary on Jn 3-4.

This structure shows Thomas's interpretation of Jn 3-4 as a study in *oikonomia.* Starting from the conversations Jesus has with Nicodemus and the Samaritan woman in Jn 3-4, Thomas shows via his *divisio textus* a model of the work of the triune God in the lives of believers. In the commentary on Jn 1 Thomas had already proposed his reading of the divinity of Christ as the underlying theme of the fourth Gospel, both as to its meaning in terms of *theologia,* the understanding of Father, Son and Holy Spirit, and in terms of *oikonomia,* the salvific work of the triune God. In the commentary on Jn 3-4 he elaborates and deepens this reading of the Fourth Gospel with regard to our fundamental relationship with God through Christ, in the Spirit that is opened up in baptism.

Jn 5-11: light and life

With regard to the commentary on Jn 5-11, I will limit my reading to an interpretation of the *divisio textus*. We have seen that Thomas grounds his *divisio textus* of these chapters in what he sees as the three things parents give to their children. Just as parents give their children life, food and instruction, so those who are spiritually reborn receive from Christ spiritual life (Jn 5), spiritual food (Jn 6) and spiritual teaching (Jn 7-11).[30] All three gifts are to be understood as spiritual gifts, given in the Spirit.

Thomas not only stresses that the gifts are spiritual gifts, he also calls them life-giving. For the first gift, the gift of spiritual life, this sounds tautological. Thomas explains it in the commentary on Jn 5:20-23, which for him is the heart of the chapter, in the sense that he develops the ways that Christ gives life, here. Thomas mentions several ways: Christ gives life through the miracles of his disciples, in the sense that what the members of his body do, can be seen as something that Christ does. Thomas refers here to the disciples's miracles that are recounted in the book of Acts. Christ gave life to some by raising them from the death during his lifetime, by the life-giving power that is in him according to his divine nature. Finally, Christ gives life by the resurrection of the bodies, which happens through Christ in his human nature, as judge.[31]

That the spiritual food that is given to the spiritually regenerated, is life-giving, is something Thomas recognizes in Jn 6:27: "Do not work for the food that perishes, but for that which endures to eternal life". The

[30] *In Io* 5:1 §699.
[31] *In Io* 5:20b-23 §755-769.

spiritual food Christ gives to those who are spiritually regenerated, is eternal life.[32]

In the chapters on spiritual teaching, Jn 7-11, Thomas reads Jn 7 as a chapter on the origin of that teaching. Jn 8-11 are about the power of the teaching of Christ, which according to Thomas, is twofold: it has the power to enlighten and to give life. Both of these are shown by Christ by words and by a miracle, which leads him to structure these chapters as speaking of the teaching of Christ concerning Christ's power to enlighten (Jn 8), and the confirmation of that by the action of giving sight to one physically blind (Jn 9), followed by the teaching on his life-giving power (Jn 10) and the confirmation of that teaching with the miracle of the raising of Lazarus (Jn 11).[33]

When he presents his *divisio textus* for Jn 8-11, Thomas gives a reason for it:

> The doctrine of Christ has the power both to enlighten and to give life, because his words are spirit and life.[34]

'His words are spirit and life' of course is a reference to Jn 6:64. Spirit, light, life-giving in the sense of creating and recreating, these are the key words of the commentary on Jn 1 that we have been discussing when we studied the commentary on Jn 1 in the preceding chapters. That chapter is for Thomas the Gospel in a nutshell, and the *divisio textus* of Jn 5-11 shows how they are the key words that he further develops while studying these chapters.

In conclusion: the structure Thomas gives to his commentary is Trinitarian in character. It points his readers towards a deeper understanding of the work of Christ and the Spirit in the lives of the faithful, and further develops the concepts of life and light, concepts that we saw were keys to understanding the commentary on Jn 1.

2. Son of the Father

In my reading of the commentary on Jn 1, we have seen that Thomas discusses the divinity of Christ in relation to the divinity of the Father primarily in the commentary of the first few verses of Jn 1. As John returns often to the topic of the relation of the Son to the Father in his Gospel, it is one of the themes Thomas develops throughout the

---

[32] *In Io* 6:26-27 §893-896.

[33] *In Io* 8:1 §1118; *In Io* 9:1 §1293; *In Io* 10:1 §1364; *In Io* 11:1 §1471.

[34] "Habet autem doctrina Christi virtutem illuminativam et vivificativam, quia verba eius spiritus et vita sunt". *In Io* 8:1 §1118.

commentary. He does this in many ways: in this section, I will present what seem to me to be the most important points. In so doing, I will show that and how the topic of the relationship of the Son to the Father is an important example of something that Thomas presents in a nutshell in the commentary on Jn 1, and subsequently develops in the rest of the commentary.

The main point Thomas stresses again and again in the commentary about the relation of the Father and the Son is their equality, whether it is discussed in terms of co-eternity, equality of power, or equal greatness. This corresponds to what according to Thomas is the main subject of the Fourth Gospel: the divinity of Christ. The consideration given to the equality of the Father and the Son has as its goal to manifest the divinity of Christ, which is the characteristic aim of the Gospel of John, according to Thomas.

At several points in the commentary, this stress on the equality between the Father and Son is developed in a soteriological sense. Commenting on Jn 17:21 ("that they may all be one; even as you, Father, are in me, and I in you, that they also may be in us, so that the world may believe that you have sent me") Thomas states that there is a twofold unity of the Father and the Son: a unity of essence and a unity of love. Human beings do not share in the unity of essence. We do, however, share in the unity of God's love, not in an equal way, but through a remote likeness. Our unity in love with God bears fruit: it causes the world to believe. "Because if my disciples are one, the world may believe that the teaching I gave to them is from you, and know that you have sent me. For God is a cause of peace, not of contentions".[35]

What Thomas explains here in terms of the love of the Father and the Son, is developed elsewhere with regard to knowledge as well. Commenting on Jn 10:15 ("as the Father knows me and I know the Father; and I lay down my life for the sheep") Thomas comments that the 'as' in this verse can be explained in two ways. It can suggest a similarity in knowledge, and Thomas suggests such knowledge can be given to a creature, referring to St. Paul: "I shall know, even as I am known" (1 Cor 13:12). In another way, the 'as' in the verse in Jn can suggest not just a similarity, but a proper equality in knowledge. Because this knowledge of the Father is comprehensive knowledge, it is a knowledge that is proper to the Son only. Thomas suggests that it is to this comprehensive knowledge that the Gospel of Matthew refers when Jesus in that Gospel says: "No one knows the Son except the Father, and no one knows the

[35] *In Io* 13:21 §2239-2241. Cf. *In Io* 17,11 §2214.

Father except the Son" (Mt 11:27).[36] It is part of this comprehensive knowledge that only the Son has of the Father to know the will of the Father that the Son should die for the salvation of the human race, Thomas argues.[37] I will not go deeper into this here, but leave it as an example where Thomas develops the equality of the Father and the Son in terms of knowledge, and relates that to soteriology.

Another example of the link between Thomas's theology of the relation of the Father and the Son and soteriology can be found in the commentary on Jn 6:38-40. Thomas starts by remarking that there are two wills in Christ, a human and a divine will. The divine will of the Son is the same as the will of the Father. To this divine will Christ subordinated his human will, something which we pray for for ourselves as well when we pray the Our Father: 'Thy will be done'. It is the will of the Father that none of those who come to Christ are lost; he desires their salvation. The reason why the Father wills to bring men to life, is that He is the fountain of life: "For it is the will of my Father, who sent me, that every one who sees the Son and believes in him, should have eternal life. And I will raise him up on the last day" (Jn 6:40). Thomas carefully unpacks this verse, stating that seeing Christ in his humanity leads to the faith that is the first step towards seeing the divine essence that the Father, the Son (and the Holy Spirit) share.[38] Again, the one divine nature and the distinction between Father and Son are linked by Thomas to human salvation. Texts like these show how closely linked Trinitarian theology and soteriology are, they show the *nexus mysteriorum* in a remarkable way.

Since the divinity of Christ for Thomas is based on the equality of the Father and the Son, the most problematic biblical texts in this regard are texts that suggest a subordination of the Son to the Father: these texts seem the strongest biblical argument for Arianism. Thomas discusses the question of how to interpret these texts in the commentary on Jn 5:19 ("The Son cannot do anything of himself, but only what he sees the Father doing"). Thomas presents two strategies for dealing with texts from Scripture which suggest inferiority in the Son with regard to the Father. The first possibility is to apply the text to Christ's assumed, human nature, but not to his divine nature. This is the way Thomas interprets "The Father

[36] In his commentary on Mt 11:27, Thomas argues that the mutual knowledge between Father and Son is based on the consubstantiality of the persons in God: it is because the Father, the Son (and the Holy Spirit, Thomas adds) share in the one divine nature that exceeds all our understanding, that they know each other with perfect knowledge. *In Mt* 11:27 §965-966.

[37] *In Io* 10:15 §1414.

[38] *In Io* 6:38-40 §923-928.

is greater than I" in Jn 14:28.[39] That however is not possible as an interpretation of "the Son cannot do anything of himself but only what he sees the Father doing" (Jn 5:19) because it would either mean that the Father had done previously what Christ in his human nature did (like walking on water), or it would mean that Christ in his human nature does what the Father had done before him (like creating the world), both of which are impossible. The first strategy, to explain with regard to Christ's human nature those verses that seem to imply inferiority in the Son fails in this case.[40]

The second strategy available is to understand statements that seem to imply inferiority by referring them to the eternal procession of the Son from the Father. Persons in God are to be distinguished according to their relations, and in this respect there is a primacy of the Father as generating the Son, and the Son as having his origin in the Father. As Aquinas states: 'For although the Son is equal to the Father in all things, he receives all these things from the Father in an eternal begetting. But the Father gets these from no one, for he is unbegotten'.[41] That is the better explanation of Jn 5:19: the Son receives his being (*esse*) from the Father, which is the reason to say 'he cannot do anything of himself'. This however has to be read without implying inequality. Read this way, the verse can be directed against a Sabellian Christology, because it states the difference between Father and Son.[42]

Having thus interpreted Jn 5:19a as referring to the origin of Christ's power, Thomas understands v. 19b ("For whatever the Father does, the Son does likewise") as referring to the greatness of Christ's life-giving power. He relates it to Jn 1:3 ("All things were made through him") in stating that limitation should be excluded in understanding Christ's power: to all things to which the Father's power extends, the Son's power extends as well. It excludes difference as well: there is no activity that the Son does, that the Father does not do. Finally, it excludes imperfection: that the Son comes forth from the Father, cannot be read as if the Father uses the divine Word as an imperfect instrumental agent: the same power with which the Father acts, is in the Son as well.[43]

Thomas gives three explanations of the greatness of Christ's power: that it should exclude limitation, difference and imperfection. It is

---

[39] *In Io* 14:28 §1970.
[40] *In Io* 5:19 §746.
[41] *In Io* 5:19 §747.
[42] *In Io* 5:19 §749.
[43] *In Io* 5:19 §752.

worth noting that all three these explanations are negative explanations, in the sense that they do not give a positive description of Christ's divine nature. Rather they exclude what does not fit our speaking of the divine nature in Christ. This is a recurring theme in the commentary: speaking of the divinity of Christ means speaking of the divine mystery, means taking away from our speech about (the divine) Christ what is human and knowable to us.

Commenting on the question of Philip in Jn 14:8 ("Show us the Father, and we shall be satisfied") Thomas asks what is wrong with Philip's wish: he had seen the Son, and if one has seen a picture, should one really be rebuked for wanting to see the thing pictured? Thomas replies with a remark by Chrysostom that the problem behind Philip's request is that he had seen the Son with his physical eyes only, and now wished to see the Father in the same way. Philip had not seen the Son in his divine nature with his bodily eyes, however, and so the wish to see the Father in that way is a wrongly directed desire. The Son in his divine nature remains unseeable with bodily eyes, and both the divinity of Christ and the unity of the two natures in Christ remain utter mystery: Thomas's Christology is a negative Christology.[44]

Commenting on Jn 8:28-29 ("Then you will understand that I AM, and that I do nothing of myself; but as the Father taught me, so I speak. He who sent me is with me; he has not deserted me, because I always do what is pleasing to him"), Thomas gives an exposition of this verse that is his teaching on the relation of the Father and the Son in a nutshell. He writes that the text shows three things that must be believed about Christ. The first is the greatness of his divinity, which can be seen in Christ using the name 'I am' for himself. Thomas explains that it means that Christ has the divine nature, and that it was he who said to Moses: "I am who I am" (Ex 3:14). A stronger statement both of the divinity of Christ and of the unity of the Father and the Son is hard to imagine.

Arianism thus out of the way, the other main misunderstanding of the divinity of Christ, Sabellianism, is immediately treated after this: in order that the distinction between the persons is not overlooked, Christ teaches: "I do nothing of myself, but as the Father taught me, so I speak", which shows his origin in the Father both in respect to what the Son does, and in respect to what he teaches, interpreting "as the Father taught me" as giving the Son knowledge by generating him as one who knows. And

---

[44] *In Io* 14:8 §1889. For Thomas's Christology as 'negative Christology', cf. H.J.M. Schoot, *Christ the 'Name' of God: Thomas Aquinas on Naming Christ*, Leuven, Peeters, 1993.

because the nature of divine truth is simple, for the Son to exist is for him to know.

Finally, the distinction between the Father and the Son being established, Thomas reads the tekst as carefully excluding all separation between the Father and the Son: "He who sent me, the Father, is with me", by a unity of essence and of love. The Father sends, and the Son is sent, but the incarnation does not imply a separation.[45]

In the commentary on John 1, the relation between the first and the second person of the Trinity was mainly discussed in the commentary on the first verses, as a theology of the Word and of the person who speaks the Word. With the relation of Jesus to the Father being such an important, recurring theme in the rest of the fourth Gospel, it is not surprising that Thomas returns to it in the commentary often as well. What is primarily developed is the understanding of the equality, as a shorthand for understanding the divinity of the Son, and the understanding of texts that seem to imply subordination and therefore undermine the divinity of the Son.

3. Glorification

The divinity of Christ, the matter of the fourth Gospel according to Thomas, is present as a constant theme discussed and reflected upon in Thomas's commentary: in the commentary on every chapter one finds remarks on how the Gospel enlightens our understanding of the divine nature of Christ. There is one exception, however: the divinity of Christ is almost completely absent as a theme in Thomas's commentary on Jn 18-19, the passion narrative.[46]

This might be considered unsurprising. The passion narrative is after all the part of the Gospel that speaks of the suffering and death of Christ, something that pertains to his human, not his divine nature.[47] On the other hand, we have seen that in his *divisio textus* of the Gospel,

---

[45] *In Io* 8:28-29 §1192.

[46] Almost absent: there are brief references to the divinity of Christ, e.g. in the commentary on the accusation the Jews bring before Pilate 'He has made himself the Son of God' (Jn 19:7), where Thomas comments that not only was doing this not against the law, but that Christ had every reason to do so because he was the Son of God by nature (*In Io* 19:7 §2387). Remarks like these, however, are brief references, rather than the more in depth reflections one finds in the other chapters of the commentary.

[47] For the relation between Christ crucified and the possible suffering of God, cf. M.-R. Hoogland, *God, Passion and Power: Thomas Aquinas on Christ Crucified and the Almightiness of God*, Leuven, Peeters, 2003.

Thomas states that in Jn 12-21 John tells his readers how Christ 'showed his divinity while dying'.[48] If that is the case, then why does Thomas not discuss it during his exposition of the passion narrative?

In this section, I want to suggest that Thomas does discuss the divinity of Christ with regard to the passion in the commentary. He does it not in commenting on the passion narrative, however, but in the remarks he makes at several places in the commentary about the Johannine concept of glorification.

What does glorification mean, according to Thomas? In general, Thomas is happy with the definition Ambrose gave of glory: 'clear knowledge accompanied by praise' (*clara cum laude notitia*): Thomas cites this definition in many of his works, and in the commentary on John he cites it no less than four times, when he discusses the important texts about glorification in the Gospel: Jn 8:54 ("It is my Father who glorifies me"), Jn 13:31 ("Now is the Son of man glorified and in him God is glorified"), and Jn 17:1 ("Father, the hour has come; glorify your Son that the Son may glorify you").[49]

The definition of Ambrose has two elements. The one Thomas stresses the most is that of something being known, becoming clear. That is the reason for Thomas to use the words glorify (*glorificari*) and clarify (*clarificari*) as synonyms, as Thomas does throughout the commentary.[50] The other element is that of praise: glorification is not just the conveying of information, there is an element of splendor, of thanksgiving to it as well.

At several places in the commentary, Thomas states that the glorification of the Son took place in three moments. The first is the crucifixion. Both in visible signs like the darkening of the sun and the rendering of the temple curtain and in the invisible sign which is his victory over the powers of darkness, Christ is glorified.

Secondly, Christ is glorified in his resurrection and ascension. Through the resurrection and ascension, the human nature of Christ is brought into the glory of his divinity, not, as Thomas explains, by having his human nature changed, but because his body now shares in the glory his soul had from the beginning of his conception.

---

[48] "Secundo quomodo Christus suam divinitatem demonstravit moriendo; et hoc a XII cap. et ultra". *In Io* 2:1 §335 (text corrected by L. Reid).

[49] E.g. *ScG* bk. III c.29; *STh* I-II q. 2 a. 3; II-II q. 103 a. 3 ad 3. In the commentary on John: *In Io* 8:54 §1278; *In Io* 13:31 §1826 and §1830; *In Io* 17:1 §2183.

[50] *In Io* 13:31 §1826.

Thirdly, Christ is glorified by the conversion of the gentiles, by all people coming to the knowledge of Him. In this knowledge of Christ, the Father is glorified as well, Thomas states, referring to Mt 11: 27 ("No one knows the Father except the Son and any one to whom the Son chooses to reveal Him").[51] This glorification for which Christ asks the Father ("Glorify your Son", Jn 17:1), shows Christ to be the Son of God: by birth, not by creation (against Arius), in truth, not just in name (against Sabellius), by origin, not by adoption (against Nestorius).[52]

It might seem odd to discuss the topic of glorification in a study on the divinity of Christ, because the glorification of Christ seems to belong to his human nature only. If Christ's divine nature would have to be glorified, it would seem like Christ at one point was not God but became God, which would be Arianism.

When Thomas speaks about the glorification of Christ, he does indeed usually speak about Christ's human nature. That is not always the case, however: Thomas does speak about the glory the Son receives from the Father. What the Son receives from the Father, is his eternal procession, his being begotten. The eternal procession from the Father does not lead to a subordination of the Son to the Father in an Arian sense, in the sense that the one who glorifies is greater than the one who is glorified. This is so, according to Thomas, because just as the Father glorifies the Son, so the Son glorifies the Father as well: "Glorify thy Son that the Son may glorify thee" (Jn 17:1).[53]

What might this glorification *in divinis* entail? If we return to the definition Ambrose gives of glory, glory as knowledge accompanied by praise, it is clear that in God glorification cannot entail an increase in knowledge. In God there is no *potentia* of knowing that is not in act, there is no lack of knowledge that has to be filled. The same is true for praise: the Father does not give the Son the praise the Son lacks, or vice versa, because in God there can be no lack. It is clear that glorification is used analogously when used for a man, or the human nature of Christ, and for

[51] These three moments of the glorification of the Son are mentioned in *In Io* 12:23 §1637; *In Io* 13:31-32 §1826-1830; and *In Io* 17:1 §2181. The second of these texts mentions a fourth glory of Christ: the glory of his judicial power, but since this explanation seems to spring from the direct textual context of the text only (the remark by Christ 'Now is the Son of man glorified' follows directly on Judas leaving to betray Christ, which Thomas interprets as a moment of judgement), and also because Thomas explicitly states that this glory of judicial power has its source in the resurrection, it seems to be less central than the other three are.

[52] *In Io* 17:1 §2181.

[53] *In Io* 8:54 §1277-1278. Cf. *In Io* 12:28 §1662; *In Io* 17:24 §2261.

God. Starting from the definition of Ambrose, speaking of the glorification of the Father by the Son and vice versa refers to a fullness of knowledge and praise that is mutually given and received from eternity.[54]

There is therefore a double glorification of Christ: one eternal, according to his divine nature and one in time, according to his human nature. Twice in the commentary, Thomas uses a remarkable metaphor for speaking about the relation between these two forms of glorification, a metaphor that is unique to this commentary, and that I have not been able to find anywhere else in Thomas's works. Thomas writes:

> As man, he had glory through an overflowing into him of the divinity, and overflowing of unique grace and glory: "We have seen his glory, the glory as of the only-begotten of the Father, full of grace and truth".[55]

Commenting on Jn 13:32, Thomas glosses:

> 'if God is glorified in him', that is, if it is true that the glory of his divinity overflows to the glory of his humanity, subsequently 'God will also glorify him in himself', give him a share of his own glory by assuming him into that glory: 'Every tongue should confess that the Lord Jesus is in the glory of the Father' [Phil 2:11].[56]

The first of these two texts is the most important. We have seen before that when Thomas uses the word 'only-begotten', it refers to Christ in his divine nature. The grace and glory of this divine nature in a way overflows into his human nature. It is this image of overflowing that links Thomas's speaking about Christ's glory according to his divine nature to the glory

---

54 In his otherwise helpful discussion of 'glorification', I think Michael Sherwin slightly underrates this second aspect. It is hard to see how in his stress on glorification as the transference of knowledge, it would be possible to speak of the glorification of the Father by the divine Word and vice versa. Cf. M. Sherwin, 'Christ the Teacher in St. Thomas's Commentary on the Gospel of John', in: M. Dauphinais, M. Levering (eds.), *Reading John with St. Thomas Aquinas: Theological Exegesis and Speculative Theology*, Washington D.C., Catholic University of America Press, 2005, p. 172-193, here p. 185-186.

55 "Secundum vero quod homo, habuit gloriam per redundantiam divinitatis in ipsum, et gratiae et gloriae singularis; supra I, 14: 'vidimus gloriam eius, gloriam quasi unigeniti a patre, plenum gratiae et veritatis' etc". *In Io* 8:54 §1278 (text corrected by L. Reid).

56 "'Deus clarificatus est in eo'; idest, si ita est quod gloria divinitatis ad gloriam humanitatis redundet, 'Deus clarificavit eum', idest, fecit eum participem suae gloriae, eum ad suam gloriam assumendo. Phil. II, 11: 'omnis lingua confiteatur quia dominus Iesus in gloria est Dei patris'". *In Io* 13:32 §1829.

of his human nature. In this way, glorification becomes a word that refers to the person of Christ according to both natures and makes it useful for our speech of both natures in Christ, and for Christ as one person: in his eternal procession, in his passion and death, resurrection and ascension, and in the coming to the knowledge of him by all people, the person of Jesus Christ is glorified.

The metaphor of the 'overflowing' of the divine nature in the human nature in Christ has a twofold significance. One often finds in the commentary on John expositions in which Thomas interprets a text from the Gospel according to both natures of Christ: we have already seen several examples of this, where Thomas makes remarks like 'according to the human nature of Christ, this verse means this, and according to Christ's divine nature it means that'. These expositions are not the easiest to interpret, because if taken to the extreme, there seems to be a whiff of Nestorianism to this kind of interpretation: is it really this simple to strictly divide the natures of Christ in an interpretation of a Scriptural text that speaks of the person of Christ? The metaphor of overflowing on its own could be problematic as well because of its platonic overtones. Read in the context of the commentary, however, it is a corrective that helps to keep the Chalcedonian balance in speaking about the person of Christ: the two natures can and must be distinguished, but not by way of separation.

Furthermore, if the glory of the humanity of Christ is caused through 'an overflowing in him of the divinity', than Christ in his humanity can never be without this glory. In the one person that Christ is, the human is never available without the divine nature. There are no 'purely human' actions of Jesus Christ, and because the human and divine nature can not be 'added up' to each other in the sense that 'more human means less divine', because the two natures of Christ are not a zero-sum game, even in his most human actions like eating or experiencing emotions, the glory of the divine nature overflows in Christ's human nature.

What does this mean for the glory of the cross? If glory means 'to make known with praise' what does the cross manifest about the divinity of Christ? My suggestion would be that on the cross Christ's divine nature is revealed as hidden.[57] On the cross, more than at any other time, only the human nature of Christ can be perceived, not because the divine nature of Christ is absent (even though Christ does not suffer according to his divine nature), but because it is revealed as hidden.

---

[57] I am grateful to J. Wissink for a helpful conversation about this interpretation.

This might sound like a paradox, if not a straight contradiction. If to reveal means to make something known that was not known before, what does it mean to say that something is revealed as hidden? If something is revealed as hidden, has something been revealed at all? A couple of remarks might be helpful, here. First, we rightly speak of a revelation when something is revealed to be the case, even if what that means remains clothed in mystery. The classic example of this is the Trinity: because God has revealed Godself to be Father, Son and Holy Spirit, in faith we do know that God is Triune, but we do not and cannot know what it means for God to be Triune: that remains utter mystery.

The other remark to be made is that while we easily understand mystery in terms of a shortage of knowledge, for Thomas mystery in God always is the mystery of excess, of abundance. The metaphor of light that we saw before is the standard one Thomas uses when speaking about this: we cannot see God, not because in God there is darkness in the sense of a shortage of light, but because the light is so abundant that our eyes are not capable of grasping it. Mystery, while it presents itself to us as hiddenness and darkness, in God is abundance, excess of light.

It is hiddenness in this sense that is manifested about the divinity of Christ on the cross. We know that He is the Son of God, how He is the Son remains mystery, more than ever on that moment where the Father seems to be completely absent. We know that He is the Word of God, how He can be that remains unknown to us, especially on this moment when his voice falls silent. What looks like death to us, reveals the mystery of God's self-giving, redemptive love. It is this hidden divine nature, which is love, that is revealed to be overflowing in Christ in the cross.

If this is true, than the almost complete absence of expositions about the divinity of Christ in Thomas's commentary on the passion narrative in Jn 18-19 is significant. In his life, Christ manifests his divine nature through his miracles and his teaching. Neither of these two are completely absent at the cross: there were visible signs, like the sun becoming dark, the rendering of the temple curtain and the opening of the graves, as Thomas acknowledges.[58] And from the cross, Christ does continue to teach, as when He gives his mother to the care of his beloved disciple to teach us to help our parents in their needs.[59] What is taught before anything else

[58] *In Io* 12:23 §1637; *In Io* 17:1 §2181.

[59] *In Io* 19:27 §2441. It is in this context that Thomas quotes the shocking text from Augustine: "Christus in cruce pendens se habuit sicut magister in cathedra".

about Christ on the cross, however, is the hidden nature of his divinity, which is God's overflowing, redemptive love.[60]

Thus far, I have discussed the first moment Thomas mentions of the glorification of the Son: in the crucifixion. I will not go into the second moment, that of the resurrection and the ascension, as it is in a way the most obvious interpretation of glorification.

It is worth going into the the third way a bit deeper, however: that Christ becomes known among the peoples. First, that Christ becomes known among the peoples is the work of the Holy Spirit. Whereas in other parts of the commentary that speak of the divinity of Christ, the relationship of the Son to the Father is what is central to Thomas's remarks, here it is the relation of the Son to the Holy Spirit. Secondly, it is here that it becomes clear how Thomas's interpretation of 'glorification' throughout the fourth Gospel is related to the commentary on Jn 1, which is the main question of this chapter of our study.

Several times in the commentary Thomas stresses that it is the Holy Spirit who glorifies the Son because he comes forth from the Son. Commenting on the characterisation of the Holy Spirit as the 'spirit of truth' in Jn 14:17, Thomas remarks that in us love of the truth arises when we have conceived and considered truth. In God, it is like that as well: just as love, the Holy Spirit, proceeds from the truth, the Word, so love leads to knowledge of the truth.[61] It is the Spirit who teaches the disciples, and makes known to them the divinity of Christ.[62] The reason why, according

---

[60] Cf. K. Rahner, 'Fragen zur Unbegreiflichkeit Gottes nach Thomas von Aquin', in: *Schriften zur Theologie*, Band XII, Zürich, Benziger Verlag, 1975, p. 306-319, and his famous earlier essay 'Über den Begriff des Geheimnisses in der katholischen Theologie', in: *Schriften zur Theologie*, Band IV, Einsiedeln, Benziger Verlag, 1960, p. 51-99. That the darkness of mystery reveals an abundance of light in God is known in mystical literature as well. For just one example among many possible ones, cf: "The true 'apophatic' approach (*apophasis* means the 'leap' towards the mystery) does not rest solely, as is often thought, in negative theology. That has only the purpose of opening us to an encounter, a revelation, and it is this very revelation, in which glory is inseparable from *kenosis*, which is strictly unthinkable. The *apophasis* therefore lies in the antinomy, the sharp distinction in character between the depth and the Cross, the inaccessible God and the man of Sorrows, the almost 'crazy' manifestations of God's love for humanity, and a humble and unobtrusive plea for our own love". O. Clément, *The Roots of Christian Mysticism: Texts from the Patristic Era with Commentary*, second edition, New York, New City Press, 1993, p. 38 (original emphasis).

[61] *In Io* 14:17 §1916.

[62] *In Io* 16:14 §2106.

to Thomas, it is the Holy Spirit who glorifies Christ, is that the Son is the principle of the Holy Spirit. Thomas formulates it as an axiom: 'For everything which is from another manifests that from which it is'.[63] Therefore the Son manifests the Father, because He is from the Father, and likewise, the Holy Spirit manifests the Son, because He is from the Son.[64] There is, in other words, a clear relationship between *theologia* and *oikonomia*, between the relationships of origin between the divine persons on the one hand, and their work in the divine *dispensatio* (to use Thomas's word for what in contemporary Trinitarian theology usually is called 'the economic Trinity'): what is made known in the *dispensatio* reflects the relationships of origin between Father, Son and Holy Spirit.

It is here that it becomes clear that Thomas develops what he initiated in the commentary on Jn 1. We saw that 'manifestation' is a key word in Thomas's understanding of Jn 1, the reason why the Evangelist speaks about the Son as 'light': light implies manifestation, revelation. It is this manifestation by Christ which makes our participation in the light possible. The Son who reveals the Father to the world, is glorified in his passion, resurrection and in the people who come to knowledge of Him because of the Holy Spirit who manifests Christ.[65] That which in the commentary on Jn 1 was started with the reflections by Thomas on the Word as manifesting the Father, is developed into a fully Trinitarian reflection on the relation between procession and mission, between manifestation and glorification in the later chapters of the commentary.

4. Conclusion

In previous chapters, we have seen how the divinity of Christ, for Thomas the central topic of the Gospel of John, determines the way he structures the Gospel, and vice versa: how the *divisio textus* leads Thomas in his commentary on Jn 1 to the divinity of Christ. We formulated the thesis that for Thomas Jn 1 is the fourth Gospel in a nutshell, and that it was to be expected that the main themes he discussed briefly there, were to be developed further in the subsequent chapters of the commentary.

The *divisio textus* of Jn 3-11 showed how Thomas develops the divinity of Christ in the commentary on these chapters by showing the grace of the Word as a model for Christian life. In that Christian life, spiritual regeneration, given at baptism and to be brought to full fruition

---

[63] "Omne enim quod est ab alio, manifestat id a quo est". *In Io* 16:14 §2107.
[64] Here Thomas uses the word *clarificet* for the Holy Spirit manifesting the Son.
[65] Cf. *In Io* 13:1 §1733.

in patria is the central point of Thomas's Trinitarian reading. The gifts of spiritual life, food and education bring divine life and light into the lives of us who have been spiritually regenerated.

The many places where Thomas speaks of the relation of the Son with the Father show how the equality between Father and Son is a development of the divinity of the Word. This equality excludes subordination, the limitation of Christ's power, difference between the Father and the Son, and imperfection: it is not a positive description of the divine nature of the Son, but by taking away what is not fitting in our speaking about Christ's divinity, leads us into the mystery of God.

The study of Thomas's interpretation of 'glorification' in Jn 13-21 showed that the glory of the divine nature of Christ overflows into his human nature: there is no 'human Jesus' without his divine nature, not even on the cross, which reveals his divine nature as hidden. It is his hidden, divine nature, which is love, that is revealed to be overflowing in Christ on the cross. All this is manifested to us through the Holy Spirit, who makes it possible for us to participate in Christ.

The *divisio textus* is in all this the structuring guide to Thomas's reading of the Fourth Gospel. It shows how for Thomas the abundance of small expositions, quotations from patristic sources and discussions of details of the text of the Gospel that together are his commentary, form a unity that speaks of the divinity of Christ. All this is mentioned and announced in Jn 1, which according to this reading is the Gospel in a nutshell, and then deepened and developed in the rest of the Gospel. The real prologue of John, for Thomas, is not Jn 1:1-18 but the whole of the first chapter. The *divisio textus* reflects this interpretation, and guides the student of Thomas through the commentary.

CONCLUSION AND SUMMARY

In this book, we studied the *divisio textus* Thomas gives in his commentary on the Gospel of John. We started with the thesis that this structure is directing Thomas's interpretation both of the Gospel as a whole and of its parts, so much so that close consideration of the *divisio textus* is necessary for a good understanding of the commentary.

We also presumed that the statement in Thomas's prologue that the Gospel of John is predominantly about the divinity of Christ is the lens through which he reads the Gospel.

Finally, we assumed that these two things would be related: that if the *divisio textus* was as significant as our thesis suggested, it would point the way to how Thomas treats the divinity of Christ in his commentary, and vice versa, that if the divinity of Christ is the topic of the Fourth Gospel, it would have an essential presence in the *divisio textus*.

Chapter 1 presented the *divisio textus* as both a didactical and a hermeneutical instrument of the biblical commentator. It is a didactical method that the commentator uses to structure his lessons, and that he can use with more or less detail, depending on the context in which he is teaching. As a didactical instrument, it aims to help the student to get a grip on the text.

The *divisio textus* also is a hermeneutical instrument that helps to understand the text as a unity and show how different parts of the text relate to one another. In the *divisio textus*, Thomas reconstructs what he sees as the structure the divinely inspired author has given to his text.

Our study of the *divisio textus* that Albert, Bonaventure and Thomas provide of John's Gospel, showed the different interpretations they have of the Gospel. Albert's *divisio* suggests a reading that is oriented towards the passion narrative, in which the notion of sanctification, so central to Albert's structure, comes to fruition. For Bonaventure, the incarnation is the lens through which he reads the Fourth Gospel. Thomas finally, in line with his remarks about the origin of the Gospel as written in response to people who denied the divinity of Christ, takes the divinity to be the object of John's Gospel.

None of the medieval commentators read Jn 1:1-18 as the 'prologue' of the Gospel: that Jn 1:1-18 is a distinct section of the text is an idea that is much more recent. Both Albert and Bonaventure read Jn 1:1-5 as a 'prologue', that speaks of the uncreated Word. After these verses the Evangelist begins to speak about the Word incarnate. Thomas's *divisio textus* is unique in the sense that it does not suggest that the main textual transition takes place after Jn 1:5, as both Albert and Bonaventure do. Instead, Thomas reads Jn 1 as a textual unity that as a whole speaks of the divinity of Christ, the central topic of the Gospel. How, according to Thomas, does the Gospel of John teach the divinity of Christ? It teaches it in a nutshell, in Jn 1, and it teaches it by showing its effects in Christ's life, death and resurrection in the rest of the Gospel. In those later chapters in the Gospel, before everything else, the divinity of Christ is shown in the way Christ's grace transforms us. The real 'prologue' to the Gospel, Thomas suggests, is the whole of Jn 1. All this is made evident by the *divisio textus*.

Thomas divides Jn 1 into three parts: a part that speaks about the divine Word (Jn 1:1-5), a part that speaks of the incarnation (Jn 1:6-14a), and a part that presents the double way in which the Word incarnate was made known to us: through seeing and hearing (Jn 1:14b-51). In chapters 2-4 of this study, we examined these parts of the commentary on Jn 1.

One of the points that Thomas's *divisio textus* of the first verses of the Gospel shows is the Trinitarian character of his reading. While he uses a framework for the first clauses that is Aristotelian, he turns the framework inside out when speaking about God. It is because divine persons in God can only be distinguished from each other according to relations of origin, that it is proper for theological thinking about the Word to start with its origin ('when' and 'where' the Word was) before discussing what the Word is. Thomas's commentary here is a discussion that is structured by the insight from Trinitarian theology that the Word can only be distinguished from the other persons in God according to the relations of origin. The *divisio textus* Thomas gives of the first verses of the Gospel shows the theological quality of his reading: Thomas's theological interpretation is the *ordo disciplinae* according to which the evangelist presents his theology.

One of the unique characteristics of Thomas's approach is that he reads the first verses of the Gospel as one side of an ongoing conversation with heretical understandings of the Word. Every *clausula* is a reaction to heretical interpretations of the preceding one. That leads to a rich tapestry of interpretations that is aimed at different heretical interpretations, read side by side. Thomas consistently shows that Scripture is to be read with Scripture, and that the one biblical text speaks differently in the different discussions in which the church fathers from the patristic era were involved. That does not mean that the text does not have its own intention, as if it were just a willing instrument in the hand of the reader. When Thomas gives a summary statement about the four clauses that form the beginning of the Gospel, he reads them as a refutation of four heresies, three which do not do full justice to the divinity of the Word.[1] That Thomas's list differs from those of Albert and Bonaventure is best understood by his understanding of the historical context of the Gospel, that is was written by John in reaction to heresies that had risen and that denied the divinity of Christ.

With regard to Thomas's use of his patristic sources, two things should be noticed. First, my reading of the commentary on Jn 1:1-5 confirms that Thomas is extraordinarily well-versed in the commentaries of the patristic era: every single clausula or verse is read within a broad context of patristic resources. Secondly, this broad use of patristic sources serves a purpose. Thomas characteristically does not choose between the different patristic interpretations of John but shows that each interpretation is useful in reaction to different possible heretical readings of the Gospel. The broad scope of different patristic interpretations is therefore not a problem, but a source for different interpretations that are useful in different contexts.

Thomas's commentary on these first verses of the fourth Gospel is a profound theology of the Word that is unique within Thomas's writings. While it has the characteristics to be an almost complete treatise on 'the Word of God', it never stops to be what it is in the first place: biblical commentary, biblical theology. This theology of the Word gives a full account of the Son of God in relation to the Father. In our speech of God, the relationship of origin as it is presented through the analogy of the Word as understood and spoken by the Father provides understanding both of the distinction between the Father and the Son, and their consubstantiality.

The importance of a theology of the Word lies not only in understanding the relation between the Father and the Son, however. Chrysostom's remark that the Gospel begins with 'In the beginning was the Word' and not with 'In the beginning was the Son' because contrary to 'son', which implies a relationship to 'father' only, 'word' implies a relation to both speaker and the person spoken to is fundamental to Thomas's reading of Jn 1:1-5. His patristic sources teach Thomas to discuss the Word *quoad nos*, to understand that from the beginning of his Gospel, John has God's revelation to us in mind. Thomas's theology of

[1] *In Io* 1:2 §64. Of the four heresies mentioned here, only the second one, Sabellianism, does not question the divinity of Christ.

the Word binds Christology, Trinitarian theology, and theology of revelation, which is why Gilles Emery rightly states that "the doctrine of the Word is incontestably the heart of Thomas's Trinitarian theology".[2]

The relationship of the Word to creation is central in Thomas's reading of Jn 1:3-5. It is through the Word and through Love that God creates the world. Creation is therefore Trinitarian in form. Thomas's thinking about the divine processions is especially helpful here. The eternal Word proceeds from the Father as spoken. With regard to creation, the Father speaks all things into being through his Word. In God, the Holy Spirit proceeds in the form of love. With regard to creation, the Father and the Word love all things through the Holy Spirit. Thus, "the eternal processions are the cause and the rationale of the making of creatures".[3]

In the commentary on Jn 1:4b-5 this relation of the Word to creation is concentrated on the relation of the Word to human beings. Here Thomas starts to unwrap his theology of the Word *quoad nos* through his reflection on what it means that the evangelist calls the Word the 'light'. The central category for Thomas here is 'manifestation'. It is because the Word comes forth from the Father and shares the Father's divinity, that it manifests the Father. It belongs to the form of the truth that is the Word that it is *manifestabilis*, that although in itself it exceeds all our human knowledge, it can be made known to us, rational beings. We can know the truth because the world is created truthfully by God, and that truth is Christ. The truth, therefore, all truth, is christoform, because it falls under the category of *manifestabilia*, it participates in the Word, who is *manifestabilis*.

A programmatic statement by Chrysostom and quoted approvingly by Thomas that John the evangelist intended to give us knowledge of the Word as directed towards the salvation of humans is the beginning of a more direct consideration of the soteriological understanding of the Word. That consideration receives its depth with the study of the way the evangelist speaks about the incarnation, which for Thomas is the topic of Jn 1:6-14a. We studied the commentary on these verses in chapter 3. In the commentary on the verses that speak of John the Baptist, Thomas presents him as a prime example of someone who participates in the light of which the evangelist has spoken before, and so becomes a witness to

[2] G. Emery, *The Trinitarian Theology of St Thomas Aquinas*, Oxford, Oxford University Press, 2007, p. 179.

[3] "Processiones personarum aeternae sunt causa et ratio totius productionis creaturarum". *1 Sent*. d.14 q. 1 a. 1c.

it. Thus 'testimony' is introduced, a concept which will remain of crucial importance both in the rest of the Fourth Gospel and in Thomas's commentary on it.

From the verses on the incarnation, Thomas understands that a lack of knowledge was a fundamental reason for the incarnation. The light became human to enlighten human nature darkened by sin, to give a full knowledge of the God that had been prefigured in the Old Testament, and to be known through himself by those who participate in Him.

The benefit of the incarnation is that we are made into children of God. The grace to become children of God is a gift that does not coerce, but that draws us into communion with God. This is another instance of Thomas introducing a concept that will be pivotal for the whole of the commentary. The concept of 'spiritual regeneration' is introduced as the fruit of the incarnation: how it works in the lives of the faithful is the topic of the commentary on Jn 3-11, especially the commentary on John 3 and 4.

As we saw in chapter 4, Thomas structures the commentary on Jn 1:14b-51 according to seeing and hearing, the two senses of testimony. The witness of Christ has seen or heard him: through these senses the mystery of the divinity of Christ is manifested to him. Thomas attentively keeps the tension between manifestation and the hiddenness of God: in Christ we do get to know God in a new and definitive way. We get to know God as Father, Son and Holy Spirit. That knowledge, however, is knowledge of a mystery, just as both the divinity of Christ and the unity of the divine and human nature in Christ remain incomprehensible to us.

In the stories of Christ's first disciples we also saw Thomas's attentiveness to process. Both when he speaks about salvation history, about what was revealed to Moses and what has been revealed in the Word incarnate, and when he speaks about the calling of the first disciples, Thomas like a good teacher has a sensitivity for the process that education is, and recognises it in Scripture.

Finally, what Thomas underscores again and again in his commentary on Jn 1:14b-51is the relation between Christology and soteriology, manifestation and salvation. The stress on the divinity of Christ is informed by a longing to understand the salvific history of Christ.

Having thus analysed Thomas's commentary on Jn 1, in chapter 5 the thesis that for Thomas Jn 1 is the fourth Gospel, in a nutshell, was tested by taking the *divisio textus* of Jn 2-21 as a guide to its interpretation. The *divisio textus* of Jn 3-11 showed how Thomas develops the divinity of

Christ in the commentary on these chapters by presenting the grace of the Word as a model for Christian life. In that Christian life, spiritual regeneration, given at baptism and to be brought to full fruition *in patria* is the central point of Thomas's Trinitarian reading. The gifts of spiritual life, food and education bring divine life and light into the lives of those who have been spiritually regenerated.

The many places where Thomas speaks of the relation of the Son with the Father show how the equality between Father and Son is a development of the divinity of the Word. This equality excludes subordination, the limitation of Christ's power, difference between the Father and the Son, and imperfection: it is not a positive description of the divine nature of the Son, but by taking away what is not fitting in our speaking about Christ's divinity, leads us into the mystery of God.

The study of Thomas's interpretation of 'glorification' in Jn 13-21 showed that the glory of the divine nature of Christ overflows into his human nature: there is no 'human Jesus' without his divine nature, not even on the cross, which reveals his divine nature as hidden. It is his hidden, divine nature, which is love, that is revealed to be overflowing in Christ on the cross. All this is manifested to us through the Holy Spirit, who makes it possible for us to participate in Christ.

The *divisio textus* is in all this the structuring guide to Thomas's reading of the Fourth Gospel. It shows how for Thomas the abundance of small expositions, quotations from patristic sources and discussions of details of the text of the Gospel that together are his commentary, form a unity that speaks of the divinity of Christ. All this is mentioned and announced in Jn 1, which according to this reading is the Gospel in a nutshell, and then deepened and developed in the rest of the Gospel. The *divisio textus* reflects this interpretation and guides the student of Thomas through the commentary.

For that reason, further studies in Thomas's biblical commentaries (and likewise, for that matter, in other commentaries that find their origins in the medieval university, such as those by Albert and Bonaventure) would therefore do well in paying close attention to the *divisio textus*, as it gives crucial insights in the theological choices the *Magister in sacra pagina* makes.

This study is but a modest contribution to the existing scholarship on Thomas Aquinas. Further avenues of research could be explored.

There is a lot still unknown about the *divisio textus*. A historical overview of its origin and development does not exist and would be very helpful for the study of medieval commentaries, including but not restricted to medieval biblical commentaries.

Focusing on Thomas's biblical commentaries, while the *divisio textus* does get more attention in contemporary studies in Aquinas, studies like this one which focuses on the *divisio textus* of a given commentary are still rare, and for many of the commentaries non-existent. It would be helpful to have more in-depth studies that look into the Biblical commentaries through the lens of the *divisio textus*, and discover more about the implications of such a view for understanding the biblical commentaries.

While this study focused on medieval biblical commentaries, it could be fascinating to bring the medieval attention for structure, visible in the use of the *divisio textus*, in conversation with the ways in which in contemporary biblical scholarship conclusions are reached about the structure of a given biblical text. What can the *divisiones textus* that theologians like Thomas Aquinas, Albert, and Bonaventure make of the fourth Gospel contribute to our understanding of the Gospel, to the way we think about its structure, and the hermeneutical importance we do or not do attribute to this structure?

This study has shown that Thomas's reading of the Gospel of John is deeply trinitarian in character, with the doctrine of the Word as the heart of this trinitarian theology. This might give new insights to contemporary research in trinitarian theology and in the systematic theological understanding of the divine Word as the *nexus mysteriorum* of Christology, Trinitarian theology and a theology of revelation.[4]

Finally, my suggestion that on the cross Christ's divine nature is revealed as hidden could be developed further. What does it mean to speak of God's hidden presence in the suffering and death of Christ? How can this hidden divine nature be understood to be God's overflowing, redemptive love?

Throughout his commentary on the Fourth Gospel, Thomas teaches his students about "the Word of life" (1 Jn 1:1); the Word that is life and that gives life. What he teaches is a profoundly biblical Christology of the divine Word: the Word that is God, and that became man to bring us to God.

---

[4] An example of a study that takes the Word of God as starting point from which it develops a complete overview of systematic theology is O.H. Pesch, *Katholische Dogmatik: Aus Ökumenischer Erfahrung*, Bd. 1/1 Die Geschichte der Menschen mit Gott, Ostfildern, Matthias-Grünewald-Verlag, 2008

BIBLIOGRAPHY

Leonine edition of the works of Thomas Aquinas

I-1	Expositio libri Peryermenias
IV-XII	Summa Theologiae
XIII-XV	Summa contra Gentiles
XXVI	Expositio super Iob ad litteram
XLII-3	Opuscula (Compendium Theologiae)

Primary Literature

Origen

C. BLANC (ed.), Origen, *Commentaire sur saint Jean I-V*, SC 120 bis, Paris, Les Éditions du Cerf, 1966

Hilary of Poitiers

P. SMULDERS (ed.), Hilary, *De Trinitate*, CCSL 62-62A, Turnhout, Brepols, 1979-1980

Basil of Caesarea

J.-P. MIGNE (ed.), Basil of Caesarea, *Homiliae et sermones,* PG 31, Paris 1857

John Chrysostom

J.-P. MIGNE (ed.), John Chrysostom, *Homiliae in Ioannem*, PG 59, Paris 1862

Augustine

F. DOLBEAU, 'Le Sermon 117 d'Augustin sur l ineffabilité de Dieu: Édition critique', in: *Revue bénédictine* 124 (2014), 213-253

W.J. MOUNTAIN, F. GLORIE (eds.), Augustine, *De Trinitate libri XV*, CCSL 50-50A, Turnhout, Brepols, 1968

R. WILLEMS (ed.), Augustine, *In Ioannis Evangelium Tractatus*, CCSL 36, second edition, Turnhout, Brepols, 1990

J. ZYCHA (ed.), Augustine, *De agone christiano*, CSEL 41, Vindobona [Wien], F. Tempsky, 1900

Beda Venerabilis

J.-P. MIGNE (ed.), Beda Venerabilis, *Expositio in Evangelium S. Joannis,* PL 92, Paris 1862

Alcuin

J.-P. MIGNE (ed.), Alcuin, *Commentaria in S. Joannis Evangelium,* PL 100, Paris 1863

John Scotus Eriugena

E. JEAUNEAU (ed.), Jean Scot, *Homélie sur le Prologue de Jean*, SC 151, Paris, Les Éditions du Cerf, 1969

Peter Lombard

I. BRADY (ed.), Peter Lombard, *Sententiae in IV libris distinctae*, 2. volumes, Grottaferrata, Editiones Collegii S. Bonaventurae ad Claras Aquas, 1971

Glossa Ordinaria

K. FROEHLICH, M. GIBSON (eds.), *Biblia Latina cum Glossa Ordinaria: Facsimile Reprint of the Editio Princeps*, 4 volumes, Turnhout, Brepols, 1992

Albert

A. BORGNET, E. BORGNET (eds.), Albertus Magnus, *Opera Omnia*, vol. 24: *Enarrationes in Joannem*, Paris, Vivès, 1899

J. CASTEIGT (ed.), *Albertus Magnus, "Super Iohannem" (Ioh. 1, 1-18)*, Leuven, Peeters, 2019

Roger Bacon

J.S. BREWER (ed.), *Fr. Rogeri Baconis opera quaedam hactenus inedita,* London, Longman, Green, Longman and Roberts, 1859

Bonaventure

A. PARMA (ed.), S. Bonaventura*,* *Opera Omnia*, vol. 6: *Commentarius in Evangelium Ioannis*, Grottaferrata, Quaracchi, Collegium S. Bonaventurae ad Claras aquas, 1893

Thomas Aquinas

R. BUSA (ed.), *S. Thomae Aquinatis Opera Omnia*, vol. 1-7, Stuttgart, Friedrich Fromman Verlag Günther Holzboog KG, 1980

R. CAI (ed.), Thomas Aquinas, *Super Epistolas S. Pauli Lectura*, editio VIII revisa (2 volumes), Torino, Marietti, 1953

R. CAI (ed.), Thomas Aquinas, *Super Evangelium S. Ioannis Lectura*, Editio V revisa, Torino, Marietti, 1952

R. CAI (ed.), Thomas Aquinas, *Super Evangelium S. Matthaei Lectura*, Editio V revisa, Torino, Marietti, 1951

A. GUARENTI (ed.), Thomas Aquinas, *Catena Aurea in Quatuor Evangelia*, nova editio, 2 volumes, Torino, Marietti, 1953

P. MANDONNET (ed.), Thomas Aquinas, *Scriptum super libros Sententiarum magistri Petri Lombardi episcopi Parisiensis*, Vol. 1, Lethielleux, Paris, 1929

Translations

J. VAN DEN EIJNDEN, J. KLOK (translation), Bonaventura, *Vleesgeworden Woord: Preken en Schriftcommentaren bij gelegenheid van Kerstmis*, Budel, Damon, 2015

R.J. KARRIS (translation), Bonaventure, *Commentary on the Gospel of John*, Saint Bonaventure, Franciscan Institute Publications, 2007

F. LARCHER, J. WEISHEIPL (translation), Thomas Aquinas, *Commentary on the Gospel of John*, Washington D.C., The Catholic University of America Press, 2010

J.H. NEWMAN (translation), Thomas Aquinas, *Catena Aurea: Commentary on the Four Gospels Collected out of the Works of the Fathers*, Oxford, 1845

M.-D. PHILIPPE (translation), Thomas d'Aquin, *Commentaire sur l'Évangile de saint Jean* Vol. I, Paris, Les Éditions du Cerf, 2002

H.W.M. RIKHOF (translation), *Over God spreken: Een tekst van Thomas van Aquino uit de* Summa Theologiae, Delft, Meinema, 1988

H. TEVEL, H. VAN REISEN (translation), Augustinus, *Geef mij te drinken: Verhandelingen 1-23 over het Johannesevangelie*, Budel, Damon, 2010

H. TEVEL, H. VAN REISEN (translation), Augustinus, *Brood om van te leven: Verhandelingen 24-54 over het Johannesevangelie*, Budel, Damon, 2017

S. TUGWELL (translation), Albert & Thomas, *Selected Writings*, New York, Paulist Press, 1988

Secondary literature

M. AILLET, *Lire la Bible avec S. Thomas: Le passage de la* littera *à la* res *dans la Somme Théologique*, Fribourg, Éditions Universitaires Fribourg Suisse, 1993

M. ARIAS REYERO, *Thomas von Aquin als Exeget: Die Prinzipien seiner Schriftdeutung und seine Lehre von den Schriftsinnen*, Einsiedeln, Johannes Verlag, 1971

C.T. BAGLOW, *"Modus et Forma": A New Approach to the Exegesis of Saint Thomas Aquinas with an Application to the Lectura Super Epistolam ad Ephesios*, Roma, Editrice Pontificio Istituto Biblico, 2002

L.J. BATAILLON, 'De la lectio à la praedicatio: Commentaires Bibliques et sermons ae XIIIe siècle', in*: Revue des Sciences Philosophiques et Théologiques* 70 (1986), p. 559-575

L.J. BATAILLON, 'Saint Thomas et les pères: de la *Catena* à la *Tertia Pars*', in: C.-J. Pinto de Oliveira (ed.), *Ordo Sapientiae et Amoris: Image et message de Saint Thomas d'Aquin à travers les récentes études historiques, herméneutiques et doctrinales*, Fribourg, Éditions Universitaires Fribourg Suisse, 1993, p. 15-36

T.F. BELLAMAH, *The Biblical Interpretation of William of Alton*, Oxford, Oxford University Press, 2011

T.F. BELLAMAH, 'The Interpretation of a Contemplative: Thomas' Commentary *Super Ioannem*', in: P. Roszak, J. Vijgen (eds.), *Reading Sacred Scripture with Thomas Aquinas: Hermeneutical Tools, Theological Questions and New Perspectives*, Turnhout, Brepols, 2015, p. 229-255

C. BERCHTOLD, *Manifestatio Veritatis: Zum Offenbarungsbegriff bei Thomas von Aquin*, Münster, Lit Verlag, 2000

C.C. BLACK, 'St. Thomas's Commentary on the Johannine Prologue: Some Reflections on Its Character and Implications', in: *The Catholic Biblical Quarterly* 48 (1986), p. 681-98

S.-T. BONINO, 'La théologie de la vérité dans la *lectura super Ioannem* de Saint Thomas d'Aquin', in: *Revue Thomiste* 104 (2004), p. 141-166

J.F. BOYLE, 'St. Thomas Aquinas and Sacred Scripture', in: *Pro Ecclesia* 4 (1995), p. 92-104

J.F. BOYLE, 'Authorial Intention and the *Divisio Textus*', in: M. Dauphinais, M. Levering (eds.), *Reading John with St. Thomas Aquinas: Theological Exegesis and Speculative Theology*, Washington D.C., Catholic University of America Press, 2005, p. 3-8

J.F. BOYLE, 'The Theological Character of the Scholastic "Division of the Text" with Particular Reference to the Commentaries of Saint Thomas Aquinas', in: J. Dammen McAuliffe, B.D. Walfish, J.W. Goering (eds.), *With Reverence for the Word: Medieval Scriptural Exegesis in Judaism, Christianity, and Islam*, Oxford, Oxford University Press, 2010, p. 276-283

R.E. BROWN, *The Gospel According to John I-XII*, New Haven, Yale University Press, 1966

D.B. BURRELL, 'Creation in St. Thomas Aquinas's *Super Evangelium S. Joannis Lectura*', in: M. Dauphinais, M. Levering (eds.), *Reading John with St. Thomas Aquinas: Theological Exegesis and Speculative Theology*, Washington D.C., Catholic University of America Press, 2005, p. 115-126

D.B. BURRELL, 'Providence', in: P. McCosker, D. Turner (eds.), *The Cambridge Companion to the Summa Theologiae*, Cambridge, Cambridge University Press, 2016, p. 156-67

M.-D. CHENU, 'Le plan de la Somme Théologique de S. Thomas', in: *Revue Thomiste* 47 (1939), p. 93-107

M.-D. CHENU, *Introduction à l'Étude de Saint Thomas d'Aquin*, Montréal, Institut d'Études Médiévales, fourth edition, 1984

O. CLÉMENT, *The Roots of Christian Mysticism: Texts from the Patristic Era with Commentary*, second edition, New York, New City Press, 1993

S. COAKLEY, 'Person of Christ', in: P. McCosker, D. Turner (eds.), *The Cambridge Companion to the Summa Theologiae*, Cambridge, Cambridge University Press, 2016, p. 222-39

C.G. CONTICELLO, 'San Tomasso ed i padri: La *Catena Aurea Super Ioannem*', in: *Archives d'histoire doctrinale et littéraire du Moyen Âge* 65 (1990), p. 31-92

M. CORBIN, *Le chemin de la Théologie chez Thomas d'Aquin*, Paris, Beauchesne, 1974

M. CORBIN, *L'inouï de Dieu: Six études christologiques*, Paris, Desclée de Brouwer, 1981

E. COVINGTON, '*Divisio Textus* and the Interpretative Logic of Thomas Aquinas' *Lectura ad Ephesios*', in: *Journal of the Bible and its Reception* 4 (2017), p. 21-41

G. DAHAN, 'L'exégèse de l'histoire de Caïn et Abel du XIIe au XIVe siècle en occident I: Notes et textes', in: *Recherches de théologie ancienne et médiévale* 49 (1982), p. 21-89

G. DAHAN, 'L'exégèse de l'histoire de Caïn et Abel du XIIe au XIVe siècle en occident II', in: *Recherches de théologie ancienne et médiévale* 50 (1983), p. 5-68

G. DAHAN, *L'exégèse chrétienne de la Bible en occident médiéval - XIIe-XIVe siècle*, Paris, Les Éditions du Cerf, 1999

G. DAHAN, *Lire la Bible au Moyen Âge: Essais d'herméneutique Médiévale*, Genève, Droz, 2009

M. DAUPHINAIS, M. LEVERING (eds.), *Reading John with St. Thomas Aquinas*, Washington D.C., Catholic University of America Press, 2005

H.-F. DONDAINE, 'S. Thomas et Scot Érigène', in: *Revue des Sciences Philosophiques et Théologiques* 35 (1951), p. 31-33

G. EMERY, *La Trinité créatrice: Trinité et création dans les commentaires aux Sentences de Thomas d'Aquin et de ses précurseurs Albert le Grand et Bonaventure*, Paris, Vrin, 1995

G. EMERY, 'Biblical Exegesis and the Speculative Doctrine of the Trinity in St. Thomas Aquinas's Commentary on St. John', in: M. Dauphinais, M. Levering (eds.), *Reading John with St. Thomas Aquinas*, Washington D.C., Catholic University of America Press, 2005, p. 23-61

G. EMERY, 'Trinity and Creation', in: R. van Nieuwenhove, J. Wawrykow (eds.), *The Theology of Thomas Aquinas*, Notre Dame, University of Notre Dame Press, 2005, p. 58-76

G. EMERY, *The Trinitarian Theology of St Thomas Aquinas*, Oxford, Oxford University Press, 2007

M. ESTLER, *Rigans Montes (Ps. 104,13): Die Antrittsvorlesung des Thomas von Aquin in Paris 1256*, Stuttgart, Katholisches Bibelwerk, 2015

A. EVEN-EZRA, 'Visualizing Narrative Structure in the Medieval University: *Divisio Textus* Revisited', in: *Traditio* 72 (2017), 341-376

R. FERRI, *Gesù e la verità: Agostino e Tommaso interpreti del vangelo di Giovanni*, Roma, Città Nuova, 2007

S.F. GAINE, *Did the Saviour See the Father? Christ, Salvation and the Vision of God*, London, T&T Clark, 2015

M.T. GIBSON, 'The Place of the Glossa ordinaria in Medieval Exegesis', in: M.D. Jordan, K. Emery (eds.), *Ad Litteram: Authoritative Texts and their Medieval Readers*, Notre Dame, University of Notre Dame Press, 1992, p. 5-27

L. GILI, 'Thomas Aquinas's Commentary on Aristotle's *Metaphysics*: Prolegomena to the Study of the Text', in: *Divus Thomas* 118 (2015), p. 185-218

P. GONDREAU, 'Anti-Docetism in Aquinas's *Super Ioannem*, St. Thomas as Defender of the Full Humanity of Christ', in: M. Dauphinais, M. Levering (eds.), *Reading John with St. Thomas Aquinas: Theological Exegesis and Speculative Theology*, Washington D.C., Catholic University of America Press, 2005, p. 254-76

H.J.M.J. GORIS, *Free Creatures of an Eternal God: Thomas Aquinas on God's Infallible Foreknowledge and Irresistible Will*, Leuven, Peeters, 1996

H.J.M.J. GORIS, 'Theology and Theory of the Word in Aquinas: Understanding Augustine by Innovating Aristotle', in: M. Dauphinais, B. David, M. Levering (eds.), *Aquinas the Augustinian*, Washington, D.C., The Catholic University of America Press, 2007, p. 62-78

M.M. GORMAN, 'Rewriting Augustine: Alcuin's Commentary on the Gospel of John', in: *Revue Bénédictine* 119 (2009), p. 36-85

S. GRADL, *Deus Beatitudo Hominis: Eine Evangelische Annäherung an die Glückslehre des Thomas von Aquin*, Leuven, Peeters, 2004

F. DE GRIJS, 'Kom en zie waar ik woon!: Aantekeningen bij een hermeneutiek van Christus', in: *Jaarboek Thomas Instituut Utrecht* 17 (1997), p. 49-61

M. HAMMELE, *Das Bild der Juden im Johannes-Kommentar des Thomas von Aquin: Ein Beitrag zu Bibelhermeneutik und Wissenschaftsgeschichte im 13. Jahrhundert,* Stuttgart, Verlag Katholisches Bibelwerk, 2012

N.M. HEALY, *Thomas Aquinas: Theologian of the Christian Life*, Aldershot, Ashgate, 2003

M.-R. HOOGLAND, *God, Passion and Power: Thomas Aquinas on Christ Crucified and the Almightiness of God*, Leuven, Peeters, 2003

M.F. JOHNSON, 'Another Look at the Plurality of the Literal Sense', in: *Medieval Philosophy and Theology* 2 (1992), p. 117-141

B.V. JOHNSTONE, 'The Debate on the Structure of the Summa Theologiae of St. Thomas Aquinas: From Chenu (1939) to Metz (1998)', in: P. van Geest, H. Goris, C. Leget (eds.), *Aquinas as Authority*, Leuven, Peeters, 2000, p. 187-200

M.D. JORDAN, 'Structure', in: P. McCosker, D. Turner (eds.), *The Cambridge Companion to the Summa Theologiae*, Cambridge, Cambridge University Press, 2016, p. 34-47

R.J. KARRIS, 'Introduction', in: R.J. Karris (ed.), *Commentary on the Gospel of John: Introduction, Translation and Notes by Robert J. Karris*, St. Bonaventure, Franciscan Institute Publications, 2007, p. 1-31

D. KEATING, M. LEVERING, 'Introduction', in: F. Larcher, J. Weisheipl, (translation), Thomas Aquinas, *Commentary on the Gospel of John*, vol. 1, Washington D.C., The Catholic University of America Press, 2010, p. ix-xxx

C.S. KEENER, *The Gospel of John: A Commentary*, 2 volumes, Grand Rapids, Hendrickson Publishers, 2003

F. KERR, *After Aquinas: Versions of Thomism*, Oxford, Blackwell Publishing, 2002

P. KLIMCZAK, *Christus Magister: Le Christ maître dans les commentaires évangéliques de Saint Thomas d'Aquin*, Fribourg, Academic Press Fribourg, 2013

A.M. TEN KLOOSTER, *Thomas Aquinas on the Beatitudes: Reading Matthew, Disputing Grace and Virtue, Preaching Happiness*, Leuven, Peeters, 2018

C.R. KOESTER, *Symbolism in the Fourth Gospel: Meaning, Mystery, Community,* Second Edition, Minneapolis, Fortress Press, 2003

J. LECLERCQ, *The Love of Learning and the Desire for God: A Study of Monastic Culture*, third edition, New York, Fordham University Press, 1982

C. LEGET, 'The Concept of "Life" in the Commentary on St. John', in: M. Dauphinais, M. Levering (eds.), *Reading John with St. Thomas Aquinas: Theological Exegesis and Speculative Theology*, Washington D.C., Catholic University of America Press, 2005, p. 153-72

C. LEGET, 'Eschatology', in: R. van Nieuwenhove, J. Wawrykow (eds.), *The Theology of Thomas Aquinas*, Notre Dame, University of Notre Dame Press, 2005, p. 365-85

D. LEGGE, *The Trinitarian Christology of St Thomas Aquinas*, Oxford, Oxford University Press, 2017

M. LEVERING, M. DAUPHINAIS (eds.), *Reading Romans with St. Thomas Aquinas*, Washington D.C., Catholic University of America Press, 2012

I.C. LEVY, *Introducing Medieval Biblical Interpretation: The Senses of Scripture in Premodern Exegesis*, Grand Rapids, Baker Academic, 2018

F. VAN LIERE, *An Introduction to the Medieval Bible*, Cambridge, Cambridge University Press, 2014

B.J.F. LONERGAN, *Verbum: Word and Idea in Aquinas*, Toronto, University of Toronto Press, 1997

H. DE LUBAC, *Surnaturel: Études historiques*, Paris, Aubier, 1946

H. DE LUBAC, *Exégèse Médiévale: les quatre sens de l'Écriture*, 4 volumes, Paris, Aubier, 1959-1965

H. DE LUBAC, *Le mystère du surnaturel*, Paris, Aubier, 1965

P.-Y. MAILLARD, *La vision de Dieu chez Thomas d'Aquin: Une lecture de l'In Ioannem à la lumière de ses sources Augustiniennes*, Paris, Vrin, 2001.

S.J. MANGNUS, 'When Thomas reads a Story…: Aquinas on Jn 4,43-54 and its Implications for reading his Biblical Commentaries', in: *Jaarboek Thomas Instituut Utrecht 2003* (2004), p. 9-29

S.J. MANGNUS, 'On Heresies and Hermeneutics: Thomas Aquinas on John 2', in: A. Ghisalberti, A. Petagine, R. Rizzello (eds.), *Letture e interpretazioni di Tommaso d'Aquino oggi: Cantieri aperti*, Torino, Annali Chieresi, 2005, p. 59-68

S.J. MANGNUS, 'Understanding God's Word: Thomas Aquinas' Explanation of John 1,1-5', in: H. Goris, H. Rikhof, H. Schoot (eds.), *Divine Transcendence and Immanence in the Work of Thomas Aquinas*, Leuven, Peeters, 2009, p. 283-297

P. MCCOSKER, 'Grace', in: P. McCosker, D. Turner (eds.), *The Cambridge Companion to the Summa Theologiae*, Cambridge, Cambridge University Press, 2016, p. 206-21

T. MCGUCKIN, 'Saint Thomas Aquinas and Theological Exegesis of Sacred Scripture', in: *Louvain Studies* 16 (1991), p. 99-120

E.L. MILLER, *Salvation-History in the Prologue of John: The Significance of John 1: 3/4*, Leiden, Brill, 1989

A.J. MINNIS, *Medieval Theory of Authorship: Scholastic Literary Attitudes in the Later Middle Ages*, second edition, Aldershot, Scolar Press, 1988

G. MLAKUZHYIL, *The Christocentric Literary Structure of the Fourth Gospel*, Roma, Editrice Pontificio Istituto Biblico, 1987

F.J. MOLONEY, *The Gospel of John*, Collegeville, Liturgical Press, 1998

D. MONGILLO, 'Giovanni l'evangelista contemplativo: Glosse sul proemio di S. Tommaso al Vangelo di Giovanni', in: L. Padovese (ed.), *Atti del IX Simposio di Efeso su S. Giovanni apostolo*, Roma, Istituto Francescano di spiritualità, 2003, p. 197-208

M.M. MULCHAHEY, *"First the Bow Is Bent in Study": Dominican Education before 1350*, Toronto, Pontifical Institute of Mediaeval Studies, 1998

M. OLSZEWSKI, 'St. Albert the Great's Theory of Interpretation of the Bible', in: W. Senner (ed.), *Albertus Magnus: Zum Gedenken nach 800 Jahren*, Berlin, De Gruyter, 2001, p. 467-478

R. PASNAU, *Thomas Aquinas on Human Nature: A Philosophical Study of Summa Theologiae, Ia 75-89*, Cambridge, Cambridge University Press, 2002

G. PERILLO, *Teologia del Verbum: La lectura super Ioannis Evangelium di Tommaso d'Aquino*, Napoli, Luciano Editore, 2003

O.H. PESCH, *Theologie der Rechtfertigung bei Martin Luther und Thomas von Aquin: Versuch eines Systematisch-Theologischen Dialogs*, Mainz, Matthias-Grünewald Verlag, 1967

O.H. PESCH, 'Theologie des Wortes bei Thomas von Aquin', in: *Zeitschrift für Theologie und Kirche* 66 (1969), p. 437-465

O.H. PESCH, 'Paul as Professor of Theology: The Image of the Apostle in St. Thomas's Theology', in: *The Thomist* (1974), p. 584-605

O.H. PESCH, 'Exegese des Alten Testaments bei Thomas', in: *Die Deutsche Thomas Ausgabe, Summa Theologica*, Band 13; Heidelberg, Gemeinschaftsverlag, 1977, p. 682-716

O. H. PESCH, *Thomas Von Aquin: Grenze und Grösse mittelalterlicher Theologie, Eine Einführung*, Mainz, Matthias Grünewald Verlag, 1989

O.H. PESCH, *Katholische Dogmatik: Aus Ökumenischer Erfahrung*, Bd. 1/1 Die Geschichte der Menschen mit Gott, Ostfildern, Matthias-Grünewald-Verlag, 2008

D.-D. LE PIVAIN, *L'Action du Saint-Esprit dans le commentaire de l'Évangile de Saint Jean par Saint Thomas d'Aquin*, Paris, Pierre Téqui Éditeur, 2006

T. PRÜGL, 'Thomas Aquinas as Interpreter of Scripture', in: R. van Nieuwenhove, J. Wawrykow (eds.), *The Theology of Thomas Aquinas*, Notre Dame, University of Notre Dame Press, 2005, p. 386-415

K. RAHNER, 'Über den Begriff des Geheimnisses in der katholischen Theologie', in: *Schriften zur Theologie*, Band IV, Einsiedeln, Benziger Verlag, 1960, p. 51-99

K. RAHNER, 'Fragen zur Unbegreiflichkeit Gottes nach Thomas von Aquin', in: *Schriften zur Theologie*, Band XII, Zürich, Benziger Verlag, 1975, p. 306-319

T. REIST, *Saint Bonaventure as a Biblical Commentator: A Translation and Analysis of His Commentary on Luke, XVIII, 34-XIX, 42*, Lanham, University Press of America, 1985

H.W.M. RIKHOF, 'Aquinas' Authority in the Contemporary Theology of the Trinity', in: P. van Geest, H. Goris, C. Leget (eds.), *Aquinas as Authority*, Leuven, Peeters, 2000, p. 213-34

H.W.M. RIKHOF, 'Trinity', in: R. van Nieuwenhove, J. Wawrykow (eds.), *The Theology of Thomas Aquinas*, Notre Dame, University of Notre Dame Press, 2005, p. 36-57

H.W.M. RIKHOF, 'Thomas on Divine Adoption', in: H. Goris, H. Rikhof, H. Schoot (eds.), *Divine Transcendence and Immanence in the Work of Thomas Aquinas*, Leuven, Peeters, 2009, p. 163-93

E.F. ROGERS, *Thomas Aquinas and Karl Barth: Sacred Doctrine and the Natural Knowledge of God,* Notre Dame, University of Notre Dame Press, 1995

E.F. ROGERS, 'How the Virtues of an Interpreter Presuppose and Perfect Hermeneutics: The Case of Thomas Aquinas', in: *The Journal of Religion* 76 (1996), p. 64-81

M.M. ROSSI, *Teoria e metodo esegetici in S. Tommaso d'Aquino: Analisi del super epistolas Sancti Pauli lectura ad Romanos, C. I, L. 6*, Roma, Pontifica Studiorum Universitas a S. Thomas Aq. in Urbem, 1992

M.M. ROSSI, 'La "divisio textus" nei commenti scritturistici di S. Tommaso d'Aquino: Un procedimento solo esegetico?', in: *Angelicum* 71 (1994), p. 537-548

M.M. ROSSI, '(L') Attenzione a Tommaso d'Aquino esegeta', in: *Angelicum* 76 (1999), p. 73-104

M.M. ROSSI, 'Mind-Space: Towards an 'Environ-Mental Method' in the Exegesis of the Middle Ages', in: P. Roszak, J. Vijgen (eds.), *Reading Sacred Scripture with Thomas Aquinas: Hermeneutical Tools, Theological Questions and New Perspectives*, Turnhout, Brepols, 2015, p. 171-198

M.M. ROSSI, *Called into a Story: An "environ-mental" Approach to Saint Thomas Aquinas as Exegete and Preacher*, Roma, Angelicum University Press, 2018

P. ROSZAK, 'The Place and Function of Biblical Citations in Thomas Aquinas's Exegesis', in: P. Roszak, J. Vijgen (eds.), *Reading Sacred Scripture with Thomas Aquinas: Hermeneutical Tools, Theological Questions and New Perspectives*, Turnhout, Brepols, 2015, p. 115-139

T.F. RYAN, *Thomas Aquinas as Reader of the Psalms*, Notre Dame, University of Notre Dame Press, 2000

M. SABATHÉ, *La Trinité rédemptrice dans le commentaire de l'évangile de Saint Jean par Thomas d'Aquin*, Paris, Librairie Philosophique J. Vrin, 2011

P. SAENGER, L. BRUCK, 'The Anglo-Hebraic Origins of the Modern Chapter Division of the Latin Bible', in: F.J. Burguillo, L. Meier (eds.), *La fractura historiográfica: Edad media y renacimiento desde el tercer milenio*, Salamanca, Seminario de Estudios Medievales y Renacentistas, 2008, p. 177-202

M. SCHEUER, *Weiter-Gabe: Heilsvermittlung durch Gnadengaben in den Schriftkommentaren des Thomas von Aquin*, Würzburg, Echter, 2001

H.J.M. SCHOOT, *Christ the 'Name' of God: Thomas Aquinas on Naming Christ*, Leuven, Peeters, 1993

H.J.M. SCHOOT, 'Holy, Holy, Holy: A Plea for the Holiness of Theology', in: *Jaarboek Thomas Instituut* 26 (2006), p. 7-33

M. SHERWIN, 'Christ the Teacher in St. Thomas's Commentary on the Gospel of John', in: M. Dauphinais, M. Levering (eds.), *Reading John with St. Thomas Aquinas: Theological Exegesis and Speculative Theology*, Washington D.C., Catholic University of America Press, 2005, p. 172-193

M.G. SIRILLA, *The Ideal Bishop: Aquinas's Commentaries on the Pastoral Epistles*, Washington D.C., Catholic University of America Press, 2017

B. SMALLEY, *The Study of the Bible in the Middle Ages*, Third revised edition, Oxford, Basil Blackwell Publisher, 1984

B. SMALLEY, *The Gospels in the Schools: c. 1100 – c. 1280*, London, Bloomsbury Publishing 1985

L. SMITH, *The* Glossa Ordinaria*: The Making of a Medieval Bible Commentary*, Leiden, Brill, 2009

R. SOKOLOWSKI, *The God of Faith and Reason*: *Foundations of Christian Theology*, Washington D.C., Catholic University of America Press, 1995

L.-T. SOMME, *Fils adoptifs de Dieu par Jésus Christ: La filiation divine par adoption dans la théologie de Saint Thomas d'Aquin,* Paris, Vrin, 1997

C. SPICQ, *Esquisse d'une Histoire de l'Exégèse Latine au Moyen Âge*, Paris, Librairie Philosophique J. Vrin, 1944

C. SPICQ, 'Thomas d'Aquin Exégète', in: E. Amman (ed.) *Dictionnaire de Théologie Catholique*, vol. 15/1, Paris, Librarie Letouzey et Ané, 1946 p. 694-738

D.C. STEINMETZ, *Taking the Long View: Christian Theology in Historical Perspective*, Oxford, Oxford University Press, 2011

E.M. SWEENEY, "Divine Revelation in the Commentary of St. Thomas Aquinas on St. John's Gospel", Unpublished doctoral dissertation, University of Navarra, 1981, typescript

M.M. THOMPSON, *John: A Commentary*, Louisville, Westminster John Knox Press, 2015

J.-P. TORRELL, *Saint Thomas Aquinas: The Person and his Work*, Washington D.C., Catholic University of America Press, 1996

J.-P. TORRELL, *Le Christ en ses mystères: La vie et l'oeuvre de Jésus selon Saint Thomas d'Aquin*, vol. 1, Paris, Desclée, 1999

J.-P. TORRELL, *Saint Thomas Aquinas: Spiritual Master*, Washington D.C., Catholic University of America Press, 2003

D. TURNER, *Eros & Allegory: Medieval Exegesis of the Song of Songs*, Collegeville, Cistercian Publications, 1995

D. TURNER, *Thomas Aquinas: A Portrait*, New Haven, Yale University Press, 2013

W.G.B.M. VALKENBERG, *Words of the Living God: Place and Function of Holy Scripture in the Theology of St. Thomas Aquinas,* Leuven, Peeters, 2000

W.G.B.M. VALKENBERG, 'Scripture', in: P. McCosker, D. Turner (eds.), *The Cambridge Companion to the Summa Theologiae*, Cambridge, Cambridge University Press, 2016, p. 48-61

R.A. TE VELDE, *Aquinas on God: The 'Divine Science' of the Summa Theologiae,* Aldershot, Ashgate, 2006

J. VERGER, 'L'Exégèse de l'université', in: P. Riché, G. Lobrichon (eds.), *Le Moyen Age et la Bible*, Paris, Éditions Beauchesne, 1984, p. 199-232

G. WARD, *How the Light Gets in: Ethical Life I*, Oxford, Oxford University Press, 2016

J. WAWRYKOW, 'Grace', in: R. van Nieuwenhove, J. Wawrykow (eds.), *The Theology of Thomas Aquinas*, Notre Dame, University of Notre Dame Press, 2005, p. 192-221

J. WAWRYKOW, 'Hypostatic Union', in: R. van Nieuwenhove, J. Wawrykow (eds.), *The Theology of Thomas Aquinas*, Notre Dame, University of Notre Dame Press, 2005, p. 222-251

T.G. WEINANDY, D.A. KEATING, J.P. YOCUM (eds.), *Aquinas on Scripture: An Introduction to his Biblical Commentaries*, London, T&T Clark International, 2005

J.A. WEISHEIPL, 'The Johannine Commentary of Friar Thomas', in: *Church History* 45 (1976), p. 185-195

D.L. WHIDDEN, *Christ the Light: The Theology of Light and Illumination in Thomas Aquinas*, Minneapolis, Fortress Press, 2014.

P.J. WILLIAMS, 'Not the Prologue of John', in: *Journal for the Study of the New Testament* 33 (2011), p. 375-386

R. WILLIAMS, *Christ the Heart of Creation*, London, Bloomsbury, 2018

J. WISSINK, *Thomas van Aquino: De actuele betekenis van zijn theologie*, Meinema, Zoetermeer, 1998

M.D. YAFFE, 'Interpretive Essay' in: A. Damico, M.D. Yaffe (eds.), *Thomas Aquinas: The Literal Exposition on Job, A Scriptural Commentary Concerning Providence*, Atlanta, Scholars Press, 1989, p. 1-65

INDICES

Scripture

Names

Subjects

FULL TABLE OF CONTENTS